# 3
# PLAYS
# BY

# PLAUTUS

Stage of Roman Theater at Sabratha,
N. Africa, ca. 180 A.D. Photo: R. Schoder, S.J.

# 3 PLAYS BY PLAUTUS

## MILES GLORIOSUS
### (MAJOR BULLSHOT-GORGEOUS)
## AMPHITRYON
## THE PRISONERS

### TRANSLATED AND WITH AN INTRODUCTION
### BY
## PAUL ROCHE

## BOLCHAZY-CARDUCCI PUBLISHERS

1984 Reprint

New Publisher and Distributor

**BOLCHAZY-CARDUCCI PUBLISHERS**
44 Lake St.
OAK PARK, IL 60302 U.S.A.

Printed in the United States of America

International Standard Book Number
0-86516-035-X

This is a Reprint of the 1968 Edition
MENTOR CLASSICS

# CONTENTS

The text used in these translations is in general that followed by Paul Nixon in the Loeb Classics edition: a text that was first edited by Leo and published by Weidmann, Berlin, 1895–96.

Line numbers refer to those in the Latin text.

# FOREWORD

## Plautus and Us

JUST AS WE need to be told in a way that grips us that man is but a contingent creature subject to sudden disrupting forces, whom it behooves to be modest in his own conceits, we need to be reminded also that this life is neither the time nor place for complete success, that struggle and near-ineptitude are the norm, and perfection only the ideal. The tragedies of Aeschylus, Sophocles and Euripides supremely convince us of the first—in a form that reduces us to tears. The perennially human comedies of Plautus accomplish the second: by holding up a mirror to our foibles and making us laugh at them.

Left to ourselves we are altogether too solemn, even about the seriousness of our plight. Yet the same material that is the breeding ground for sorrows is, on the obverse, a tissue of incongruities and a treasury of human relationships, almost all of which are funny. It is not so much that our failures are absurd, as that our almost militant expectation of perfection in everything is idiotic.

Laughter is the unfailing salve, the right antidote to false proportions. Laughter is our sense of the imperfect: our tolerance of the truth. If ever a truism was self-evident it is that laughter keeps us sane. Yes, laughter shakes up the liver, increases the circulation, releases the glands, punctures pomposity and reduces self-inflation to a heap. At its deepest level it implies a patience with—almost a welcome of—partial success instead of triumph. It implies a metaphysics of enlightened pessimism which is both liberating and consoling because it balances our expectations of the possible with our acceptance of the real.

The genius of Plautus was that he seized those stock human situations which have been a joke since the time of Adam, developed them from the Greek New Comedy, and used them for a tolerant view of man: a view scaled down to the littlest man among us. His characters may only be a distraught father,

a ne'er-do-well son, a clever servant, a fatuously important
soldier—or even a greedy courtesan or pander—but *not* one
of the great and therefore unlike us. It matters not at all that
he was a Latin and wrote his plays over two thousand years ago.
The essence of the human scene remains the same. And even if
he were no longer funny—which is far from true—we still
should read and play him because he was the one, predominantly, who made comedy what it is today. He inspired the
farce, the burlesque, the slapstick, from the third century B.C.
till the Middle Ages; and after the Renaissance became—with
his compatriot Terence—the founder of western comedy as we
know it now: even the model of such plays as *The Comedy of
Errors*, Molière's *The Miser*, Giraudoux's *Amphitryon 38*—
right down to *The Boys from Syracuse* and *A Funny Thing
Happened on the Way to the Forum*.

And so Plautus, on a less lofty but no less necessary plane
to that of the great Greek tragedians, makes it easier for us to
go on coping with our fate day after day. Unlike them, by his insistence on realized rather than idealized human nature, he
is finally an optimist and makes a belief in happy endings a
symbol of the trivial yet sublime.

PAUL ROCHE

*Aldermaston, England*

# INTRODUCTION

## Plautus and Comedy

TITUS MACCIUS PLAUTUS, to give him the full name he assumed on being granted Roman citizenship, was born about 254 B.C. in the small town of Sarsina in Umbria, where his father was a farmer. He came to Rome while still a lad and seems to have attached himself, first as a stagehand and then an actor, to a company of players. Perhaps he played the part of clown— *maccus* is the word for it in Latin—in those early Italian farces known as *Fabulae Atellanae*. These were short plays with slap-stick plots, enlivened by song and dance and some indecencies, centered on a few stock characters. His own nickname was Plautus or Flatfoot. There is no evidence that he, like Terence a generation after him, began life as a slave, but the vitality and sympathy with which he drew slaves' characters shows how well he understood their lot. In any case, a troupe of players in those days was not only recruited chiefly from the ranks of slaves and freedmen, it was very much the property of the *dominus gregi* or manager-producer, who could threaten with the whip or reward with free drinks. He it was who commissioned plays or bought them outright from authors and con-tracted with the public officials for performances on given festivals. He also directed and staged them.

But it is doubtful if anyone could have lived solely by being an actor at that time. Plays such as they were—rustic high jinks with mime, song and dance—were not put on at whim but only at stated times: public holidays, military triumphs and the funerals of great men. Before the year 200 B.C. this probably did not amount to more than a dozen times a year, the season lasting from April until November. Nevertheless, Plautus seems to have saved enough money by some means or other to set himself up in business as a merchant trader; he lost all his investment and was forced to become a laborer in a flour mill. It was during this occupation, tradition has it, that he set to good use his intimate knowledge of the theater and began to translate and adapt plays from the Greek New Comedy of the late fourth century.

Rome at that time was in the first flush of her enamoration with Greek culture. Hardly a score of years had passed since she had subjugated the whole of Italy and though she was still in the middle of her wars with Carthage and had not extended her influence over the rest of the Mediterranean, she was already mistress of the Greek cities in her own deep south. Her soldiers and statesmen were impressed with the far more civilized and sophisticated way of life they found there. They went to the splendid theaters and saw Greek plays, and when they came home they brought with them educated slaves for their households and Greek tutors for their sons.

One such tutor to a senatorial family was Livius Andronicus, an Italian Greek from Tarentum and some thirty years older than Plautus. He translated Homer's *Odyssey* into Latin and proceeded to adapt several tragedies and comedies from Greek originals. Almost contemporaneously Gnæus Nævius did the same and also created the native historical play: the *Fabula Prætexta*. But almost nothing of the works of these important and prolific writers has survived. It is to Plautus we must go and to his twenty extant adaptations of Greek New Comedy (out of a total of over a hundred plays) if we are to know what Roman comedy was like before the time of Terence.

The discovery of the plays of Menander, Diphilus, Philemon and other Greeks was a godsend to the Romans who, it must be remembered, were still treading the path of early rectitude—not to say of primness—with which they began their disciplined career to power. Rome was being drained by the Punic Wars, morality was stern, public expenditure careful and private, limited by the sumptuary laws.[1] Now, through Greek New Comedy and the exuberant manipulation of Plautus, a new range of characters and situations was opened. Furthermore, by keeping the whole thing ostensibly Greek while in reality injecting it with the manners and preoccupations of Italian middle-class society, the Roman playwright could make the plays the mirror both of his times and his own wishful thinking, and let the Romans have their cake and eat it. Prostitutes, pimps and prodigal sons, conniving slaves who abetted the amours

[1] Clothes were limited to homespun and the number of courses at meals restricted.

of reckless young men, witty parasites and desperate fathers, easily tricked panderers and senile dotards—all could be enjoyed provided they were not Romans but Greeks.

Unfortunately, none of the plays that Plautus translated has come down to us from the original Greek, and so it is impossible to prove textually what we are 99 percent sure of from internal evidence: that he did far more than merely translate. He adapted and amalgamated, reworked dialogues, changed characters and shaped new scenes. Put at its briefest, his genius was to wed Greek New Comedy to native Italic farce; he brought to this task not only dramatic imagination but an entirely fresh deployment of several theatrical techniques.

The Greeks themselves had gradually let go of the chorus proper of Aristophanes. The chorus had already begun to slip —to become a pretty, melodramatic interlude—under Euripides; by the time of Menander it had nothing to do with the play but served as a kind of music-cum-dance intermission to mark the divisions of dramatic action. The circle of the *orchestra* where the chorus had deported itself was cut in half and the altar of Dionysus removed. The play was no longer a liturgical act. Now Plautus, still without the chorus, re-introduced song and dance as an integral part of the performance. He invented a rich variety of metrical patterns to carry the language, and harnessed sung lyrical passages to the music of the flute. Straight dialogue, spoken—the *diverbia*—alternated with more elaborate passages called *cantica* or "recitative," which were sometimes recited and sometimes sung (if lyrical) against a soft musical background of flute, lyre and tympanum (the kettledrum). The whole was written in verse: a six-foot iambic line usually for the *diverbia,* and a galaxy of iambic, trochaic and dactylic meters for the *cantica.* What remained constant was the quality of the language: rarely literary but seldom slangy—the everyday speech of the early Romans at its best.[2]

Comedy as Plautus left it, both in genre—farce, burlesque, operetta, extravaganza—and content—close family life, amor-

---

[2] E. F. Watling makes a good point in the introduction to his excellent translations of Plautus when he says that attempts to translate the Plautine dialogue into an English metrical form are hampered by lack of any equivalent stage convention. However, I think he goes too far when he brands the Gilbertian lyric as a particularly unsuitable model. There are plenty of places in Gilbert and Sullivan opera where the same natural and colloquial idiom runs through both the dialogue and the lyrics, as in Plautus.

ous mix-ups, domestic hullabaloo, and sweet young things in love—looks oddly familiar after twenty-two hundred years. A Roman comedy of 200 B.C. and a Broadway musical comedy of 1968 A.D.—"the gulf between," to quote the late Edith Hamilton, "can be passed without exertion. Save in respect of time only, it is neither wide nor deep. This swiftly changing world we must all run so hard to keep up with suddenly looks strangely static."[3]

## Plautus: Yesterday and Today

Edith Hamilton's words are true, and yet there remains a difference and a difficulty. The audience that flocked to his plays —an audience of all classes including women, children and even slaves—saw these hackneyed scenes for the first time. Ours is a sophisticated audience: dramatically unimpressed by over two thousand years of imitation and variation by uncountable playwrights. It is not that Plautus himself needs changing or even adapting, except for some cutting here and there: his words are as funny as ever, given—as I shall presently stress— the correct poetic emphasis and timing. No, it is that when we come to reconstitute the art of Plautus what is wanted is imagination in recasting the comic situation.

I feel inclined to suggest that the less conscious we are of the Roman stage the better. Our knowledge of ancient drama can become a hindrance if it merely leads to a display of scholarship or to an arty hankering after masks, wigs, scænæ, and porticos, or an insistence on the traditional costumes and colors: white for an old man, multicolored for a youth, yellow for a courtesan, a chlamys for a soldier, a short tunic for a slave, and so on. These things conceivably could be helpful but they are only incidentals. We must use our mass of facts discreetly and choose only those elements of theatrical circumstance that are still convincing.

To begin with, Plautus's lengthy prologues are tiresome whatever way we look at them, and so are the built-in ingenuously elementary stage directions—"the door is creaking, here he comes." But we must remember that the first were necessary as the unique means of preparing the ground for dramatic irony

3 *The Roman Way*, Mentor, 1959.

—more than half the secret of his humor—and the second because there existed no drop curtain to divide the scenes into their various entrances and exits. Finally, both were necessary because no printed handbills or programs explained time, setting and dramatis personæ. Characters had to introduce themselves and each other. Therefore, Plautus makes doubly sure that the dullest among the spectators knows what is going on. Sometimes he seems almost to announce that a joke is on its way, has arrived, is come and gone. However, even here I counsel a director not to be too enlightened. I have often found that the most sophisticated way of dealing with an apparent naïveté is to leave it as it stands and give the modern audience the chance of a "double take." The reward sometimes is a new laugh.

As to other things: sets and scenery at this time were of the simplest: a long wooden platform for the temporary stage (which possibly accommodated one or two altars), and a backdrop of two or three house-fronts with a passage between them to represent a street. It was outside these houses that the action took place. Anything that was supposed to have happened inside was described in the dialogue. The actors were four or five in number, all male until the time of Julius Caesar, and though they did not usually duplicate parts in the manner of the Greeks there were seldom more than three on the stage at once. Whether masks were worn or not in the time of Plautus has not been settled beyond question. Modern opinion tends to think they were. We do know that the actors in the Greek comedies on which the *palliatæ* were modeled *did* wear masks, and that they were in use in the Roman theater by the first century. As I have said, there was no drop curtain and no division into acts or scenes, though the former was recommended by Horace in the first century B.C. and the second regularly appear in the manuscripts of Plautus and Terence. The divisions in the scripts could easily represent those times in the Greek originals when the stage was empty and taken over by a choral interlude. Finally, asides, soliloquies, eavesdropping, violations of dramatic illusion for the sake of a joke, were all part of the convention. I believe that if such elements are used with gusto and without apology, a modern audience will take them in its stride.

When it comes to the theaters, it is curious to reflect that though permanent theaters had long been common in southern Italy, Rome itself was not given a stone theater until as late as 55 B.C., when Pompey built the one named after him, seating about 27,000 people. Even so, it seems that benches for

the spectators were not introduced until 44 B.C. (and these
only of wood), though this is now disputed. At any rate, by
11 B.C.—about 173 years after the death of Plautus—Rome
could boast three theaters, with a total seating capacity of
about 50,000: "an insignificant number as compared with the
255,000 of the Circus Maximus but impressive when set beside
the largest theaters of the modern world: the Opera in Paris
with 2,156 seats, the San Carlo in Naples with 2,900, the Scala
in Milan with 3,600, or even the 5,000 seats of the Colon at
Buenos Aires. The smallest theater of Imperial Rome was still
twice the size of the largest modern American theater; and these
dimensions bear witness—if nothing else did—to the fact that
the Roman's love of the theater, though less consuming than
his passion for the races, was still manifest."[4] The later Roman
emperors vied lavishly with one another in commissioning
new theaters all over the Empire: buildings of a magnificence
the world is not likely to see again. There is no doubt, however,
that the very size of these edifices contributed not a little to
the decadence and final disappearance of legitimate theater.

Today, in the comparative intimacy of even our largest
theaters, I should not be surprised if in fact we could get closer
to the spirit of Plautus than was possible during the later Re-
public and during the days of Imperial Rome. The growing
passion for size and spectacle that swamped the plays wrenched
the focus of the audience from closeness-to-human-nature and
fixed it on sensationalism. By the time of the Emperor Claudius
—some hundred and sixty years after the death of Plautus—
the Roman calendar contained no less than 159 days expressly
marked as holidays: days on three-quarters of which theatrical
representations could be given. But by then both tragedy and
comedy were in their death throes, passing through a deleterious
series of metamorphoses: from mixed song-and-dialogue to
opera, operetta to music hall, mime to pantomime, ballet to
mere acrobatics, helped finally to their demise by the sacrifice
of all inherent excellence to the star system and competitive
ratings.

By the second century A.D. people still went to see Plautus
and Terence acted, but rather out of deference to tradition
than for pleasure. As early as 160 B.C. when Plautus himself
still had another four years to live, the public deserted the
theater where the *Hecyra* of Terence (the *Mother-in-Law*)

4 Jérôme Carcopino: *Daily Life in Ancient Rome.*

was being performed, for one of the gladiatorial combats. From the time of Nero onward no playwright wrote for the theater unless it were for private readings to fellow authors: dismal proof, if ever there was, that there cannot be great plays unless there be great audiences.

## The Way to Plautus

If we are to avoid making Plautine comedy a bore or worse, the first thing to realize about these plays is that they were not written as "literature": they were not written to be read but played. If they are in fact considerable works of literature, it is because Plautus was an artist with an instinct for the common touch as sure as Shakespeare's and knew to a syllable how to communicate the spoken word. His language was perfectly shaped to one purpose: to arrest and entertain a far from captive audience.[5] Sense, association, and the sound of words —all that complex of idea and sonic organism we call poetry— Plautus used with copious insight and fluent invention. I am not suggesting he wrote perfect plays. On the contrary, his plays are uneven and sometimes flawed with careless structure, haphazard plots and incomplete characterization. Some of them might not rate a C plus in a "creative drama" course. But they have the kernel, the soul of whatever makes art real, next to which mere textbook craftsmanship is nothing.

In the matter of choosing and timing words to make a joke, Plautus was a genius.

Again and again I found myself laughing at his Latin, slapping it straight into English and then wondering, rather vapidly, where the laughter had gone. Well, it took only a good look at the Latin to see where: it had slipped like quicksilver through my missing syllables—the rhythms, the shades of emphasis, the cadences that were not there. I had murdered it with the wrong sound and the wrong pace. So I analyzed a little more and tried again, with my sights set on some very clear objectives. The verse of Plautus is a plum-pudding of oral devices to capture the right sound at the right moment. His language is spontaneous, rapid, energetic, idiomatic and

---

[5] In the hurly-burly of a festival crowd he probably had to compete with ropedancers, tightrope walkers, boxing matches, chariot races and all the fun-and-games laid on for a public celebration.

elegant. He uses almost as much assonance, consonance and alliteration as Gerard Manley Hopkins. He coins words and grotesque phrases, and can never resist a pun. Unless you speak him aloud—even in translation—you are killing him as surely as you kill a bar-room joke when you write it out. What Plautus fabricates is great verse. The way he says something tinkles in the ear long after the message is conveyed. And even when he is being boisterous there is a lapidary memorability about his colloquial Latin that leaves the English standing.

It goes without saying that my attempts to capture some of the quality that makes Plautus live are based on fixing him with a searching regard, or rather, riveting him with my ear. In trying to follow him pre-eminently in pace I have never taken longer to say anything than *he* took—at least analogously, given the difference of tongue. I have modeled myself on his audial effects, resisted the temptation, I hope, to invent, and tried to render into English (and sometimes American) not merely what he said but the way he said it. I should like my words to be put to the same test as his: the ear. Plautus stands or falls by the way he sounds.

# AMPHITRYON

for Aunt Ginny:
Virginia Traphagen

# THE CHARACTERS

**MERCURY**

*A god, Jupiter's son and servant*

**SOSIA**

*Servant of Amphitryon*

**JUPITER**

*A god*

**ALCMENA**

*Wife of Amphitryon*

**AMPHITRYON**

*Commander-in-chief of the Theban army*

**BLEPHARO**

*A sea-captain*

**BROMIA**

*Maid of Alcmena*

**THESSALA**

*Maid of Alcmena (silent part)*

**(PORTERS** *and* **SERVANTS**—*silent***)**

## TIME AND SETTING

The scene is a Greek street in the seaside town of Thebes.[1] In the background stands a house more imposing than the rest—Amphitryon's. The time is just before dawn on the morning of Amphitryon's return from the wars. Jupiter some months before had had an affair with Alcmena, impersonating her husband. Now he is enjoying another love-night. The dawn has been conveniently delayed for him and he is at this moment locked in embrace with Alcmena—who in point of fact is pregnant by both her husband and the impostor. Meanwhile, Mercury disguised as Sosia dances attendance on his amorous father; with a plumed hat on his head, a scarf tied around his neck, and carrying a bundle on a stick, he walks jauntily on to the stage and addresses the audience with perky self-confidence.

# PROLOGUE

MERCURY   If you want my blessing on your businesses,
    Bargains, lucky deals in buying and selling,
    Help in everything: success
    In speculations—home and foreign—
    Fine fat profits *in perpetuo*
    From everything you've done (or not yet done)
    And nothing but good news, sensational
    Reports of general good for you and yours . . .        10
    You've guessed of course the gods have granted me
    The patent for goods news and profits—
        [*Takes a deep breath*]
    As I say, if you want my firm support in this—

[1] It made no matter to Plautus that the real Thebes was not on the coast.

Please keep still while we act this play.
Then you can judge it fair and squarely.
        [*Perkily again*]
I'll tell you now who sent me, why I came.
Simultaneously I shall announce my name:
Jove sent me, my name is Mercury.
        [*Pauses for effect*]
20      Yes, my father sent me to you with a plea.
He knows of course you would comply with a command
And show the proper reverence and awe to Jupiter,
But he wants me to approach you coaxingly
With a nice kind ingratiating speech.
        [*Cups his hand for a stage whisper*]
This Jupiter, you see, who made me come here
Can't bear trouble any more than you:
*He's* got a human father and a human mother too.
No wonder he's a little nervous—
30      Same as I am, this Jove's son . . .
When things go wrong with him *I* catch it too.
[*melodramatically*]   So, with peace in my hands I bring
        you peace.
        [*Drops the pose*]
Hang it all—what I'm asking's such an easy decent
        little thing!
I'm asking decent people decently to do the decent
        thing.
Naturally one can't ask decent people to do the inde-
        cent,
And to ask the indecent to do the decent
Is sheer nitwittery—
They don't care a damn or even know what *is* the decent
        thing.

Now attention, please, everyone:
Listen to me.
You ought to want what we want—oughtn't you?
We deserve no less from you and the state, my father
40      and I . . .
But why should I remind you
(As I've seen those others do in tragedies:
Neptune, Virtue, Victory, Mars, Bellona—
Rehearsing marvels that they've done for you)

Remind you of the things my father's done—
And he ruler of the gods, the universal architect?
It's not like him at all to tax good people
With the good he's done them.
No, he takes for granted that you're grateful—
Worth his services.

So then—first I'll tell you about the favor I've come to
   ask.                                                              *50*
Later, I'll expound the plot of this—er—tragedy . . .
       [*Pretends to be taken aback*]
What? Frowning because I said it's tragedy!
I'm a god. I'll change it for you:
Transform this selfsame play from tragedy to comedy
   and never blot a line.
That's if you want me to: yes or no?
       [*Pauses, then claps his hand to his forehead*]
What a blamed fool I am!
I'm a god and know already what you want.
I understand your mind exactly.
We'll have a mixture: tragicomedy.
After all, with kings and gods upon the boards,
Comedy out-and-out would never do.                                     *60*
How about it then? . . . There *is* a slave's part in it . . .
All right—as I said—we'll make it tragicomedy.

And now for that favor Jove instructed me to ask:
He wants inspectors to go combing through the house
   from seat to seat
And if they spot a claque canvasing for anyone,
They're to confiscate their togas as security—
Right there in the house.
      [*Sternly wagging a finger*]
If any man tries to rig the prize[2] for actors or for other
   artists,
Whether by letters, personal appeal or go-betweens,                    *70*
Or even through officials of the state,

2 Forced applause, "fixed" by an actor or his clique, was an abuse
easy to promote in the rough-and-tumble setting of 3rd and 2nd
Century Roman drama. Plautus as a playwright (and also, probably,
as an ex-actor and an extant actor-manager) knew all the tricks and
had to devise ways of circumventing an actor's bringing unfair influence to bear upon an audience or on the judgment of a prize-
giver.

Jupiter decrees the selfsame statute holds
As when parties are convicted
Of trying to sneak themselves or others into public office.
*Worth* won your wars, he says,
Not soliciting and jobbery.
The same rules, then, for actor or great man.
Why not, when worth must win, not lobbying?
If things are in the hands of honesty
80  Straightforwardness is all the lobbying you want.

And here's a further mandate from my father:
Let the actors have inspectors too,
And if any actor hires claquers to clap himself
Or tries to filch applause from someone else,
He'll have his costume beaten off his hide.
[*smiling*] No need for you to wonder why
Jove's so careful of the actors in this play;
No need at all: he's one himself.
What? Surprised?
As if this were a new departure—
90  Jove an actor! Why, just last year
When the players called upon him from this very stage
He came and helped them out.[3]
And so, as I say, today,
In this very play,
Jupiter himself performs and I along with him.

Now your attention, please: the plot.
         [*Gestures toward the backdrop*]
This city here is Thebes.
Over there in that house lives Amphitryon,
Argos-born of an Argive father.
His wife's Alcmena, King Electryon's daughter.
At the moment this Amphitryon's at the front,
100  Commander of the army—
Thebans and Teleboians being at loggerheads.
Just before he left to join his men, however,
This same character got his wife, Alcmena, pregnant.
         [*Grinning rather sheepishly*]
Now I think you know already what my father's like:

---

[3] We have no way of knowing what the play in question was, or
whether it was one of Plautus's own, but clearly Jove was produced
as a *deus ex machina.*

How uninhibited he's apt to be in cases of this sort,
And what a lover he can be when once his fancy's
    caught.
Well, he carries on with her—Alcmena—
Husband unawares,
Husband's body borrowed,
And leaves there on his own account
A pregnancy with his embrace.
So Alcmena—get it straight—                                          *110*
Is with child by each of them:
Her husband and almighty Zeus.
            [*Nods toward the house*]
My father's right there now, inside, in bed with her,
Enjoying himself with her up to the hilt;
That's why this night's been made so long . . .
Disguised as Amphitryon, of course, you understand.
        [*Looks down at himself apologetically*]
Now don't be too surprised at this strange decor of mine:
Coming here in front of you got up like a slave.
This is a new version of the old worn-out tale,
So I'm new too.
Well then, at this moment, there inside
Is the man himself—my father, Jupiter—                               *120*
Changed into the spitting-image of Amphitryon,
Whom all the servants take him for. [*chuckling*]
Oh yes, he's a real quick-change artist when he wants.
*I've* taken on the looks of Sosia, the slave
Who went off with Amphitryon to the wars.
This way I can lend a hand to my—er—loving father
Without the servants asking who I am
When they see me scurrying about the house.
They'll think I'm one of them, a slave.
Nobody'll dream of asking who I am or why I came.          *130*

So Father's there, inside, having his heart's desire:
Wrapped up with his redhot flame.
He's telling her what happened at the front;
She thinks it is her husband,
Not of course a blooming cuckolder.
            [*Smiling to himself*]
*Now* my father's going on about the way he sent the
    enemy battalions flying,
Oh, and the prizes galore that fell to him:

Prizes Amphitryon really did receive
And we absconded with . . . haha!
Everything comes easy to my father.

140   Well, today's the day Amphitryon returns
Fresh from the front with his faithful slave,
Whose living image I parade.
To make it easier for you to tell us each apart,
*I* shall always sport these little plumes upon my hat
While my father's hat will have a golden tassle:
A mark Amphitryon will lack—
Signs invisible to all the house but not to you.
          [*The sound of a somewhat shaky voice coming
                    up the street.* MERCURY's *eyes light up*]
It's Sosia, Amphitryon's slave,
Coming from the harbor with a lantern.
150   Just wait till he gets here:
I'll bundle him off from the house.
Come and see.[4]
When Jove and Mercury start putting on a show,
It's worth your while to go.
          [*Slips behind a pillar*]


# ACT I

SOSIA *comes ambling along the street, swinging his lantern
and singing—to keep his courage up. He is dressed exactly
like Mercury but has no feathers in his hat.*

SOSIA
    Is there any braver man about, more debonair—
Roaming abroad this dead of night, though well aware
    Of what our teen-aged toughs can do and dare?
          [*Thinks he hears a noise and jumps*]
What if three strong coppers came and locked me up,
    Put me in a cell no bigger than a cupboard,
    Took me out tomorrow, administered the whip?

---

[4] In the early days of Roman drama, with no proper theater or
provision for the players, the playwright had to coax his audience
to him in a corner of the bustling forum. On a public holiday, with
every kind of activity going on, one can imagine how keen the
competition for attention must have been.

I couldn't say a word,
My boss would be no help,
Not a soul who wouldn't quip:
Let him have it, quick.
Eight hefty bruisers then to pound me
Like a blooming anvil. Yes, confound me!          *160*
Back from abroad
And what a public welcome—Gawd!
[*Flings down his bundle disgustedly*]
It's this damned impatience of my boss:
Routing me out this time of night by force—
From the port . . .
He could have waited for the day—of course!
[*Sits disconsolately on a step*]
That's the trouble serving a tycoon—
A rich man's slave is worse than a poltroon.
Night and day there's always something new:
Something to go and say, something to go and do
Just beyond the rest you had in view.
And the plutocrat, the master
Never lifts a finger:                              *170*
Takes for granted that his slightest whim
Can easily be met,
It's all the same to him.
He never thinks of all the sweat.
Oh, to be a slave is so unjust!
You fetch and carry, fetch and care—
It's so unfair—
Just because you must.

MERCURY [*to the audience*]
His menial state!
That's quaint!
Seems to me
I'm the one who ought to lodge complaints:
This morning free
And now my father's lackey,
Yet he's the one—
Born scullion—
Who does not think it fun.

SOSIA [*remembering he has not said his prayers*]
My my my!
Born scullion from birth! . . .

          Did I ever stop to think
          Of giving heaven thanks
              For my survival?
          If I get what I deserve
          For such a selfish attitude
          It's a hired man to carve
          My face up on arrival.
              My my my!
          All those happy turns
          And I've never made returns
          Or shown a scrap of gratitude.

MERCURY [*to the audience*]  Rather uncommon that—
    knowing his deserts—what!

SOSIA [*brightening at the recollection of recent events*]
    The thing I never thought could happen,
    The thing not a man-jack-of-us expected—
    Has gone and happened:
    We're back at home safe and sound,
    Our victorious army's homeward bound,
    The enemy is downed.
    Yes, we wiped them out, the lot;
    And as for those bitter walls that rained death down
*190*    On us poor Thebans—
    They're breached at last
    By our soldiers' bravery and dash
    Under the brave and stalwart sway
    Of our glorious Amphitryon, my boss.
    [*heroically*] He has furnished forth his countrymen
        with booty, land, renown;
    He has fixed King Creon firmly on the Theban throne.
    He has . . . ? [*scratches his head*]  oh, yes—has sent me
        on ahead to tell his wife
    How the Commonwealth has triumphed
    Under the brave, unique and stalwart sway of—himself.
        [*Getting up*]
    Hm! Here I've got to think a little:
    How best to put it when I see her.
    A lie or two worked in won't be
    Exactly out of character for me.
    Actually, when they were at their hardest fighting
    *I* was at my hardest running.

Oh well, I'll just pretend that I was there                 *200*
And tell her what I've heard declare . . .
But first, to find the words and manner that I fabricate,
I'll practice on myself a little here.
This is what I'll state:
            [*Puts down his lantern and makes a bow*]
When we first arrived there, madam,
The moment we put foot on *terra firma,*
Amphitryon picks out his most illustrious men
And sends them to the Teleboians with this challenge:
If they're willing without a blow, without a war,
To hand him over both the plunder and the plunderers
And give him back all they've carried off,
Then he is prepared to take his army home at once,
The Argives shall depart their land
And leave them to prosperity and peace.
Be they not so willing, however,
To grant him what he wants,
Then he will proceed with all his might and men
To crush their town.                                        *210*
            [*Pauses for further invention, then runs on glibly*]
When Amphitryon's ambassadors
Had told this to the Teleboians word for word,
Those lusty warriors
Glorying in their prowess and sword
Answered our delegates with rude disdain and jeered:
                    "We can well take care
                     Of ourselves in war.
                     So you'd better quit
                     And take your army, quick."
Forthwith the delegates relayed him this retort,
Forthwith Amphitryon marches out
His total army from the fort.
The Teleboians mobilize in turn
Their grand battalions glittering from the town.
Then both sides full strength advance:
Men in formation, formations in formation.                  *220*
*Our* regiments deploy, *their* regiments deploy,
Face to face in favorite ploys.
The two generals then stride out toward the middle,
Parley in-between the ranks,
And then agree:
That whichever loses in the struggle

Shall surrender town and territory,
Altars, homes, their very soul and body. [*working him-*
      *self up*]
This done, the trumpets blare on either side.
Earth shakes. The shout is raised on either side.
On either side the generals say their prayers.

230   On either side they give their soldiers cheers.
                [*Dancing about with thrust and parry*]
                Then it's every brave man
                With what every brave man
          For himself with his valor can muster.

                Sword clashes on sword
                And the splintering lance
          In the air torn to shreds like a duster.

                The sky seems to shout,
                The air pants with mist:
          Men striking and stricken and dropping,

                Till slowly the strength
                Of our prowess prevails:
          Foe falling in heaps without stopping.

                Successful and savage
                We press and we ravage,
          None gives any ground but would rather

240             Lose his life than his post
                Falls just where he must
          So keeps the formation together.
                      [*Takes a deep breath*]
                My master sees
                And immediately
                He orders the
          Right wing of the cavalry
          To charge from the right
                The cavalry do
          They swoop with a gallop and shout
          Right into the fight from the right
          To mangle and trample our foe underfoot
                And wrongs are put right.
                      [*Stands panting but proud*]


MERCURY [*to the audience*]   So far not a single solitary
      word of fiction uttered:

I was there myself during the whole affair,
Yes, and my father also saw the fight.

SOSIA [*gathering himself together again*]
    So they pitch into flight
    A thing to excite                                    *250*
Our men. And the poor Teleboians

    Now showing their rears
    Have them stuck full of spears
And Amphitryon's chief of destroyers.

    With his very own swing
    He hacks down their king
Pterelas. Oh, and the fighting

    Is fought on and on
    From dawn till the wane
Of that terrible day and the evening.
      [*Breaks off to reflect*]
Yes, of course! I remember that: I went without my
  lunch.
      [*Gets going again*]
    Nothing but night
    Put a stop to the fight
And there came to our camp in the morning
      [*Suddenly doleful*]
    The princes of their people
    From the city keening
    Hands spread out beseeching
    Pardon for their sinning.
    Give themselves, their persons,
    Town and their possessions
    Both profane and sacred
    Together with their children
    To the Theban keeping.
Oh, and as a prize for bravery, my boss,
Amphitryon, was presented with a golden cup:          *260*
The very one from which King Pterelas
      Once used to sip.
        [*Wipes his forehead*]
Phew! That's just how I'll tell it to the Mistress.
Now to carry out the orders of my boss
And press on toward the house.
      [*Picks up lantern*]

[*The ensuing speeches of Mercury and Sosia are carried
on as asides*]

MERCURY

Aha! Coming this way,
I'll go and intercept.
I don't propose to let this man
Get near his home today.
No sir! I'm his double and can play
The very deuce with him.
In fact
Now that I've got his shape and form
I'll have to ape his conduct and his habits too:
Low-down, tricky, full of shiftiness;
Drive him from his doorstep with his favorite tool:
Plain dirty-work and nastiness.
[*Turning toward* SOSIA]
Now what's he up to staring at the stars?
270     I'll watch and make a note of what he does.

SOSIA   Great Scott!
If one can be sure of a thing I'm absolutely sure
Nocturnus went to bed quite drunk last night. Great
Bear
Hasn't budged a fraction in the heavens.
And the Moon's the same—not moved an inch—as
when she rose.
Orion's belt and the Evening Star aren't set,
Nor the Pleiades.
The constellations stand stock still.
Night's not giving way to Day at all.

MERCURY [*looking up at the sky*]
Keep it up, good Night:
Give Father what he hankers for—
A perfect performance in a perfect cause,
With a hundred per cent perfect profit.[5]

SOSIA   I doubt I've ever seen a longer night;
Except that time they gave me stripes
280     And strung me up and left me swinging.

5 The Latin of this passage is: *optumo optume optumam operam das,
datam pulchre locas.* What is one to do with it?

This night, I swear to God, beats even that.
And the Sun I swear's asleep—asleep and soused:
Drank too much at dinner . . . ha ha ha!

MERCURY   Really?
Wretch, you think the gods take after you?
You gibbet-bait—I'll give you something to remember.
Come a little nearer—get a sampler:
     you'll feel sorry.

SOSIA   Now where's that crowd of lady-chasers
Who can't abide bedding down alone?
Tonight's a lovely night for raking—
Raking in your money's worth from expensive ladies.

MERCURY
Dad at least is wisely following
     this man's recipe to the letter:
In the lap of—locked and wallowing—
     his ladylove, Alcmena.                               *290*

SOSIA [*suddenly remembering*]
     As yes—Alcmena,
          I've got to go and tell her
               the Boss's news.
                    [*Sees* MERCURY *and stops short*]
Who's that fellow standing by the house—
     this time of night?
          I do not like!

MERCURY [*contemptuously*]   No one easier to frighten.

SOSIA   Strikes me that fellow's ready
     To grab the coat from off my back.

MERCURY [*grinning*]   Why, he's scared!
     Now for tricks.

SOSIA [*cringing behind a lamppost*]
                    I'm a goner[6]! Got
                Goosepimples in my teeth.

6 In Latin: *Perii*—I have been ruined, finished etc. Lionel Casson's
"goner" is exactly right. *Plautus: Six Plays,* Doubleday, 1963.

He's going to greet me home,
Greet me with his fists.
Kindhearted of him—sure!
Since Boss has kept me up
All night long,
He's going to knock me off
To sleep all day.
Oh, I'm as good as gone!
By Hercules, just look:
How big and strong!

MERCURY
I'll speak up loud
*300*     so he can hear me:
          make him twice as terrified.
                    [*With melodramatic fierceness*]
Come on, my fists—
    up and at 'im!
        It's been ages since
You've tucked away
    into nice fat guts.7
        Was it yesterday—?
Seems æons ago—
    when you laid out four men
        stone-cold naked, *four.*

SOSIA
I'm petrified!
    He's going to change my name
        from "Sosia" into "Number Five."
Four men
    "stone-cold naked four"
        he does insist.
I'm pretty sure
    I'm going to swell the list.

MERCURY [*belts up his tunic and flashes punches around
    him*]
Splendid! Now you're talking!

SOSIA   He's belting up—getting ready.

7 An attempt to keep the play of words in the Latin, *ventri victum:*
feeding his hungry fists and scoring a victory over a belly.

MERCURY   He shan't escape a thrashing.

SOSIA   Shan't! Who shan't?

MERCURY   Any man who comes this way: he'll feast on
     fist.

SOSIA   Not me. I've no appetite this time of night,
     Just had my dinner.                                    *310*
     That's a supper you can throw the starving if you had
        the sense.

MERCURY [*opening and shutting his fist admiringly*]
     Quite a weighty piece of fist, this!

SOSIA   I'm as good as out:
        he's weighing fists.

MERCURY   What if I send him to sleep
     with a nice soft soothing slug?

SOSIA   Send me to sleep! . . .
        you'll save my life.
     Haven't slept a wink for three nights running.

MERCURY [*feints, swings, stops and looks at his fists*]
     Terrible!
     We're doing awful.
     Come on, fists, knuckle down
     To the job of jabbing jaws—
     The merest graze
     And someone ought to have a different face.

SOSIA   So this man's going to overhaul me:
        fix me up a new face.

MERCURY [*dangerously swinging*]
     One direct hit
        makes faces boneless.

SOSIA   Hm! Seems to want to fillet me—like a fish.
     Down with human filleters.
     If he catches sight of me I'm done for.                *320*

MERCURY    Fee fie fo fum! I smell a man.

SOSIA    Oh hell! Did he get a whiff of me?[8]

MERCURY [*sniffing the air*]
　　He must be near,
　　　　though once he was far.

SOSIA    The fellow's a clairvoyant.

MERCURY    My fists are champing.

SOSIA    Champ them on the wall first
　　before you let them exercise on *me*.

MERCURY [*stops throwing fast jabs and cocks his ear, bur-
　　lesquing the style of grand opera*][9]
　　A little voice comes winging to mine ears.

SOSIA    Oh, my god, my little dicky voice!
　　I should have clipped its wings.

MERCURY    The jackass is simply begging
　　for a load of trouble.

SOSIA    I'm not—and I haven't got—any kind of ass.

MERCURY    Straddle his saddle!

SOSIA    Well I never!
　　I'm all done up with the sea-trip,
　　　　seasick still and struggling
　　　　　　even empty-handed:
　　Don't get it into your head
330　　　　that I can take on loads.

MERCURY [*pretending to be surprised*]
　　I'm sure I'm right: I heard somebody talking.

SOSIA    Saved! He doesn't see me.

8 It could also be translated: "Hey! I didn't make a smell, did I?"
9 One of Lionel Casson's imaginative and timely stage directions. I
have found his general alertness to the settings extremely helpful.

"Somebody," he says.
Well, I know for a fact
    my name's not Somebody but Sosia.

MERCURY [*burlesquing grand opera again*]
Ah yes, to the right
    methinks there strikes
        a voice upon mine ears.

SOSIA [*edging away*]
Struck him, did my voice? Oh dear!
    He's sure to strike me back.

MERCURY [*sarcastically*]
Splendid! He's coming nearer.

SOSIA [*stands rooted where he is, gabbling*]
I'm numb, dumb, in a dither:
    Don't ask me where I am.
I'm stuck in a rut and I shiver:
    Poor Sosia's in a jam.
Yes, Sosia's mission and Sosia
    Here go down together.
        [*Waits for worse, but seeing nothing happen
            he takes a hesitant step forward*]
I'll put on the brashiest swagger,
        He'll think I'm a dangerous man
        And perhaps he'll lay off his hand.                340
            [MERCURY *and* SOSIA *are now facing
                each other in front of Amphitryon's
                house*][10]

MERCURY [*in his grand opera manner*]
Wither goest thou with Vulcan
        bottled up inside yon lantern?

SOSIA [*brazenly mimicking him*]
Wherefore ask thou, man-deboner,
        fisty filleter of faces?

---

[10] The meter of the ensuing dialogue is basically trochaic with four
stresses: $\acute{\smile}\smile\acute{\smile}\smile\acute{\smile}\smile\acute{\smile}\smile$.

MERCURY [*wheeling on him*]
    Slave or free?

SOSIA [*airily*]    Whichever suits me.

MERCURY    Is that a fact?

SOSIA    Yeah, that's a fact.

MERCURY    It's a fact you're fit for flogging.

SOSIA    That's a lie.

MERCURY    Which I shall make you
    Say is true by and by.

SOSIA [*nervously*]
    Whatever for? . . . What good is that?

MERCURY [*imperially*]
    I want to know *where* you're going,
    *Whose* you are, *where* you came from.

SOSIA [*impudently*]
    Coming this way—master's orders—
    Am his servant—any wiser?

MERCURY    Damn your cheek, you good-for-nothing!
    I'll screw your tongue out now for that.

SOSIA [*fluttering his eyelids with simpering girlish embar-
    rassment*][11]
    No screwing, sir. She is a virgin
    Properly chaperoned by me.

MERCURY [*unmoved*]
    Still more drivel! What are you doing
    Hanging around these premises?

350    SOSIA    Well, what are *you?*

11 See note 9.

MERCURY   King Creon stations
All-night sentries here at night.

SOSIA [*very superior*]
Nice of him to keep an eye on
This place of ours while we're away.
[*waving him off*]
You can go now . . . Let him know that
The family household staff is back.
[*Tries to pass him toward the door*]

MERCURY [*blocks him with an arm*]
*You* family staff? That's news to me.
Buzz off at once before I put this
Family servant through some very
Unfamiliar paces.

SOSIA [*hurt*]   This is where I live, I tell you.
I'm the servant of these people.

MERCURY [*beckons him with a finger*]
Want to know something, eh?
*If* you don't remove yourself
I'm going to set you up in style.

SOSIA   How exactly?

MERCURY   Well, just let me
Lay my hands upon a truncheon:
You won't go walking, you'll be carried.

SOSIA [*imploringly*]
But I swear I really am
A family servant of this family.

MERCURY [*raising a fist*]
Want to see how soon it takes
To dress you down if you don't scatter?                    *360*

SOSIA [*reproachfully*]
What! Block me from my house
When I'm coming home from overseas?

MERCURY [*with a jeer*]
  This your house?

SOSIA   Yes, I say.

MERCURY [*swooping*]
  Then who's your master?

SOSIA   Amphitryon:
  Commander of the Theban armies;
  Married to Alcmena here.

MERCURY   Is that so? What's your name then?

SOSIA [*grandly*]
  Sosia's what the Thebans call me:
  Davus is the sire I'm sprung from.

MERCURY [*surveying him with a curl of the lip*]
  Well, you made a bad mistake then
  Coming here with your pack of lies,
  Your monumental cheek and darned deceits.

SOSIA [*innocently*]
  Oh no, sir, not with darned deceits:
  I came here with a darned jacket.

MERCURY   What! Still lying, when you came here
  With your feet and not a jacket. Ha ha ha!

SOSIA [*forcing a laugh*]
  Of course, you're right, sir. Ha ha ha!

MERCURY [*switching off the laughter*]
370   Then of course get thrashed for fibbing.

SOSIA   Which of course I much object to.

MERCURY   That of course is immaterial—
  Not a matter for discussion:
  My "of course" is backed by fact.
      [*Delivers* SOSIA *a wallop on the nose*]

SOSIA [*holding his nose*]
  Please! Please! Mercy! Mercy!

MERCURY [*giving him a jab in the solar plexus*]
  So you have the gall to tell me
  *You* are Sosia when that's who I am?

SOSIA [*doubled up*]   Murder! Murder!

MERCURY                 Absolutely
  Nothing to what is still in store.
        [*Continues to pummel*]
  Who d'you now belong to?

SOSIA                 You, sir.
  Yours by right of deed of fist.
        [*Shouts down the street*]
  Theban people—rescue! Rescue!

MERCURY [*silencing him with a slap on the face*]
  Bellow, would you? There, you jailbird!
  Now inform me what you're here for?

SOSIA [*in a small voice*]
  Just for you to use as punchbag.

MERCURY   And now you are . . . ?

SOSIA         Amphitryon's Sosia.

MERCURY [*hitting him again*]
  Another thump for talking nonsense.
  *You* his Sosia? That's who I am.

SOSIA [*under his breath*]
  I wish to heaven that you were
  And I instead were doing the drubbing.                     *380*

MERCURY   Muttering now?

SOSIA         Oh no, I won't, sir.

MERCURY   Who's your master?

SOSIA            Who'd you like?

MERCURY    Well, tell me this: who are you *now*?

SOSIA   No-one, no-one *you* don't want, sir.

MERCURY    You said you were Amphitryon's Sosia.

SOSIA [*sniveling*]
    Then I made a bad mistake, sir.
    All I meant was, I was closely
    Er—connected with Amphitryon.

MERCURY [*folding his arms*]
    There, you see, I knew we never
    Had a Sosia at home but *me*.
    You made a slip.

SOSIA             I wish your fists had.

MERCURY [*with sweet reason*]
    The Sosia you said that *you* were
    Is the Sosia I say that *I* am.

SOSIA [*trying to save his identity*]
    For god's sake, mister, let me have a
    Word in peace without being clobbered.

MERCURY [*severely*]
    No, not peace—an armistice:
    If you've anything to say.

SOSIA [*digging in his heels*]
    Unless there's peace, *I'm* not talking:
390  There's too much power in your punches.

MERCURY [*shrugging*]
    Say what you like. I'll not hurt you.[12]

SOSIA   Word of honor?

12 Actors, please note that with this line the rhythm ($\smile\smile\underline{\phantom{x}}\underline{\phantom{x}}\smile\underline{\phantom{x}}\smile$ still
4 stress) becomes predominantly dactylic ($\underline{\phantom{x}}\smile\smile$), until line 462.

MERCURY   Word of honor.

SOSIA   What if you fool me?

MERCURY [*solemnly*]   Then may Sosia
Feel the anger of Mercury.

SOSIA [*blurting it out with his old cockiness*]
Take note of this, then—now that I freely
Speak my own mind: *I* am Amphitryon's
Servant Sosia.

MERCURY [*in incredulous mock outrage*]
                                 What! Not again?

SOSIA [*hurt consternation*]
We made a truce. We struck a treaty.
I tell the truth.

MERCURY [*advancing*]   Be thrashed for it.

SOSIA [*doggedly*]
Suit yourself—do whatever suits you.
Your fists are much too strong for me.
Whatever you do do, just the same,
          [*Raising his voice*]
*I'll* not go back on my word, by Hercules!

MERCURY [*in ultimatum*]
And *you* can live for a month of Sundays
Before you'll prevent *my* being Sosia.

SOSIA [*obstinately*]
And you, by Jiminy, you won't either
Stop me being our servant here.
Except for me we haven't at home
A single solitary Sosia.                              *400*

MERCURY [*shaking his head*]   The fellow's crazy.

SOSIA [*defiantly*]   That's what *you* are.
       [*Turns to the audience*]
See here now, hang it all!

Aren't I really Amphitryon's Sosia?
Didn't our ship put in this night
From Persicus port with *me* on board?
Aren't I standing in front of our house?
Don't I dangle a lamp in my hand?
Aren't I talking? Aren't I awake?
Didn't this fellow just give me a bruising?
[*groaning*]   *I'll* say he did!
My miserable jaw still aches . . .
Then what am I waiting for? Why don't I step
Right inside my house this minute?

MERCURY [*blocking his way*]
What d'you mean—*your* house?

SOSIA   That's what I said.

*410*   MERCURY   What you've just said is absolute poppycock.
No one but *I* am Amphitryon's Sosia.
Only last night from Persicus port
Our ship weighed anchor . . . We captured the town
Where Pterelas reigned. We smashed the grand
Teleboian battalions. Amphitryon
With his own right hand
Cut King Pterelas down in the battle.

SOSIA [*dumfounded*]   I can't believe my ears as I hear him.
He's reeling it off just as it happened.
        [*Turns to* MERCURY *with a sudden inspiration*]
Tell me this: what was the prize
Amphitryon won from the Teleboians?

MERCURY [*immediately*]   The golden cup King Pterelas
used.

SOSIA [*gaping*]   He's said it right . . . And where is the cup?

*420*   MERCURY   Inside the cabinet sealed with Amphitryon's
seal.

SOSIA   The seal? Tell me that.

MERCURY   The rising Sun in his four-horse chariot . . .
Trying to trick me, eh, you blighter?

SOSIA [*to the audience, hopelessly*]   Hell, that clinches it!
I've got to find me another name.
But where on earth has he seen it all from?
        [*Thinks desperately, then wheels around*]
Wait a minute: I'll test him with this,
Something I did when all by myself—
Not a soul in the tent—
Something he'll never, but never, unfathom.
            [*With the air of one slapping down his trump
    card*]
*If* you are Sosia, what were you doing
In the tent at the height of the battle?
Answer me that and you've got me beaten.

MERCURY [*tossing it off nonchalantly*]   There was a keg of
    wine: I drew off a jugful.

SOSIA [*reeling*]   He's on the right track.

MERCURY   I swigged the lot:
Wine as neat as it came from its mother.          *430*

SOSIA [*sits down on the step, flabbergasted*]   That's the
    truth. I guzzled down
A whole jugful of neat wine . . .
This fellow most likely was there at the bottom.

MERCURY [*grinning triumphantly*]   Well, have I proved
    that you're not Sosia?

SOSIA [*in a cold sweat*]   You really mean to say I'm not?

MERCURY [*nonchalantly*]   How can I really say you *are*
    When that's who I am?

SOSIA [*jumping up and shouting*]   But I swear by Jupiter
    *I* am,
And that's not a lie.

MERCURY [*mimicking him*]   And I by Mercury swear it:
    That Jupiter doesn't believe you.
He'd take my bare word for it any day
Rather than yours with an oath.

SOSIA [*shattered*]   Then for god's sake, will you tell me:
If *I'm* not Sosia, who am I?

MERCURY [*shrugging*]   Look, mister:
When *I* don't want to be Sosia,
*You* can be Sosia—sure!
But seeing *I'm* Sosia now,
Either get out or get a beating,
440        You nameless nobody!

SOSIA [*stepping back to survey him*]   Well I'll be damned!
Now that I gaze at him next to myself,
(And I know what I look like—I've often peeped
At myself in the glass), he might be *me:*
Same hat and coat . . . Yes, easily:
Same leg and foot, haircut, height,
Same nose and lips, cheeks and chin—
He's got the lot: same everything.
Now if he's got a whiplashed back—
He is me, and that is that.
          [*Screws up his eyes in reflection*]
Yet when I come to think of it,
I'm positive I'm still the same
Man I always was . . . I *am.*
          [*With growing conviction*]
I know my boss; I know our house;
I've got my senses sound and sane.
To hell with what this person says:
I'm going to knock at my front door.
          [*Marches toward the door*]

MERCURY [*blocking him*]   Ah-ah! Where are you off to?

SOSIA   Home.

MERCURY [*with a dry laugh*]   Even if you jumped aboard
Zeus's four-horsed chariot,
450        You wouldn't now escape your lot.

SOSIA [*sullenly*]   Can't I take my mistress news
My master's ordered me to take?

MERCURY   Take your mistress what you like,

Only keep away from ours.
    [*With a wave of dismissal*]
Don't annoy me any more—
Or you'll pick the pieces off the floor.

SOSIA [*backing away*]   No no, I'm going . . . Oh, gods
    immortal,
Where did I lose myself? Where on earth
Could I have undergone mutation?
Where did I drop my personal shape?
Maybe I left it behind—
Back at the port—forgot.
This fellow is carrying about
Looks which once on a time
I thought entirely mine.
It's gone and happened alive
To me instead
Of when I am dead.
        [*Picks up bundle and shuffles off*]
I'll go to the harbor and tell my master
What's going on . . . O excellent Jupiter,                    460
What if my boss don't know me either?
Can you bring it about? Then today
I'll shave off my topknot and clap
On a freedman's cap.13
        [SOSIA *departs for the harbor*]

MERCURY [*sauntering forward with a grin*]   You see, my
    little game has gone quite well:
I've shifted a piece of nuisance from the door
And let my father go on lolling with his love.
Now when our friend gets back there to his master,
And tells Amphitryon how his servant Sosia
Sent him packing from his own front door,
He'll think he's lying, naturally—
Never came here as he ordered.
        [*Chuckles*]
I'll muddle up the pair of them,
Befuddle them from head to foot—                              470

13 Slaves were not allowed to wear their hair long. When given their
freedom they put on the *pileus,* a close-fitting felt cap. Sosia must
mean that he'll willingly shave off whatever hair he has, just to get
his head inside the *pileus.*

Amphitryon's whole household too—
And keep it up till Father with his filly
Has had his fill.
Not till then shall people know the truth
And Jupiter put back the sweet content
Alcmena and her husband had before.
Amphitryon, you see, is going to storm at her
And say she's played him false.
Father'll then step in and calm the ferment.
          [*Leaning toward the audience*]
Now a word about Alcmena,
Something I've not told you yet:

480    She's on the point of giving birth to twins—two boys:
One a nine month's child, the other seven;
Junior has the senior father,
And vice versa, you understand.
For Alcmena's sake, however, Father's so arranged
They'll both arrive together:
One labor making do for two.
But, as I told you, Amphitryon in the end
Will have it all explained to him . . .

490    What does it matter anyway?
No one's going to think the worse of poor Alcmena:
It wouldn't do—now, would it?—to let a human being
Get saddled with the consequences of a god's
Little indiscretions and excesses.
          [*Turning his head*]
Excuse me, please . . .
I hear the front door going.
Look: the sham Amphitryon's coming out,
Together with the wife he's got on credit.

          [*He gestures toward the house from which* JUPI-
          TER—*in disguise*—*and* ALCMENA *emerge hand
          in hand.* MERCURY *takes up his stance as* SOSIA]

[ALCMENA, *dressed in a soft morning gown, her hair not
yet done up, is radiant with the full bloom of womanhood.
She is more than a sumptuous female; her eyes shine with
that simple devotion to her husband which invests even the
most beautiful women with a new gentleness and purity.
Her consort is a fine powerful man in robust early middle-
age: a commanding figure and all that we should expect of*

*a victorious general. He wears a military cape in swash-*
*buckling style, carries a marshal's baton and has on his*
*head a pith helmet with a golden tassle. As they come out*
*of the house he takes one of* ALCMENA's *hands in his and*
*raises it to his lips*]

JUPITER   Goodbye, Alcmena darling, bless you.
   See to everything as always.
   Be careful not to overdo it:
   Your time is nearly up, you know.                    *500*
   Now I've got to go from here . . .
   Welcome the little one, my dear.

ALCMENA   What on earth, my husband, is this business
   Which makes you break away from home so brusquely?

JUPITER [*kissing her hand again*]   Not boredom with *you*
      or home, my dearest,
   Absolutely not—but when a
   General isn't with his army
   Things go much more wrong than rightly.

MERCURY [*in a stage whisper to the audience*]   *He's* got a
      smooth technique, has this one.
   Does me credit, my old man:[14]
   Just watch the way he'll soften her up!

ALCMENA [*pouting*]   Oh yes, I'm finding out exactly
   Just how much you think your wife worth.

JUPITER [*fondly*]   Isn't it enough that you're the only
   Woman in the world to me?
      [*Kisses her*]

MERCURY [*aside, jerking a thumb heavenward*]   Careful,
      sir!
   Just let the lady up above
   Catch sight of your performances down here,          *510*
   And I guarantee you'd rather be
   Amphitryon than Jupiter.

ALCMENA   Experience, not description, sir,

14 Mercury was the patron god of thieves.

Is something I would much prefer.
You're off before you've warmed your bed:
Here yesterday at dead of night,
Gone today—does that seem right?

MERCURY [*to the audience*]    I'd better sidle up to her and
   talk . . .
Do my stuff for Dad.
         [*Steps up to* ALCMENA]
Cross my heart, ma'am,
There's not a mortal man alive
Dotes on his wife—I do believe—
The way he dotes on *you*.

JUPITER [*rounding on him*]    To hell with you!
Don't I know your antics? Out
Of my sight. What call have you—
You little pest—to come butting in
With your big loud mouth?
I'll take this cane and I'll . . .

ALCMENA [*putting out a restraining hand*]    No no, don't!

JUPITER [*to* MERCURY *between his teeth*]    Just breathe a
*520*    syllable . . .

MERCURY [*to the audience, dryly*]    There you are!
The flunky flunks his first attempt to flunk.

JUPITER    Sweetheart, as to what you say—
You needn't be so cross with me.
I left my army on the sly:
Stole these moments just for *you*.
I wanted you to be the first
To have the news and first from *me*
Of how I've triumphed for the state.
And now I've told you everything
And surely wouldn't have unless
I loved you more than anything.
         [*Kisses her on the forehead*]

MERCURY [*to the audience, grinning complacently*]    Just
   as I said he would, eh, what?
Petting away the poor thing's fears!

JUPITER   Now I must slip back before
  The regiments get wind of this
  And make the story rife:
  Of how I put the public welfare
  Well behind my wife.

ALCMENA [*beginning to cry*]   Yes, you've fixed things well
    for her:
  Left behind a wife in tears!

JUPITER [*kisses her eyes*]   There now! Don't spoil your
    pretty eyes.
  I'll soon be back.                                    *530*

ALCMENA   A long long "soon."

JUPITER [*tenderly*]   It's not as if I *liked* going off and
    leaving you.

ALCMENA [*dabbing her eyes*]   So I perceive:
  Leaving me the same
  Evening that you came.
      [*Clings to his arm*]

JUPITER [*gently disengaging himself*]   You must not try
    to hold me back.
  My time is up.
  I want to leave the town
  Before the light of dawn.
      [*On a sudden impulse, he opens the flap of his
      military great-cloak and takes out something
      which he unwraps*]
  For you, my dear—this cup:
  Given to me for bravery.
  King Pterelas once sipped from it,
  Whom my own right hand struck down.
  It's yours, Alcmena, now:
  A gift from me.

ALCMENA [*taking it delightedly*]   That's so like you, dear!
  What a gorgeous gift . . .
  From what a gorgeous giver!

MERCURY [*prompting* JUPITER *from behind*]

You say: "Not at all:
A gorgeous gift for a gorgeous girl."

JUPITER [*wheeling on him*]   Not you again!
Can't you get lost—
You sneaking little twerp?
        [*Raises his baton*]

ALCMENA [*catching his arm*]   Please, Amphitryon!
540   Don't be cross with Sosia because of me.

JUPITER [*still glowering at* MERCURY]   Anything you
please.

MERCURY [*to the audience, jerking a thumb at* JUPITER]
Love turns him, you see,
Into a monster of ferocity!

JUPITER   Anything else, my darling?

ALCMENA   Only that you love me while away:
I'll still be yours—
Though I am not there to say.
        [*A prolonged kiss*]

MERCURY [*interrupting*]   Let's be off, Amphitryon—
It's getting light.

JUPITER   Go on ahead then, Sosia;
I'll follow in a trice.
        [MERCURY *departs.* JUPITER *gives* ALCMENA *a
        last embrace*]
Anything you'd like?

ALCMENA   Y-yes,
Come back soon.

                [*She breaks away into the house*]

JUPITER [*calling to her*]   Of course!
Before you've even guessed.
Don't, darling, be depressed.
        [*He hears the door slam, and stands looking up
        into the fading stars*]

> And now good Night who waited for me,
> I send you off: give place to Morning.
> Let the daylight shine on mortals
> Bright and light,
> And since your stay
> Was longer than your last, sweet Night,
> I'll put back parity
> And make a shorter day.
> Let Morning follow Night
> As I'm away
> To follow after Mercury.                          *550*

> [JUPITER *waits till the dawn comes*
> *up with a rush; then—smiling—he*
> *disappears*]

# ACT II

*It is half an hour later and now broad daylight.* AMPHI-
TRYON—*dressed exactly like Jupiter but not sporting the
tassle from his hat—hurries eagerly toward his home, with*
SOSIA (*who is making the journey for the third time*) *lag-
ging behind. In the rear are porters carrying luggage, including a small conspicuous cabinet.*

AMPHITRYON    Get a move on, man: keep up with me.

SOSIA [*scrambling*]
    Right behind you, sir:
        as close as I can be.

AMPHITRYON [*turning around and glaring at him*]
    It's my opinion you're the damnedest liar.

SOSIA [*injured innocence*]
    Why, sir—whatever for?

AMPHITRYON    You tell me things that are not, were not,
    won't be—ever.

SOSIA [*reproachfully*]
    There, you see,

> that's you all over:
> Won't trust anyone around you . . .
> never.

AMPHITRYON [*warming up*]
> What's that? Watch it, mister!
>> By Hercules I swear
> I'll have that twisting tongue of yours
>> cut out of you, you twister.

SOSIA [*hurt but resolute*]
> Since I'm yours,
>> do whatever
> Suits your fancy
>> but you'll never
> Frighten me from saying exactly
>> what goes on here.

560

AMPHITRYON [*sarcastic and seething*]
> You damned vagabond!
>> Do you dare
> Tell me you're at home
>> while you're standing *there?*

SOSIA   It's a fact, sir.

AMPHITRYON   Fact be damned!
> The gods and I will see to that.

SOSIA [*shrugging, insolently*]
> I'm all yours—
>> it's in your hands, sir.

AMPHITRYON [*fuming*]
> What! you scum—
>> do you presume
> To make fun of me, your master?
>> Do you have the nerve
> To tell me what's impossible:
> Something no one's ever seen or done,
> That one man in two places can be one?

SOSIA [*shrugging*]

That's how things are:
   just as I assert.

AMPHITRYON [*feeling for his baton*]
   Be damned to you—by Jupiter!

SOSIA   But, Master, what have I done?
   Why should I be hurt?                              *570*

AMPHITRYON   Hypocrite!
   You have the gall to ask me that—
   And try to make a fool of me?

SOSIA [*earnestly*]
   You'd curse me rightly
      if I were.
   But what I'm telling you is true.
      That's the way things are.

AMPHITRYON [*throwing up his hands*]
   The man's drunk.
      That's what *I* think.

SOSIA [*glumly*]   I wish I were!

AMPHITRYON [*icily*]   You needn't wish: you are.

SOSIA   *Me*, sir?

AMPHITRYON   *You*, sir.
   Where did you get it from?

SOSIA   So help me—nowhere.
   Not a drop.

AMPHITRYON [*in despair*]
   What can one do with a chap like that?

SOSIA [*losing patience*]
   Haven't I told you ten times over
   I'm at home and I swear
   Next to you here:
   The very same Sosia?

Now do you hear me?
Now is it clear—
Am I putting it plainly?

AMPHITRYON [*a long pause.* AMPHITRYON *takes a step back*]
Get away from me.

580 SOSIA   Whatever for?

AMPHITRYON   You've got the plague.

SOSIA   What an idea!
I'm perfectly fine:
I really am as right as rain.
  Amphitryon!

AMPHITRYON [*swinging his baton*]
You won't feel quite so fine or well
If ever I make it home myself:
        You'll feel like hell.
            [*Starts to go, turns and surveys*
            SOSIA *with distaste as he stands
            there gaping*]
        Now do you mind coming along?
            Boss-baiter,
            Nonsense-maker,
            So completely gone
            That even after
    Neglecting orders of a master
    You can follow up with laughter
            Right in his face.
        Your yarn's impossible,
            Incredible
        And you're a disgrace.
        I'll soon make you learn
            You scum,
        How fast your lies return
        On your own bottom.

SOSIA [*shaking his head in sorrow*]
                Amphitryon,
            It's a sad sad thing
590         When a gentleman's man

> Speaks him all the truth he can
> And gets a flogging.

AMPHITRYON [*trying to apply sweet reason*]   Hell's bells!
  Work it out, man,
  Term by term:
Under what possible scheme
  Here and now
Can you be here and at home:
  Explain me that!

SOSIA [*with dogged innocence*]   But I *am*
  Here and now
Precisely here and there;
And I don't for the life of me care
Who thinks this exceedingly rare . . .
It's no more a wonder to me than to you, sir.

AMPHITRYON   What do you mean?

SOSIA   Just what I declare:
It's no more a wonder to me than to you . . .
So help me god, I couldn't believe
Myself at first—this Sosia here—
And then belief became crystal clear
Because of that Sosia over there.
He reeled off every item pat
That happened to us on the field of battle.
He went and stole my shape, my name:                     *600*
One drop of milk's not more the same
To all the rest than *I* to I am.
      [*Stops to think*]
You see, when you sent me on ahead this morning
From the harbor, home, at dawn, just a little
While ago. . .

AMPHITRYON   Get on with it, man!

SOSIA   Long before I reached the house
  There I was before I got there.

AMPHITRYON [*exploding*]   What the deuce! Are you sane?

SOSIA    As sane as I am standing here.

AMPHITRYON [*strokes his chin, muttering*]
    Ever since this fellow left me
    Something sinister has touched him.

SOSIA [*breaking out hysterically*]    Ha ha ha!
    Touched all right:
    Pounded to pieces!

AMPHITRYON    Who pounded you?

SOSIA [*still laughing hysterically*] Why, *I* did.
    The I who's now at home.

AMPHITRYON [*gripping him by the shoulders*]
    Hold on, man: Now just what I ask you.
    First: this Sosia—who *is* he?
    That's all I want to know.

SOSIA [*promptly*] Your own servant.

AMPHITRYON [*with a groan*]
    No no! Even one of you's too many.
610    And I swear since the day I was born
    That except for you I've never
    Had another servant Sosia.

SOSIA [*pulling himself together*]
    Well then, Amphitryon, I'll tell you this:
    When you get home you're going to find
    An extra Sosia—same as I'm.
    His Dad is Davus, same as mine,
    His age and shape with mine combine.
    What need of words? The point is nice:
    Your Sosia's twinned—you've got him twice.

AMPHITRYON [*nonplused*]
    Strange, very strange . . .
        But did you see my wife?

SOSIA    Your wife? Ha! I wasn't even let inside the house.

AMPHITRYON    Who stopped you?

SOSIA [*rubbing his bruises*]
  The same blame Sosia I told you of:
  The one who smashed me up.

AMPHITRYON [*roaring*]
  But who IS this Sosia?

SOSIA [*roaring back*]
  I AM I SAY.
  How many times do I have to tell you?

AMPHITRYON [*helplessly*]
  But what *are* you telling me?
        [*An idea occurs to him*]
  Say, have you been asleep?

SOSIA [*shocked*]
  Not on your life!                              *620*

AMPHITRYON [*diplomatically*]
  I mean, perhaps in sleep you might
  Have seen him—that other Sosia,
    In which case . . .

SOSIA [*drawing himself up*]
  I do *not* sleep on duty, sir.
        [*Punches out the words*]
  With eyes wide open, wide awake, I saw him,
  Wide awake I'm telling you now,
  And wide awake I got my pummeling . . .
    And *he* was wide awake.

AMPHITRYON    Who was?

SOSIA [*in despair*]
  The Sosia I told you of.
  Please, won't you understand?

AMPHITRYON [*weakly*]
  How the hell could anyone?
  You talk such tommyrot.

SOSIA [*ominously*]
      All right, you'll soon see what I mean
      When you meet that other Sosia.

AMPHITRYON    Very well! Come along with me.
      I'll look into this thing immediately.[15]
                  [*Moves off, with* SOSIA *following in the direction
                                                     of his house*]
      [*Further down the street, before* AMPHITRYON'S *house, the
      door opens and* ALCMENA *walks out disconsolately with her
                                                                maid*]


                           SONG[16]

*630*                      How little there remains of joy in
                           Life—its puny round of living—
                           Next to all the certain sorrow;
                           And how common

                           To our human lot that heaven
                           Settles it that sadness quickens
                           On the heels of laughter always.
                           Yes and after

                           Just a little touch of pleasure
                           Double pain and ill should follow.
                           This I'm learning close to home now
                           In my heart. Oh!

                           Just the briefest moment given,
                           Just a night to see my loved-one,
                           Then at break of day to have him
                           Gone so sudden.

                           How alone I feel I am now
*640*                      When the one I love excelling
                           All, has left me. Ah! More bitter
                           Is his going

15 Leo brackets the following verses (629–632)
AMP: See that they bring everything I've ordered from the ship.
SOS: Sir, I've taken care of everything.
You know I don't mix drink with duty.
AMP: Well, I just hope none of your delirium comes true.
16 The basic meter is trochaic: ́∪ ́∪ ́∪ ́∪  3 lines
                                ́∪ ́∪        4th line

Than I felt his joy in coming.
> [*She pauses to dab her eyes, then looks
> up, and her face brightens. The music
> changes*][17]

Oh but I am happy
At least that his struggle is over and he
Returns to his home all covered in glory.
This is my consolation.

I'll always let him go
If he always comes back to me here as a hero.
Oh yes—his going I'll undergo
Full of resolution

Through the thick and the thin
If my prize at the end is to hear of him win:
My husband a champion.
That is enough for me.

Oh valor's beyond compare:
Greater than anything—greater far.
Health, life, home and children are                   650
Safe (with freedom and country)
Where there is valor.

Valor comprises everything:
A valorous man has every blessing.
> [AMPHITRYON *and* SOSIA *come into sight*]

AMPHITRYON   She can hardly wait to have me home—I
bet you.
She loves me so and *I* love her . . .
And after things have gone so well:
The unbeatable enemy beaten, ha!
When no one thought they could be.
We did it, by Jove, we did it—
Under me of course—
In the very first encounter . . .
Oh I know it! She can hardly wait to have me home.

[17] The basic meter is anapaestic:
$$\acute{}\cup\acute{}\cup\acute{}\cup$$
$$\cup\acute{}\cup\cup\acute{}\cup\cup\acute{}\cup\cup\acute{}$$
$$\cup\acute{}\cup\cup\acute{}\cup\acute{}\cup\cup\acute{}\cup$$
$$\acute{}\cup\cup\acute{}\cup\acute{}\cup$$

SOSIA   And me?
There's another little lady who can hardly wait.

ALCMENA [*catching sight of them from a distance*]
Why, it's my husband.

AMPHITRYON   Come along, Sosia.

ALCMENA [*bewildered*]
660   What's he back for, after saying
he had to hurry off?
Testing me perhaps and trying
to see how much I miss him.
Bless him! *I* shan't object
to having him home again.

SOSIA [*sees* ALCMENA *and stops dead*]
Amphitryon, we'd better hurry
back to the ship.

AMPHITRYON   Whatever for?

SOSIA   No one's going
to give the home-returners breakfast.

AMPHITRYON   Now where did you get that notion from?

SOSIA   We've arrived too late.

AMPHITRYON   What?

SOSIA [*pointing*]
Alcmena's standing there outside
with a very well-filled look.

AMPHITRYON [*smiling all over*]
Oh, she was pregnant when I left her.

SOSIA [*making a face*]
That's the end!

AMPHITRYON   What's the matter?

SOSIA   *I* come home just in time
    to haul the water for the baby's bath.
    It's the ninth month—if your reckoning's right.     *670*

AMPHITRYON [*laughing*]
    Come on, cheer up!

SOSIA [*savagely*]
    Want to know how cheerful I feel?
    Just let me grab a bucket,
    Just let me get started,
    And if I don't squeeze the life out of that
        damned well—
    Never trust my word again.

AMPHITRYON [*still amused*]   All right! All right!
    I'll give the job to someone else, come on.

ALCMENA [*to herself, still trying to figure out his quick
    return*]
    Anyway, it would be more wifely, I suppose,
    If I went to meet him.
        [*She steps forward and* AMPHITRYON, *with play-
        ful gallantry, prepares to receive her into his
        arms*]

AMPHITRYON   Amphitryon greets his darling wife with
    joy:
    Unique in Thebes—or so her husband thinks—
    And virtuous too; as every Theban citizen will tell.
        [*Drops the pose*]
    How are you, darling? Glad to see me back?
        [ALCMENA *stares at him*]

SOSIA [*aside*]   Glad? I never saw anyone more so:
    Welcomes him like a stray mongrel.     *680*

AMPHITRYON   And to see you so filled out, my dear! It
    does me good . . .
    So beautifully filled out.

ALCMENA [*in dismay*]   For god's sake will you tell me

Why you are making fun of me
With all these greetings and salutations
As if you hadn't seen me just a little while ago,
As if you'd just this minute come home from the front!
Why are you talking as though you hadn't seen me
For a long long time?

AMPHITRYON [*thunderstruck*]   A long long time, my dear?
Heavens above! I've not clapped eyes on you
Until this instant.

ALCMENA [*coolly*]   Why deny it?

AMPHITRYON   I was taught to tell the truth.

ALCMENA   What a pity to forget it, then!
Or are you trying to pry?
Just what made you rush back here?
*690*   Did some omen hold you up? Or the weather?
A little while ago you couldn't wait to join your men.

AMPHITRYON [*mystified*]   A little while ago?
How little while ago was that?

ALCMENA [*sarcastically*]   Inquisitor! . . . A very little while
ago—just now.

AMPHITRYON   "A very little while ago—just now"?
What can you possibly mean by that?

ALCMENA [*frigidly*]   What do *you* think?
Can't I have my little game as well?—
Since you insist you've only just arrived
When you've already come and gone!

AMPHITRYON [*shaking his head*]   The poor thing's rambling.

SOSIA   Sh! Wait a little. Let her sleep it off.

AMPHITRYON   You mean she's dreaming—wide awake?

ALCMENA [*with vigor*]   *I'll* say I'm wide awake!

And I was wide awake not long ago—
Why, just at dawn—
When I saw that man and you.

AMPHITRYON [*promptly*]   And where was that?

ALCMENA   In this house: the house you live in.

AMPHITRYON [*fiercely*]   *That* you never did.

SOSIA [*with a cautionary hand on* AMPHITRYON]   Hold on,   *700*
   sir:
What if the ship sailed right into town from port
With us on board asleep?

AMPHITRYON [*exasperated*]   *You're* not siding with her,
   are you?

SOSIA [*in an earnest whisper*]   Well, don't you know:
These raving mænads when they're raving—
You mustn't cross them . . .
Or you'll make the crazy things still crazier
And get yourself torn in two.
Humor them and then they'll let you go
With just a single blow.

AMPHITRYON [*sharply*]   She's going to learn a thing or two
   from *me*
If you want to know:
Refusing to welcome me home decently!

SOSIA   You'll only stir up a nest of hornets, sir.

AMPHITRYON   Oh, shut up!
   [*Looks severely at* ALCMENA]
Alcmena, I wish to ask you something.

ALCMENA [*with placid disregard*]   Anything you like.

AMPHITRYON [*sternly*]   What's come over you, my dear?
Is this a silly prank—or are you serious?

ALCMENA [*wincing*]   My own dear husband.

What can have entered your head
710    To make you ask me such a question?

AMPHITRYON [*self-pityingly*]    Because before you always
   used to welcome me,
Like an honest wife, pleased to see her husband.
Now I come back home and find
A very different frame of mind.

ALCMENA    Good gracious me!
When you arrived here yesterday
I welcomed you the moment you appeared.
I asked you immediately
How you were, my dear,
And seized your hand and kissed you.

SOSIA [*impudently*]    So, yesterday you welcomed him, eh?

ALCMENA    Yes, and you too, Sosia.

SOSIA [*to* AMPHITRYON, *shaking his head*]    Amphitryon,
I had hopes that she would bear you a son,
But she's not *with child*.

AMPHITRYON    With what, then?

SOSIA [*flapping his hands over his ears*]    March hares!

ALCMENA [*outraged*]    March hares, indeed! My health is
   fine.
720    And if heaven hears my prayers, I'll bear a son.
      [*Turns on* SOSIA]
   As for you, sir, you crooked crystal gazer,
   If my husband does his duty
   You'll be beaten to a jelly . . .
   Just what you deserve.

SOSIA [*at first cheekily, then—catching the look in*
   ALCMENA's *eyes—tapering off into respect*]
   On the contrary, madam, in your condition
   You're the one who's going to feel beaten to a jelly[18] . . .
   18 The pun in the Latin is on *malum*: "evil," and an "apple."

I mean something—er, er—eaten like a jelly,
Or a raw apple,
Is what you need to stop you feeling seedy.

AMPHITRYON [*impatiently*]   So yesterday you saw me here?

ALCMENA [*with a sigh*]   Yes—for the tenth time.

AMPHITRYON   In a dream, perhaps?

ALCMENA   Not at all. I was wide awake. And so were you.

AMPHITRYON   Heaven help us!

SOSIA   What's the matter?

AMPHITRYON   My wife's gone mad.

SOSIA [*helpfully*]   Just the liver acting up, sir.
It always sets them going.

AMPHITRYON [*ignoring him*]   Dammit, woman, when did
you first feel it coming on?

ALCMENA   Oh, what's the use? I'm perfectly sane and
sound.

AMPHITRYON   Then why do you keep on saying you saw   730
me yesterday?
We only disembarked last night?
I had my dinner on board
And that's where I spent the rest of it.
I haven't set foot in this goddam house
Since I left for the war with my army—
And beat the Teleboians.

ALCMENA [*flabbergasted*]   The idea! You had dinner with
*me* and slept with *me*.

AMPHITRYON [*eyes popping*]   What—did—you—say?

ALCMENA   The simple truth.

AMPHITRYON [*bitterly*]   Far from it, if it's the only thing
   I know.

ALCMENA [*unruffled*]   At the first chink of day,
   You went off to join your men.

AMPHITRYON [*hopelessly*]   How on earth? . . .

SOSIA [*helpfully*]
   She's only trying to remember it right, sir,
   And recall her dream . . .
            [*Waggles a finger at* ALCMENA]
   Madam, the moment you woke up this morning
   You ought to have taken a present of salt and incense
740   To Jupiter god of jinxes and said a prayer to him.

ALCMENA [*seething*]   Be hanged to you!

SOSIA   And to you, madam. It would do you good . . .
      [*Quails again before her look*]
   To go and look into it.

ALCMENA [*smoldering, to* AMPHITRYON]
   That's the second time he's been impertinent
   And you let him get away with it.

AMPHITRYON   Quiet, Sosia . . . So, Alcmena,
   I said goodbye to you this morning
   At the first chink of day, did I?

ALCMENA [*tossing her head*]   Well, if it wasn't you two,
   Who gave me all the front-line news?

AMPHITRYON [*ominously*]   Don't tell me you know that too?

ALCMENA   Naturally I do. I got it straight from you:
   How you stormed the mighty town
   And with your own hands
   Struck King Pterelas down.

AMPHITRYON [*reeling*]   *I* told you that?

ALCMENA   You did. With Sosia here standing by.

AMPHITRYON [*wheels on* SOSIA]   Did *you* hear me say such
things this morning?

SOSIA [*playing for time*]   Now where could I have done
that?

AMPHITRYON   Ask *her,* not me.

SOSIA [*shuffling*]   To my knowledge, I wasn't present at
any such event.

ALCMENA [*with an icy smile*]   Strange how he avoids con-
tradicting you!

AMPHITRYON [*sternly*]   Sosia, come here and look me in
the eye.                                                                  750

SOSIA [*blinking*]   I'm looking, sir.

AMPHITRYON   Now I want the truth,
Nothing but the truth—no shilly-shallying.
Did you ever hear me speak a single syllable
Of this rigmarole of hers?

SOSIA   For god's sake—are you crazy too?
Asking me a thing like that!
Aren't I seeing her for the first time—
Same as you?

AMPHITRYON [*triumphantly*]   How's that, m'lady? Do you
hear him?

ALCMENA [*shrugging*]   I do indeed—telling lies.

AMPHITRYON [*throwing up his hands*]   What, you won't
believe him or even me—
Your own husband!

ALCMENA   Only because I believe myself more than anyone,
And I know the facts: they're as I say.

AMPHITRYON [*sarcastically*]   According to which I arrived
here yesterday!

ALCMENA    And left—do you deny it?—today.

AMPHITRYON [*roaring*]   Of course I deny it.
I am arriving home to you
For the very first time now.

ALCMENA [*with chilling assurance*]   And perhaps you'll
    also deny—do tell me—
That this morning
760   You presented me with a golden cup:
One you said they gave you at the front.

AMPHITRYON [*exploding*]   Hell and damnation!
I never presented nor pronounced
Any such thing . . .
        [*Doing a double take*]
Hey, but I *did* think of giving it to you—
And still do—
Who the deuce could have told you?

ALCMENA [*coolly*]   I got it straight from you—
Just as I got the cup.

AMPHITRYON [*dithering*]   Wait, now—please!
        [*Whispers in consternation to* SOSIA]
Sosia, I can't make out how the devil she knows
Of my getting hold of that gold cup.
Unless of course you came and met her
And told her everything much earlier.

SOSIA [*shocked*]   Good heavens, no, sir!
I never told her a thing:
Never saw her till this moment,
Now, with *you*.

AMPHITRYON [*in despair*]   What am I dealing with?

ALCMENA   Would you like to see the cup?

AMPHITRYON [*weakly*]   I would.

ALCMENA   Certainly.
        [*Claps her hands*]

Oh, Thessala,
Go and bring out the drinking cup my husband
Presented me this morning.                            *770*

AMPHITRYON [*between his teeth to* SOSIA]  Sosia, come
over here.
          [*They go into a huddle*]
It'll be the most fantastic thing in this whole fantasy
If she turns out to have that cup.

SOSIA
Now you wouldn't fall for that, sir, would you—
Seeing I've got it here in this little chest—
          [*Pats a small roped box*]
All nicely sealed up with your own seal?

AMPHITRYON   Is the seal intact?

SOSIA [*holding up the cabinet*]
Look for yourself.

AMPHITRYON [*examines it and breathes a sigh of relief*]
Fine! Exactly as I left it sealed.

SOSIA [*relaxing*]   Sir, what I'd like to know is:
Why don't you have her certified?

AMPHITRYON [*mournfully*]   I damn well should.
She's damn well possessed.

          [THESSALA *walks in exhibiting the cup*]

ALCMENA [*waving her hand toward it with a triumphant
smile*]
Any explanations needed?
Your drinking cup—see?

AMPHITRYON [*reaching out his hand as in a dream*]
Give it to me.

ALCMENA   Go right ahead!
Take a good look at it—
See if you can contradict a fact—
You flagrant contradictor!

I'm going to show you up.
Is this the thing they gave you there or not:
This cup?

AMPHITRYON [*taking it with a shaky hand*]
780    God almighty—what am I gazing at?
It's the cup, the crazy cup!
Sosia, I'm all washed up.

SOSIA [*gulping*]
Hell, either she's the world's champion witch
Or it's still in there—your cup.
      [*Pats the box again*]

AMPHITRYON [*fumbling with impatience*]
Quick, man: unlock the box.

SOSIA [*apprehensive*]    Unlock the box? Why bother?
It's sealed all right;
Everything's as right as rain:
You've produced an Amphitryon,
I've produced an extra Sosia,
And now if the cup's produced a cup—
We've all reproduced ourselves again.

AMPHITRYON    Well, we've got to open up and see.

SOSIA    Then see the seal for yourself, sir:
I don't want you afterwards blaming *me*.

AMPHITRYON [*trembling with impatience*]
Oh, go on—just open it.
She's out to make us gibbering idiots.

ALCMENA [*acidly*]    Really!
790    Then where's this little present from
If not from you?

AMPHITRYON [*snorting*]
That's exactly what I mean to discover.

SOSIA [*bursts open the lid*]
Jupiter, great Jupiter!

AMPHITRYON [*leans over*]   What?

SOSIA [*standing back*]
   There's no cup at all in this box.

AMPHITRYON [*going pale*]   What am I hearing?

SOSIA   The facts.

AMPHITRYON [*grabbing him*]
   Facts that'll string you up
   If there's still no sign of that cup.

ALCMENA [*taking the cup and waving it under* AMPHI-
   TRYON's *nose*]
   There's signs of this one at any rate.

AMPHITRYON [*savagely*]   Who gave it to you?

ALCMENA   The man who's asking.

SOSIA [*slapping his forehead and turning on* AMPHITRYON]
   Why, *you!* You're trying to catch me out.
   You ran on ahead yourself:
   Sneaked in from the ship another way,
   Took out the cup yourself and gave it her;
   Then sealed up the box again . . . you sneak!

AMPHITRYON [*surveying* SOSIA *with disgust*]
   That does it!
   Even *you*—abetting her delusions . . .
        [*With a deep sigh, turns wearily to* ALCMENA]
   So we arrived here, did we, yesterday?

ALCMENA   Yes,
   And as we arrived you greeted me
   And I gave you a kiss.                                    800

SOSIA [*to the audience*]   To my way of thinking,
   The rot set in with that kiss!

AMPHITRYON   Go on, go on.

ALCMENA   You took a bath.

AMPHITRYON   Yes, and after my bath?

ALCMENA   You sat down to dinner.[19]

SOSIA   Magnificent! Now we're getting somewhere.

AMPHITRYON   Stop interrupting . . . Go on with your story.

ALCMENA   Dinner was served, you had it with me—
   Right along beside me . . .

AMPHITRYON [*suspiciously*]   On the same couch?

ALCMENA   The very same.

SOSIA   Ai, ai! This little junket looks bad.

AMPHITRYON [*irritably to* SOSIA]
   Just let her get on with her case . . .
   What happened after dinner?

ALCMENA   You said you were sleepy.
   The table was cleared.
   We went off to bed.

AMPHITRYON [*still more suspicious*]   Where did you sleep?

ALCMENA   In the same bed as you, of course—
   In our bedroom.

AMPHITRYON [*rocking his head in his hands*]
   Oh my god! That's the end!

SOSIA   What's the matter?

AMPHITRYON   She's as good as killed me.

ALCMENA [*concerned*]   Darling, what is it?

19 The Latin, naturally, is *accubuisti*: "you reclined" (to dinner).

AMPHITRYON [*turning away*]    Don't you speak to me.

SOSIA    But what is it, sir?

AMPHITRYON [*sobbing it out*]    I'm finished.                *810*
    She adds adultery to all the rest
    While I'm away.

ALCMENA [*really shocked*]    But darling, heavens above,
        you my husband—
    How can you say such a thing?

AMPHITRYON [*with chilling sarcasm*]    Your husband, eh?
        Fake wife!
    None of your fake names for me.

SOSIA [*naïvely*]    It's a mess, isn't it, if he's lost his husband-
        hood!

ALCMENA [*deeply hurt*]    What have I done to be talked
        to like that?

AMPHITRYON [*thundering*]    What have you *done?* You
        blurt out your crime and ask *me!*

ALCMENA [*pitifully*]    But what crime have I committed—
        being with you,
    The man I married?

AMPHITRYON [*shouting at the top of his voice*]    So it was
        with *me,* was it?
    Of all the brazen shamelessness!
    You might at least pretend to have some decency.

ALCMENA [*with wounded dignity*]    What you've accused
        me of . . .
    In my family, we do not do such things.                *820*
    If you think you'll catch me in adultery,
    You never never will.

AMPHITRYON [*snorting*]    Well, by all the immortal gods!
        [*Turns to* SOSIA]
    *You* know me, anyway, don't you, Sosia?

SOSIA [*surveying him dubiously*]    Hm! . . . On the whole.

AMPHITRYON [*pressing onward*]    I dined on board yester-
    day, didn't I,
In the port of Persicus?

ALCMENA [*coldly*]    *I've* got witnesses as well to back me
    up.

SOSIA [*looking at both of them, nonplused*]    This whole
    affair, sir, has me beaten . . .
Unless of course there is another
Amphitryon who when you're gone,
Fills in completely for you—does your job.
That so-called Sosia was a shocker,
But this Amphitryon the second
Is a knockout.

AMPHITRYON [*helplessly*]    It's impossible to say what
    spell's
830    Been cast over the unhappy woman.

ALCMENA [*solemnly stretching up her hands*]
          By the King of Kings of heaven
            And Juno queen of every home,
          Whom I worship and have given
            All the reverence that I own,
          I swear that next to you no other
          Human being has touched me ever,
            To smirch my honor.

AMPHITRYON [*woefully shaking his head*]
I wish it were true.

ALCMENA [*bitterly*]
    It *is* the truth
       but truth is useless
Since you won't
       believe me now.

AMPHITRYON [*acidly*]
You're a woman: you perjure easily.

ALCMENA [*with sorrowful dignity*]
     A woman's conscience, yes, is easy
     When she's done no wrong at all:
     With right she speaks up bold and freely
        For her own soul.

AMPHITRYON [*sneering*]
     "Bold and freely"—I should say so!

ALCMENA   As honor should.

AMPHITRYON   Honor? Pooh! That's *your* description.

ALCMENA [*solemnly*]
     Sir, I do not look upon a dowry
       As others do, it is for me:
     Honor, self-control and purity      *840*
       And fear of god and love
     Of parents, peace within the family,
       Serving you and out to serve
        Those who so deserve.

SOSIA   My word! She's a perfect paragon
   If what she says is true.

AMPHITRYON [*hopelessly*]   Hell! I'm so confused
   I hardly know my own soul.

SOSIA [*taking over*]   Hell! You do—sir: you're Amphi-
    tryon.
   Don't go and lose the use of *that*:
   People are getting so changed around
   Ever since we came back from abroad!

AMPHITRYON [*sternly but wearily*]   Rest assured, Alcmena,
   I shall proceed with this inquiry.

ALCMENA   By all means do. I welcome it.

AMPHITRYON   Do you really?
     Then what do you say if I fetch your cousin
       Naucrates from the ship?

He and I shared a cabin . . .
*850*      If he denies my partnership
In all you say, what do you think
Would be the fairest thing to do?
Can you give a reason why
I should shrink
From divorce—
To punish you?

ALCMENA

None, of course:
If I've made a slip.

AMPHITRYON

Then that's agreed.
Sosia, show the porters in.
I'll go and fetch Naucrates from the ship.

[AMPHITRYON, *with a hangdog look, disappears down the street.* SOSIA *directs the
slaves with the baggage into the house,
is about to follow them, sees* ALCMENA
*and sidles up to her*]

SOSIA

Look, now that nobody's here but us,
Tell me seriously:
Is there really
Another Sosia inside like me?

ALCMENA [*who has been provoked beyond tears*]
Oh, get out of my sight—toad!
Perfect double of your master.

SOSIA [*in cheeky sullenness*]
If that's an order:
Certainly—*ma'am*!
[*Walks jauntily into the house*]

ALCMENA [*sadly to the audience*]
It's a scandal, it's fantastic,
Leveled at me from the blue:
Fabricated, false and drastic—

And by my husband too.
Well, whatever it is, I hope my cousin,
Naucrates, has the clue.                                    *860*
                    [*She goes forlornly into the house*]


# ACT III

*Some time later:* JUPITER *enters, looking pleased with himself. He bows to the audience.*

JUPITER  I'm the Amphitryon with the servant Sosia—
The Sosia who changes into Mercury
When it's found to fit.
I live [*waves his hand airily upward*]  in the supernal
    attic,
And turn into Jupiter when I feel like it.
Whenever I direct my passage here however,
I become Amphitryon
And change my outfit in a trice.
Now I'm here to serve your pleasure:
Clinch this comedy and simultaneously
Help Alcmena out—the guileless thing,                       *870*
Charged by Amphitryon with infidelity.
After all, it wouldn't be exactly nice
To let poor Alcmena in
For something that was all my doing.
So for the moment, I make myself Amphitryon,
As I did before . . . Today I mean
To drive this family round the bend.
Of course I'll clear the whole mess up—
In the end,
And come to Alcmena's rescue just in time,
Arranging for a double lying-in
(With a single pangless breach)
Of her husband's brat and mine.
And, in case I need him,
Mercury has orders to be in reach.                          *880*

    [*Directs his gaze to the door of the house, from*

which ALCMENA, *attended by a maid, exits*
*carrying a packed bag. She looks miserable*]

ALCMENA    No, I can't stay in this house:
  Not after being called immoral—
  A wanton adulterous woman, oh!
  By my husband too,
  Who bawls out denial of the simple facts
  Then insists on fictions which I simply don't admit;
  And thinks I'll take it all in my stride.
  Well, I won't.
  I won't put up with such a filthy libel.
  Either he says he's sorry, or I leave him;
  Yes, swears he's sorry for the horrid things
890  He's hurled at me and which I don't deserve.

JUPITER [*dryly to the audience*]
  Hm! I'll have to make events
  Go the way she wants them,
  If I'm to bring this delightful paramour of mine
  Back to—er—[*grinning*] my senses . . .
  Yes, my conduct's got Amphitryon in a mess
  And my little late flirtatious exploit
  Embroiled the innocent, and now
  I'm the innocent myself and have to face
  The rumpus and the dressing down she got from *him*.

ALCMENA [*seeing him*]    Ah, there's the man who made his
      poor wife miserable
  With an outrageous libel.

JUPITER [*approaches her with his arms out*]    My dear—
      my wife—I want you—I want to talk to you . . .
        [ALCMENA *turns on her heel*]
  Why are you turning your back on me?

ALCMENA [*in cold fury*]    It's my nature.
900  I can't stand the sight of enemies.

JUPITER    Come, my dear—enemies?

ALCMENA    I mean exactly *that*. It's true.
  Unless you turn this truth too into a lie.

JUPITER [*putting an arm around her*]   You're much too
   angry, darling.

ALCMENA [*facing him, eyes flashing*]   Keep your hands off
   me—if you can.
   I should have thought
   That if you had a particle of sanity or sense
   You would not bandy words, in joke or earnest,
   With a woman you consider and assert is loose—
   Unless you're ten times sillier than a silly goose.

JUPITER [*soothingly*]   Well, even if I *said* it, that doesn't
   make it so,
   And I don't consider you *are* anyway.
   No, I've come back to apologize
   For I never felt so sick at heart                        *910*
   As when I heard you were in a rage with me.
   "Then why did you say it?" you'll ask.
   I'll tell you why:
   It wasn't that I thought you loose—
   No, not for one moment,
   I was only trying to test your feelings:
   See what you'd do, how you'd take it.
         [*Forces a laugh*]
   Really it was all a joke—what I said just now—
   A bit of fun. Ask Sosia.

ALCMENA [*unimpressed*]   Then why not go ahead and
   fetch Naucrates—
   To prove—ha ha!—you've never been here?

JUPITER   If something's said in joke, my dear,                *920*
   It isn't fair to take it seriously.

ALCMENA [*bitterly*]   I know one thing: that joke cut me
   to the quick.

JUPITER [*pressing a kiss on her hand*]   Alcmena, by this
   own right hand of yours,
   I beg you, I implore you, let me be forgiven,
   Pardon me. Don't be angry with me.

ALCMENA [*snatching away her hand*]   My good character
   makes nonsense of your charges,

And seeing I kept clear of all misconduct
Allow me to keep clear of misconducted talk.
Goodbye.
You keep your things. Give me back mine.
And now will you tell my escort to follow me?
    *[Turns to go]*

JUPITER  Are you sane?

ALCMENA   Tell them or not—I'm off.
930    My own honor will escort me.

JUPITER *[on his knees]*  Wait. I'll swear it any way you
    want:
That I'm convinced I have a virtuous wife.
And if I've told a lie
I ask you, great Jupiter,
    *[Winks at the audience]*
To curse Amphitryon forever.

ALCMENA *[crying out in spite of herself]*  Oh no: bless
    him, bless him!

JUPITER *[rises and takes her hand]*  I think he will:
I've just sworn a very solid oath . . .
You're not angry still?

ALCMENA *[unable to hide her feelings]*  Not any more.

JUPITER  That's a good girl!
    *[Takes her in his arms]*
Ah! how common in the human round
For us to meet with pleasure then with pain:
940    Tempers flare up between, then grace comes back again.
And should a quarrel of this sort occur
And should it be by grace smoothed out once more,
We are closer to each other then
Than we ever were before.

ALCMENA *[with a reproachful smile]*  You never should
    have made such charges from the start,
But since you've now apologized in full,
I'll take it in good part.
    *[After a long embrace they separate, smiling]*

JUPITER [*as if remembering*]   Oh, have the ritual vessels
     laid out for me.
   While I was at the wars I made a vow
   To thank the gods for a safe return—
   I mean to fulfill it now.

ALCMENA   I shall see to it
          [*She claps her hands, summoning* BROMIA *and*
          THESSALA]

JUPITER   And call Sosia here:
   He's to go and fetch Blepharo the captain of my ship to
     lunch . . .                                                950

              [*The two maids,* BROMIA *and* THESSALA, *ap-
              pear.* ALCMENA *whispers to them and they
              reenter the house.*]

JUPITER [*smiles at the audience*]   In point of fact, he's
   going to get no lunch at all, poor mutt.
   He'll see Amphitryon hauled away from here, to boot,
   By me—and by the scruff.

ALCMENA [*with a bemused smile*]   I wonder what he's doing talking to himself? . . .
   Ah, there goes the door. It's Sosia coming out.
          [SOSIA *presents himself with military alacrity*]

SOSIA   Amphitryon, sir—all present and correct.
   Give the order and the order's done.

JUPITER   Sosia, you're in perfect time.

SOSIA [*surveying them*]
          So there's peace at last between you two?
          What a joy it is, what pleasure
          To see you two relaxed together!
             And I've always thought
             A decent servant ought
             To take his cue
             From what his betters do,
             Match face for face:                             960
             Somber when they're sad,
             Hilarious when they're glad . . .

Do tell me, sir,
Are you two happier?

JUPITER [*sharply*]    Don't be silly!
You know very well it was all a joke.

SOSIA [*gaping*]    All a joke—huh? I thought it was in dead
earnest.

JUPITER [*impatiently*]    Everything's explained. Peace is
made.

SOSIA [*beaming*]    That's grand, sir.

JUPITER    I'm going inside to carry out those holy vows
of mine.

SOSIA    A good thought, sir.

JUPITER    Go and convey to Captain Blepharo
My personal invitation
To come here from the ship
For an after-service luncheon.

SOSIA [*dashing into the wings*]    I'll be back before you
even think I'm there.

JUPITER    Just hurry back.

ALCMENA    You don't still want me, do you, dear?
970    I'll go in now and see what must be done.

JUPITER [*amorously*]    Yes, yes—get things ready
As quickly as you can.

ALCMENA [*blowing him a kiss as she goes*]    Come, the
moment you want, inside.
I'll see to it you won't be held up long.[20]

20 At the risk of appearing crude and even prurient I use these two
sentences to show what a rich quarry Plautus probably is to anyone
wishing to analyze his sexual implications. Is there any justification
in the Latin for the rather raw double-entendre which I make pos-

JUPITER   My perfect little wife! Just what I like to hear.

[ALCMENA *goes into the house*]

JUPITER [*turns to the audience, chuckling*]
        So I've fooled them both—
            servant and lady—
                fooled the pair.
        They take me for Amphitryon,
            what an error!
        [*Beckons into the sky*]
        Hi there! My divine one!
        Immortal Sosia!

sible in my rendering of his: *Quin venis quando vis intro? Faxo haud quicquam sit morae.* (line 972)? I believe that there is. Even on a priori grounds it would be as unusual for Plautus to miss an opportunity—given the nature of the plays and the rough-and-tumble audience he was trying to please—as it would for any scholar not to miss the surely innumerable instances when we don't know enough about the colloquial connotations of his words to spot the punning. There were several legitimate words for the sex act but we can only guess at what the slang expressions were. I use these two sentences to suggest that Plautus's plays were possibly (and probably) stuffed with them. Here, the very strong emphasis put on *intro* (inside) by its position should warn us. Add to that the word *venis* (come), which is almost a perfect homonym for *venus* (love, carnal activity), and I believe the suspicion of a salacious ambivalence is well-founded. It is not necessary and not possible to prove that "come" has the same slang connotation in both Latin and English.

As to the second sentence: *Faxo haud quicquam sit morae:* (I shall arrange it so that there is scarcely the slightest delay), my fairly direct translation of the Latin does not also directly translate the supposed innuendo. Such a coincidence of denotation, connotation and association between two languages is rarely achieved without strain. But it gets at it another way. Here are some of the known associations (purely sonic and apart from the obvious) of the words Plautus uses:

*fax* - a torch, a link, a fireball, the flame of love.
*mora* - an obstacle, obstruction.
*morum* - a mulberry (even more Freudian than *fax*).
*moris* - (genitive of *mos*) set behavior, work-to-rule.
*morus* - a fool.

There are also more remote erotic echoes hidden in the root *mor-:*
*mordeo* - to bite, penetrate into, waste, devour.
*mordus* - biting.
*mors* - death, dying.

I submit that even if Plautus was not aiming at a double meaning, he has achieved it—at least to the subconscious ear of the Latins.

           Appear.
       Oh yes, you hear me—
           Though you are not near me:
       Keep Amphitryon away
           the moment he comes here—
       And by any strategy you care.
       Amuse yourself with him
           while I am having fun
       With this wife of his
*980*            Which I have on loan . . .
       You know exactly what I mean.
           See that it is done . . .
       Oh, and *you* can be M.C.
           while I sacrifice to *me*.

       [JUPITER *goes eagerly into the house.* MER-
       CURY *enters at breakneck speed, sweeping all
                                    before him*]

MERCURY
       Hey, get out of my way,
           get out, get off the street!
       Don't any of you have the nerve
           to get in the way of my feet!
           [*Stops and looks at the audience*]
       Well, dammit, doesn't a god like me
       Have every bit as much to say
       When people get in his way
       As a twopenny-halfpenny slave
       In any comedy,
       Who thunders his abuse
       Just to say the ship is safe
           Or the cross old man is there? . . .
       And *I'm* doing the word of Zeus.
       In fact right now I'm here
       To obey,
*990*        So get out—get out—get out—out of my way.
           [*Runs a little farther and stops*]
       My father's calling—
           I'm coming:
       I listen to his mighty whim;
       Like a perfect father's son
           am *I* the son to him.

In love affairs I back him
   from behind, stand by
To cheer him on, give sound advice
   and cry:
Well done!
Whatever my father thinks is good
   becomes for me the best.
He's full of love . . . so wise and right
   to do it with such zest.
      [*Turns and grins at the audience*]
As every man should—
If it brings him any particle of good.
      [*Cuts a little caper, then resumes with a let's-get-
      down-to-business air*]
He wants Amphitryon—does Dad—
   made a fool of now.
I'm in the mood, spectators,
   just you witness how
I'll fool him good
   under your very noses:
Pretend I'm stewed,
   my head done up in posies.
      [*Jerking a thumb at* AMPHITRYON's *house*]
Yes, I'll climb upon that roof
   and gloriously from there
Fling back our man                *1000*
   the moment he comes near.
I'll make him soused though sober,
   and then that slave of his
Will bear the brunt, that Sosia,
   and be accused of this.
What does it matter to me?
I've got to humor my dad
   and keep him happy.
      [*Alertly gazing down the street*]
But here's Amphitryon coming:
   Now to see the fun.
If you'll take the trouble to watch
   you'll see how it is done.
So I'll run inside
   and decorate myself
      like a plastered sot,

Then go up on the roof
and buzz him from this spot.

[MERCURY *bustles inside.* AMPHITRYON *with a
dismal face plods wearily toward the front
door*]

AMPHITRYON

That damned Naucrates that I wanted
simply wasn't on the ship.
I couldn't find a single person
*1010*          who'd even seen him at his home,
Or in the city, though I've plodded
through the plazas, gyms and drugstores,
At the market, at the butcher's,
in the playing-fields and the forum,
At the doctor's, at the barber's,
in the churches—I'm exhausted
Searching for him. Oh, Naucrates,
you're impossible to find!
I'll go inside and press my wife for
further details on this case.
Who was the man to whom she made an
adulterous present of her body?
I'd sooner die than give up getting
to the bottom of this bloody
[*Tries the front door*]
Business . . . Well, I'm damned, it's bolted!
How absolutely ducky!
Fits the rest of it quite nicely!
[*Begins to pound on the door*]
I'll bang away. Open up there!
Ahoy! Anyone at home?
Isn't anyone—confound it!—
*1020*          going to open up this door?

[MERCURY *appears on the roof. He has a
wreath on his head and stares down, tottering
and grinning*]

MERCURY   Who'sh on the doorstep?

AMPHITRYON [*snorting*]   I am.

MERCURY   Whash yer mean: "Iam"?

AMPHITRYON [*pounding and shouting*]   Just—what—I—
said.

MERCURY [*shaking an empty bottle at him*]   My, my!
Jupiter's not going to like you—and all those gods in
heaven—that's for sure: breaking down doors!

AMPHITRYON [*unable to believe his ears*]   What! . . . What
are you getting at?

MERCURY   It's what *you're* getting at: a life of hell.

AMPHITRYON [*with sudden recognition*]   Sosia!

MERCURY [*truculently*]   Yes—Sosia. D'yer 'spect me to
forget it? Now what d'yer want?

AMPHITRYON [*exploding*]   You criminal! What do I want?
. . . Actually ask me that? What do I want?

MERCURY   I'm asking *you*. You've practically drummed
that door off its hinges, dunderhead! . . . Think the state
hands out free doors? Take that silly look off your face,
stupid. What d'you want, anyway? Who are you?

AMPHITRYON [*spluttering with rage*]   You, you sod! Dare
ask me that? Who am I? You cat-o-death-tails! I'll scorch
the bottom off you for that.

MERCURY [*shaking his head regretfully*]   You must have
burnt your candles at both ends as a young man.

AMPHITRYON   What the devil?

MERCURY   Because now you're begging me to trim you—
you old drip . . . Ha ha ha!

AMPHITRYON [*shaking his fists up at the roof*]   Soon you'll
be punning on a stake—you palavering piece of mincemeat!

MERCURY [*lifting a bucket of water piously to heaven*]   I'll
remember you in my prayers.

AMPHITRYON [*looking up*]    What's that?

MERCURY    Here's a libation . . .
*1034*21    To your very good damnation!21

AMPHITRYON    God rot you!

MERCURY    Jupiter bless you—
  With overflowing . . .
        [*Just as* MERCURY *is about to unload his bucket,*
        AMPHITRYON *moves away*]

AMPHITRYON [*brandishing his baton*]
  I've got a sacrifice for you too:                             ‡
  Torture, ruffian . . . then stringing-up.                     ‡

MERCURY    Look, Mister—er—Scum,
  I don't know who you are
  And I don't for the life of me care,
  But if you think this'll get you a free meal,
  You'd better get a new idea—Bum!

AMPHITRYON [*prancing up and down with fury*]    Free
      meal! . . . Bum! Come down off that roof.
  Just let me lay my hands on you—
  You'll soon see who I am.

MERCURY [*coolly*]    That's what I fear.
  I'd rather see from here.

AMPHITRYON    God in heaven! . . . What a disgrace!

MERCURY    Keep still, man:
  I can't make out your face.

---

21 Here there is a gap in the manuscripts—all based on one lost
source—of between two and three hundred lines. About twenty of
these have been rescued, gleaned from ancient commentators and
grammarians, and in the following eleven pages I have written them
into what I hope is a workable substitution for the missing scene.
Plautus's own text resumes on page 98 with line 1035. I have put a
cross against the lines in my invention which belong to the extant
twenty.

AMPHITRYON [*stops for a moment, but at the wrong end for*
     MERCURY's *bucket*]   I am Amphitryon:
   Your owner and commander
   Of the Theban army.

MERCURY [*rests his bucket*]   Fancy that, now!
   That's why you come banging down good people's doors
   In the middle of the morning.

AMPHITRYON   But I *am* Amphitryon;
   Conqueror of the Teleboian might.
   The very same who with a single swing
   Cut down Pterelas their king.
   And I'll prove it too.

MERCURY   I should just think so!
   Look at you—what a sight!
   Why, you couldn't swat a fly:
   You bedraggled, panting, bleary old goat . . .
   Besides, the clothes you've stolen are too big for you.

AMPHITRYON [*almost inarticulate*]   You drunken monkey!
   *I'll* teach you who I am.
   I'll teach you how to recognize your master.

MERCURY   The nerve!
   Putting on the airs and costume of a real field-marshal!
   Off with you, impostor!
   The true Amphitryon's my master.
          [*Picks up his bucket again*]

AMPHITRYON   Is he really now?
   Well, will you kindly tell your master
   That he has a great admirer
   Who would like to have a word with him.

MERCURY   Admirer? You're not the kind that he would
     fancy.
   Anyway, Master's busy‡ . . . Write a letter.

AMPHITRYON [*breaks out again*]   O-oh! Just let me get
     hold of you:
   I'll—I'll break a pot of redhot ashes on your head.                    ‡

MERCURY [*poising his bucket*]    Thanks, but I think I'll stay
  up here instead.

AMPHITRYON [*shouting*]    I'll have you whipped:
  Whipped into a sunset—flaming red.

MERCURY    I'm a gentleman's man.
  I think you'd better go, while you can.                                ‡

AMPHITRYON    By Jupiter! I'll tear you down from there.
  [*Begins pounding at the door immediately beneath*
  MERCURY]

MERCURY    By Jupiter—
  Look up a little, will you? . . .
  What you need to cool you down                                         ‡
  Is a pail of water.

> [*As* AMPHITRYON *looks up the full load of* MER-
> CURY's *bucket descends upon him.* MERCURY,
> *hooting with laughter, disappears from the roof,
> leaving* AMPHITRYON *dripping and spluttering on
> the doorstep. At this moment* ALCMENA *emerges*]

ALCMENA    Well I never!
  What's my husband up to now?
  He said he was going to sacrifice to Zeus:
  Must have been to the rain-god Pluvius.

AMPHITRYON [*with unrestrained anger and sarcasm*]    Ah,
    you m'lady, standing there,
  I know it's no concern of yours
  What your miserable ex-husband has to suffer,
  But for old times' sake at least
  You might offer
  To get him something dry to wear.

ALCMENA [*stunned*]    "Miserable ex-husband"! What do
    you mean?
  It matters very much.
  Hardly half-an-hour ago we were together,
  And in the closest touch.

AMPHITRYON   In the closest touch?
You with *me*, of course!

ALCMENA   Naturally, who else?

AMPHITRYON [*roaring out in pain*]   Oh the insidiousness!
The sheer effrontery!
You send me off to prove your innocence
And once my back is turned                                    ‡
Return yourself to strumpetry.                                ‡

ALCMENA [*in bitter disillusion*]   But you said yourself—
swore solemnly—                                               ‡
We did not need Naucrates: it was all a joke.                 ‡
And I forgave you, though you'd hurt me to the quick.

AMPHITRYON [*stamping around in near hysteria*]   And you
forgave me! You forgave me!
Ha ha ha ha ha!

MERCURY [*popping his head over the roof*]   He thinks he's
dancing round the Maypole, madam.
Dear, dear, poor man! Possessed!                              ‡
He'd better see a doctor                                      ‡
And have his sanity assessed.                                 ‡

AMPHITRYON [*still stamping with rage and frustration*]
Ah, there's the man that's going to pay
By digging sixty six-foot ditches twice a day.                ‡

ALCMENA   No, no! Sosia has his faults,
But for you and me, alas, he's not to blame.

AMPHITRYON   He's a swindling, insolent, congenital
twister.
Don't intercede for such a trickster.                         ‡
No wonder he and you take sides again!

ALCMENA [*beginning to retreat to the door*]   You are under
some delusion: sick, sir.                                     ‡
For mercy's sake go to a doctor                               ‡
And have it treated—quick, sir.                               ‡

AMPHITRYON [*acidly*]   I may be wet, but I am fit.
As for you, ma'am, it's beyond my ken
How almost at the hour of lying-in
You can entertain the thought of other men.

ALCMENA [*bitterly*]   Yes, the hour of my lying-in:
The very moment that you choose
To perjure yourself before almighty Zeus
And cover your wretched wife with nothing but abuse.

AMPHITRYON   No doubt you keep me standing at my own
      front door
To provide an escape for your disgraceful paramour.

ALCMENA   Oh outrageous man!
It's no good telling you the truth:
Perjured even in apology!
Your mocking reconciliation was no use.

AMPHITRYON   And you unjust woman,
Caught in the most flagrant lie,
With whom I used to live . . .
There's nothing left to prove.

ALCMENA [*running into the house*]   If that's all you have
      to say—goodbye.
You can stay there still:
False mocking man I used to love!
I've had my fill.

> [*She slams the front door. Meanwhile* SOSIA
> *comes down the street, bringing* BLEPHARO *for
> lunch.* BLEPHARO *is a man of few words: an
> honest, lumbering sea-captain*]

SOSIA [*surprised*]   Why, Master's already on the doorstep,
Waiting to welcome you. How nice!

BLEPHARO [*surveying him*]   Looks as though he's swum
here from the harbor.

SOSIA [*stepping up to the forlorn silent* AMPHITRYON]
Amphitryon, my master,
However did you get so wet?

AMPHITRYON [*rounding on him in incredulous fury*]  What!
   Not you again?
How do you dare
Present yourself to me right here?
Wart! Blot! You should be dead.
Who gave you the courage—
You hag-begotten drunken sot?
I'll teach you to go throwing pails of water at a master's
   head.
        [*Begins to clobber* SOSIA *with his marshal's
        baton*]

SOSIA  Oh oh oh! No, don't.
I never did. The injustice of it.
Theban people—mercy! Help!

AMPHITRYON  Go on, yelp.
What were you threatening to do, and did,
When I pounded on that door? . . .
Just you try
To make your escape . . .
If you run away, you die.

SOSIA  Much sooner, sir, if I stay.

AMPHITRYON  Who gave you leave to go up on that roof?
Who gave you leave to get completely stoned
And in that sodden state, you oaf,
Hurl down insults on your own
Master—and a pail of water?

SOSIA [*outraged*]  Are you mad, sir?
Here am I—
Trudging back and forth to the harbor
Since the middle of the night . . .
Here I bring you Blepharo, and what the deuce!
All I get is clobberings and abuse.
Does that seem right?

AMPHITRYON [*suddenly restraining his baton*]  Hm! It's
   true you've brought Blepharo the Captain here:
Why, I cannot tell—
But I suppose it *is* a kind of proof

You couldn't very well
Have been drunken on the roof.
Queer—very queer!

SOSIA [*in a flash*]    It's that other Sosia, the nasty,
Yes, of course.
I fear—I fear
He's been lurking in the house.
He's waiting to destroy me.
God help the lot of us!

BLEPHARO    It always seems to me
There's much less trouble at sea.

AMPHITRYON    Greetings, Blepharo. Glad to have you with
us.

BLEPHARO    An invitation
to lunch on land
is an innovation
I can't withstand.

AMPHITRYON [*fumbling for words*]    Ah, yes, Blepharo—
lunch on land!
A real old salt, eh, ha ha, what!
Your appetite was always grand.
[*Closes with* SOSIA]
What's this about luncheon, Sosia?
*I* never said a thing . . .
The way that man tucked in
On board when we were seasick
Was enough to turn an iron stomach.

BLEPHARO [*rubbing his hands together*]    It'll be a lovely
change from garlic and bread—
as indeed I had a hunch
when Sosia came and said:
"The General asks you home for lunch."

AMPHITRYON [*to himself, bitterly*]    There's an extra Sosia
somewhere drunk,
And now—upon my life!—
An extra Amphitryon, a brutish runt,

Who not only goes off with my wife
But invites in sailors home for lunch.

BLEPHARO    No doubt at all the keen sea breeze
Makes the sharpest appetite there is.

SOSIA    No doubt at all,
The mistress at this moment's being specific
To the cook on what we're going to bite.
Roasted fowl perhaps, or a fine fat quail.

BLEPHARO    Or perhaps an eel in aspic?

AMPHITRYON [*ruefully*]    She's being specific all right:
The way she slammed that door was quite terrific . . .
Now then, Sosia, if you're innocent
Slip round the back and let us in.
I'm no master and no victorious warrior
If I go into my own house by the servants' door.

SOSIA [*backing away*]    Are you serious, sir?
There lurks inside a Sosia—a monster.

BLEPHARO [*encouragingly*]    A fine fat chicken is a lovely
    sight,
And a capon, plump, exactly right.

SOSIA    That's all very well,
But a capon's what
I become the minute
I step into that spot.

AMPHITRYON    That's how *I* feel:
The spot is hot.

BLEPHARO    But, Amphitryon,
I came for luncheon.

AMPHITYRON    I know, I know . . .
Into the house with you, Sosia,
By the back way . . .
Unless you want to feast on truncheon.

SOSIA [*moving off with a doomed look*]    Truncheons seem
    to be the order of the day:
His or yours—I suppose it doesn't matter;
It's all the same to *you* . . .
Not yet afternoon—and I'm black and blue.

        [SOSIA *disappears round by the servants' entrance.*
        AMPHITYRON *walks up to the front door and gives
        it another mighty blow. As he does so* JUPITER
        *strides up behind him from the street and seizes
        him by the scruff*]

JUPITER    Got him—by the collar of his neck.                 ‡
    A notorious burglar caught—                               ‡
    And in the very act.                                      ‡

AMPHITRYON [*swinging around and managing to catch*
    JUPITER *by the throat*]
    Not on your life!                                         ‡
    Theban citizens, oh, look!                                ‡
    The lascivious swindler who broke into my home            ‡
    And dragged into disgrace—my wife.                        ‡

JUPITER [*still gripping* AMPHITRYON]
    Importunate intruder! Front-door breaker!
    Ruiner of peaceful lives!

AMPHITRYON [*still throttling* JUPITER]
    Impostor! Monster lecher! Hidden blight!
    You ruiner of honest wives—
    Do you dare come into the public sight?                   ‡

JUPITER    You ruttish brute.

AMPHITRYON    You lustful goat!

JUPITER    You randy copy-cat!
    You'll rue it—
    Dressing up like me to do it.

AMPHITYRON [*surveying himself and* JUPITER *aghast*]    My
    God—we're both alike!
    Same face, same cloak,
    Same beard, same baton . . .

Oh I feel weak:
Impersonation.

JUPITER    Don't blame *me*
For rampant lechery
If you think I'm copying.
In point of fact, you're copying *me*:
And that's a sin.

AMPHITRYON    Blepharo, you at least can tell apart
The true Amphitryon
From glaring upstart.

BLEPHARO [*nonplused*]
Goddammit, where does one begin?
   I see they are
      more alike
         than two halves of a pear.

JUPITER    Stalwart Blepharo, I'm the real Amphitryon
Who invited you to luncheon.

AMPHITRYON    That's a lie.
I'm the real Amphitryon.
Anyway, *I*
Have the stouter truncheon.

JUPITER    Quails in aspic, Blepharo, anything you like.

AMPHITRYON    New sails, Blepharo: new sails for your
   ship.
Choose *me*.

JUPITER    Choose *me*.

AMPHITRYON    Choose one of us.

SOSIA [*aside*]    I *say!* Things *are* humming.

JUPITER [*mockingly*]    Choose each of us in turn:
   Choose both of us.

AMPHITRYON    Get a move on, Blepharo, I'm waiting.

JUPITER [*smiling*]    Make up your mind, Blepharo. Which
    of us?
Think of luncheon.

AMPHITRYON [*smiling*]    Or my truncheon.

BLEPHARO [*to the audience*]    What am I to do?
    There's nothing in between the two.
    They fill me first with threats, then with smiles.
    They both look military.
    They both look untrustworthy.
    And they both look as though they've spent a night out
      on the tiles.
        [*There is a long pause.* BLEPHARO *looks from one
        to the other, paralyzed with uncertainty.* JUPITER
        and* AMPHITRYON *exchange a glance almost of
        sympathy. A small crowd of on-lookers has
                      gathered*]

JUPITER    It's my opinion,
    If I may have a word in private
    With the false Amphitryon,
    The man's nothing but a lumbering sea-lout.

BLEPHARO    Save your breath.                                    ‡

AMPHITRYON [*desperately*]    Blepharo—good, dull Ble-
    pharo—
    Can't you tell the real one?                                ‡
    The true Amphitryon begs you
    Not to be a washout.
        [*After a further silence,* BLEPHARO *bursts out
        with bottled-up bewilderment and frustration.
        Plautus's text resumes*]

1035 BLEPHARO    Oh, go and sort yourselves out.
    I'm off: I've got work to do.
    I've never in all my life
    Seen such an amazing muddle . . .
    That's my considered opinion.

AMPHITRYON [*seizing his arm*]    Blepharo, for mercy's sake,
    stand by me.

BLEPHARO    Goodbye! What's the point of standing by
When I don't know which of you to stand by to?
    [*Turns on his heel.* AMPHITRYON *runs after him*]

JUPITER [*to the audience, eagerly*]
I'm going in myself . . . Alcmena's giving birth.
    [*Slips unnoticed into the house*]

AMPHITRYON [*shuffling back*]
I'm finished.
    [*Sits down hopelessly on the curb*]
Whát am I góing to dó? My suppórters[22]
Yés, and my állies, have áll run óut.                    *1040*

I'm damned if I'll let this monster get off with
Making a fool of me—no matter who he is.

I'll go straight to the King this minute and tell him
What's going on. I'll punish, by Jupiter,

That Thessalonian twister today
Who's sent my whole family out of their senses.
    [*Looks round in dismay*]

Now where has he gone to? Hell and damnation!
Inside, I bet you—straight to my wife . . . Oh!

Is there in Thebes a more miserable cuckold?
What shall I do? . . . Quite disregarded,

The butt and the mutt of any who chooses.
Right—I'll smash my way in the house then.

I'll make into mincemeat whomever I meet there:
Footman or maid or wife or seducer,

Father or grandpa—there in the hall.                    *1050*
Nothing'll stop me, not even Jupiter:
My mind's made up . . . Into the house then!
    [*Just as* AMPHITRYON *hurls himself against the
door, there is a stroke of lightning and a clap of
thunder. He falls to the ground as if dead and the
thunder and lightning continue*]

22 Basic meter dactylic: $\angle$UU$\angle$U/$\angle$UU$\angle$U: 4 beats to a line.

# ACT IV

*A few minutes later, the maid,* BROMIA, *bursts out of the
house half demented. She does not notice the sprawling
body of* AMPHITRYON *over which she nearly stumbles.*

BROMIA

Oh dear! Oh dear!
It's dead and buried, gone:
My wish for life, my zest, my hope . . .
I've lost the lot.

The sea, the earth, the heavens wait
To crush me and annihilate
Me utterly. Oh dear! I fear
I don't know what

To do. Such goings on have gone
On inside this house. I'm done
In . . . Some water, quick. I'm sick:
I'm finished.

A splitting head; I cannot hear
Or even focus anywhere.
There isn't a girl that looks and *is*
*1060*                    So diminished.

It couldn't be worse . . . Such happenings
Madam's suffered—oh the things
*She* went through today . . . The way
When she was ready

For the pangs of birth, invoking heaven,
A hammer and clamor enough to deafen,
Of lightning and thunder—oh the wonder!—
Crashed sudden and heavy.

Exactly at that terrible clap,
We fell in our tracks—we fell down flat,
And somewhere about a mighty shout
Uttered: "Alcmena,

Help is coming, do not fear:

He by whom the heavens are
Is visiting your household, mercy
    In his demeanor.

Rise up, all of you," he said,
"Who've fallen down in terror and dread."
Then up I hopped from where I'd dropped;
    The house was on fire—

Or so I thought—such was the blaze.
Alcmena called, and still in a daze
But alarmed for her I ran to discover
    What she required.

Lo and behold, she'd given birth
To twins, two boys, but when on earth    *1070*
She'd done it, none of us could see
    Or even guess.

      *[She suddenly notices* AMPHITRYON]
Heavens above! What have we here?
An old man lying by the door . . .
Seems to be lightning-struck. Great Scott!
    I do believe so—yes!

Still as a corpse: all laid out prone.
I'll go and see . . . Lord, it's my own
Master, my boss, Amphitryon.
    *[Stoops over* AMPHITRYON *and shouts in his ear]*
    Amphitryon!

AMPHITRYON *[groaning]*   I'm dead.

BROMIA   Oh, do get up!

AMPHITRYON   I'm annihilated.

BROMIA   Give me your hand, sir.

AMPHITRYON   A-ah! Who's that touch?

BROMIA   Your little maid, Bromia.

AMPHITRYON *[sitting up]*   My nerves are shot. God, what
    a clap!

Jove knocked me out . . .
I think I'm just coming back—
From the land of the dead . . .
What are *you* doing outside here?

BROMIA [*clutching her head*]   It rocked us too, did that
same shock.

1080   O-oh! O-oh, the things I've seen inside your house!
I haven't got my senses back.

AMPHITRYON [*clasping her*]   Steady, steady—tell me quick
Do you know for sure I'm your boss, Amphitryon?

BROMIA   Why, yes, sir.

AMPHITRYON [*earnestly*]   Take another look.

BROMIA [*beginning to giggle as she surveys the absurd
dishevelment of her master*]   Of course, you are!

AMPHITRYON [*heaving a sigh from the depths*]   She's the
only sane one in the house.

BROMIA   Don't be silly! They're all quite sane.

AMPHITRYON [*savagely*]   *I'm* not. I'm absolutely raving . . .
After what my wicked wife has done.

BROMIA [*shocked*]   No, Amphitryon, I won't have that.
You mustn't call her that.
She's a lovely person and I'll make you know it.
It doesn't take much evidence or proof,
And to begin: she's just given birth
To two twin boys.

AMPHITRYON [*jumping up*]   Did you say *twins*?

BROMIA   Twins I said.

AMPHITRYON [*slapping his forehead*]   Lord, bless me
heaven!

BROMIA [*breathlessly*]   And that's not half.

Just wait and hear how much
The gods have blessed you and your wife.                    *1090*

AMPHITRYON   Oh, please go on!

BROMIA [*breathlessly*]   Well, when Alcmena felt her time
   had come
And the labor pains were on,
She washed her hands, covered her head, and afterwards
(As women in childbirth do)
Prayed for help to the immortal gods,
And then
Suddenly there was the most tremendous clap.
At first we thought your house was coming down:
Your whole house flashed like something made of
   gold . . .

AMPHITRYON [*interrupting*]   Will you please get on with
   it and let me go.
You've tantalized me quite enough . . .
What happened next?

BROMIA   While all this was going on
None of us heard
So much as a sigh or whimper from your wife,
Not one—
And that's how it was . . . an absolutely pangless birth.

AMPHITRYON [*torn between hurt feelings and concern*]   At
   least I'm glad of that,                                   *1100*
Whatever I think she's done.

BROMIA [*sharply*]   You leave that alone, just listen.
As soon as they were born—the boys—
She told us to sponge them down;
We began, and then—
Oh the size and strength of the one
I was washing! None
Of us could even wrap him round.

AMPHITRYON [*half in sarcasm, half in earnest*]   The whole
   thing sounds preposterous.
If it's true I have no hesitation

In pronouncing that my wife's
Been aided and abetted from above.

BROMIA [*clapping her hands with excitement*]   And, here's
   something
You're going to say is much more marvelous still:
I'd just tucked him in his cradle when
Two enormous snakes, with crests on them,
Came coiling down into the patio pool.
And there they reared their heads.

AMPHITRYON   Phew!

BROMIA   Don't be scared.
1110   The snakes scanned us with their eyes,
Took us in, and the moment they spotted the two boys
They made for them.
I backed away,
Pushing and pulling the cradles along—
Frightened for the boys' sakes
And petrified for my own—
While the snakes kept coming on—
Keener than ever.
Then that first boy—the one I told you of—
Saw the snakes
And was up and out of his cradle in a flash
And went straight for the brutes,
Gripping one in each fist.

AMPHITRYON [*wiping beads of sweat from his forehead*]
An absolute horror story!
Your mere description of it sets me quivering.
What happened then? Go on!

BROMIA [*after a pause—almost whispering with wonder*]
The boy actually strangles both the snakes.
And while he's at it,
We hear your wife's name clearly called . . .

1120 AMPHITRYON [*sharply*]   Yes, yes—who called her?

BROMIA [*her eyes shining*]   The king of gods and men—
Almighty Jupiter. And he declares

He has shared her bed in secret, unawares,
And that the baby which has killed the snakes is his,
The other yours.

AMPHITRYON [*struck silent for several seconds; and then
   with conviction*]
My god! I don't resent it in the least.
No sir!
Not sharing out my joys with Jupiter.
         [*With new enthusiasm*]
Go into the house,
Have spotless ritual gear laid out for me:
I mean to make a generous sacrifice
To Jove for peace.
         [BROMIA *hurries out*]
And I'll summon Tiresias, the seer,
And ask him what he reckons should be done,
And tell him everything
That has begun . . .
         [*A prolonged clap of thunder*]
Ah, what's that? Thunder!
How tremendous!
God protect us!                                     1130
         [*As the sound of the thunder dies away, the
         voice of* JUPITER *comes powerfully and clearly—
         but not without an element of mock solemnity—
         over the air*]

JUPITER
              Be happy, Amphitryon: I am here
              To help your home and family.
              There's nothing you need fear,
              So every prophet, every seer—
                    Dismiss.
              I'll tell your future, tell your past
              Infinitely better than these last—
                    For I am Jupiter—
              And first, I'll tell you this:
                 I took Alcmena's body
                    Borrowed it a bit,
                       Slept with her
                       And gave her
                          A baby

Son from it.
Simultaneously
She became *enceinte*
As well from you,
Who'd gone off to the front.
And in one delivery
She bore the two.
The one that springs from me
Shall by his life
Win immortal glory
1140                      All for you.
Now go back again
To the graces of your wife,
Alcmena,
Who does not merit any blame:
She was driven
By my power.
[*A faraway peal of thunder*]
So I retire
Into heaven.

AMPHITRYON

I'll do what you order.
Please keep to your promise.
[*His eyes light up*]
And now I go
Inside to my Alcmena,
And shall dismiss
1145                   Old Tiresias.
[*Walks toward the audience*]
Sweet audience, please
Some good applause!
Clap loud and clear
For Jupiter.

# Major
# Bullshot-
# Gorgeous
## (Miles Gloriosus)

for Martin Paul Duncan—
when he is of age.

# THE CHARACTERS

MAJOR BULLSHOT-GORGEOUS (Pyrgopolynices)
  *A soldier*
SHABBY SUCKPOT   (Artotrogus)
  *His hanger-on*
DODGER   (Palaestrio)
  *Servant[1] of Halcyon but temporarily in the
  household of the Major*
MR. PROLIX   (Periplectomenus)
  *An old gentleman of Ephesus*
POX   (Sceledrus)
  *Servant of the Major*
GOLDILOCKS   (Philocomasium)
  *Girl-friend of Halcyon and abducted by the
  Major*
HALCYON   (Pleusicles)
  *Young Athenian in love with Goldilocks*
PENNY   (Lucrio)
  *Servant of the Major*
MADAM LOVE-A-DUCK   (Acroteleutium)
  *A merry widow[2]*
MILPHIDIPPA   (Milphidippa)
  *Her maid*
SMALL BOY   (Puer)
  *In the household of Mr. Prolix*
CARIO   (Cario)
  *Cook of Mr. Prolix*
  (*also* ORDERLIES *and* PORTERS)

---

1 In Latin, *servus:* the English "slave," which carries too many other connotations.
2 In Latin, *meretrix:* the English "courtesan" or "prostitute"—again far too strong a word, usually.

## TIME AND SETTING

A street in Ephesus, a Greek town in Asia
Minor. Two large houses next to each other:
MAJOR BULLSHOT-GORGEOUS's and MR. PRO-
LIX's. The exit on stage left leads into town;
that on the right to the port. The time is about
ten o'clock in the morning.


# ACT I

*Enter* MAJOR BULLSHOT-GORGEOUS *from his house, followed by* SHABBY SUCKPOT. *Orderlies carry in a shield that
would fit a giant of six foot three. The Major is far from
that but his self-satisfied face wears a look of almost militant glory as he struts up and down with dangling sword.
He swishes his black-and-scarlet military great-cloak about
him as he turns.* SHABBY SUCKPOT, *small, scruffy, syco-
phantic but intelligent, dodges in and out of the Major's
legs, mimicking him at his heels.*

MAJOR

    Make sure my damn shield's bright.
Give it a sheen like the sun in a cloudless sky:
  A light that in the hurly-burly of the fight
    Shoots into the faces of my foes—
        Straight in the eye . . .
          Right?
        *[Everybody bows and nods. The* MAJOR
        *smiles, pulls out his sword and strokes it]*
        Right!
  This good steel of mine,
  I mean to cheer him up.
  He mustn't fret and pine
  Dangling here all day long
  Without a goddam thing
  To do . . . Poor Bladey!

All you want
Is to make good mincemeat
Of . . . [*wheeling around with a flourish*]
Where is Shabby Suckpot?
. . . of the enemy.
> [*Lunges at the air as* SHABBY SUCKPOT
> *scuttles from behind*]

SUCKPOT   He's right behind you, sir:
10   Right next to this strong successful man with his stamp
     of a prince,
     I mean you, sir:
     This hero Mars himself isn't a match for.

MAJOR [*sheathing his sword with sublime self-absorption*]
     Who was that fellow I saved at the battle of Maggoty
     Meadows?
     Where the commander-in-chief was Bigbangbonides
     Allmixedupides—
     The grandson of Neptune.

SUCKPOT [*instantly inventing*]   I remember.
     You mean the one with the solid gold armor.
     Ha! You just puffed away his battalions with a breath:
     Like a gust of wind among leaves and roof-straws.

MAJOR [*with a lofty wave of his hand*]   Hell, that was
     nothing! . . .
     Not really.

SUCKPOT   Hell's bells—absolutely nothing!
     Not to those other exploits I could tell of
20   Which . . . [*aside*] you never did.
> [*Turns to the audience with a grimace as* MAJOR
> BULLSHOT-GORGEOUS *stalks upstage with his
> back turned*]
     If anyone
     Ever saw a louder-mouthed more stupendous liar,
     He can have *me* for a present:
     Self-sold into slavery lock-stock-and-barrel . . .
     Ahem! Yes—if it weren't for one thing:
> [*Licks his lips*]
     I'm crazy about his pickled olives.

MAJOR [*wheeling around again*]   Where've you got to?

SUCKPOT [*popping up behind him*]   Right here, sir . . .
  Take that elephant in India, by Jiminy!
  The way you pounded its front paw to pieces with one
    punch.

MAJOR [*eyeing him narrowly*]   Front paw—eh, what?

SUCKPOT [*quickly*]   Front backside, I meant to say.

MAJOR [*loftily*]   It was the merest tap.

SUCKPOT   Don't I know it! If you'd really tried
  You'd have gone through its hide, its inside, its whole
    skeleton:
  You'd have put your arm clean through the elephant.    *30*

MAJOR [*with disarming modesty*]   I'd rather not talk of
  it now.

SUCKPOT [*ponderously ironic*]   Dear me, no! It isn't worth
    your while
  To talk to little *me* of all your wonder-work,
  I know it well.
  [*to the audience with a sour grin*]   It's my tummy lands
    me in for all this tommyrot:
  I've got to let the stuff seep into my ears
  Or my teeth'll have nothing in which to steep.
  I've got to back him up in every goddam lie he tells.

MAJOR [*importantly*]   What was I saying?

SUCKPOT   Aha! I know exactly—as if you'd said it.
    [*Racks his brains*]
  Dammit, so you did, sir! . . .
  I remember you *did*.

MAJOR   Did what?

SUCKPOT [*desperately*]   Well . . . whatever it was you did.

MAJOR   Do you . . .

SUCKPOT [*leaping in*]   Have a writing pad? Yes, and a pen.
  [*Hurriedly produces a waxed tablet and stylus from
  the folds of his tunic*]

MAJOR   You're a genius at putting soul and soul together:
  Yours to mine.

SUCKPOT [*looking him straight in the eye*]   Well, it's only
  right, sir.
40  I've got you studied through and through,
  And I take the trouble to sniff out your wishes
  Even before you've wished them.
      [*Begins jotting things down*]

MAJOR [*fishing for more tall stories*]   And you remember
  things, eh?

SUCKPOT   Yes sir! I remember things.
  [*totting up his list*]   A hundred in Cilicia—add fifty.
  A hundred in Go-in-and-grabia,
  Thirty Sardinians, sixty Macedonians—
  That's the list of human beings
  You've polished off in a single day.

MAJOR [*dryly*]   Which makes the grand total of human
  beings . . . ?

SUCKPOT [*rapidly totting up on his fingers*] Seven thousand.

MAJOR [*smugly*]   Yes, it ought to come to about that.
  Your sum's correct.

SUCKPOT [*ingratiatingly*]   And nothing recorded, either:
  It's all kept in the head.

MAJOR [*approvingly*] You've certainly got a good
  memory.

SUCKPOT [*to the audience with a sigh*] It's fodder
  prodded.

MAJOR [*patting him on the back*]   Well, just go on as you
  are

And you can stuff yourself:                                        *50*
You can always share my table.

SUCKPOT [*rubbing his hands*]   Ah! What about that time in
     Cappodocia
When you would have slain five hundred men at once—
In a single blow—
If your damn sword hadn't gone dead.

MAJOR [*with a toss of the head*]   Oh, those—
They were measly footsloggers,
So I let them live.

SUCKPOT [*hand on his heart*]   Why should I tell you
What is known to the whole race of man:
You are the one and only Major Bullshot-Gorgeous
     on earth—
Unbeatable for bravery, beauty and big deeds,
And loved by all the ladies.
          [*Flutters his eyes*]
     And how can they be blamed?
You're so darned good-looking.
Those girls for instance yesterday
Who jerked me by the sleeves . . .

MAJOR [*halting in his stride*]   Ah! What did they say to
     you?

SUCKPOT   They kept quizzing me.
"Surely that's Achilles?" says one of them.                        *60*
"No, it's his brother," says I.
"No wonder he's so beautiful!" says t'other:
"And such a gentleman.
Just look at that hair—it's ravishing . . .
Aren't they lucky, the girls that go to bed with him?"

MAJOR   They really said that, eh?

SUCKPOT [*deadpan*]   Well, didn't they both beseech me
To bring you past them today as if you were on parade?

MAJOR [*trying to yawn*]   Oh what a bore it is to be so
     beautiful!

SUCKPOT [*nodding vigorously*]   You can say that again.
They're an absolute pest, the women:
70      Teasing and wheedling and almost screaming
To be allowed to see you.
They send for me so mercilessly
I can hardly attend to your affairs.

MAJOR [*pompously*]
I think it's time for us to go toward the forum.
I want to pay those tyros I enlisted yesterday.
King Seleucus, you know, pressed me earnestly
To raise and enlist recruits for him.
I've decided to devote my day entirely to the King.

SUCKPOT [*with a tortured grin*]   Well, let's go.

MAJOR   Orderlies, fall-in and follow.

> [*The* MAJOR *sweeps off, with* SHABBY SUCKPOT *and
> the orderlies prancing and gesticulating in his wake*]


# ACT II

## PROLOGUE

DODGER *enters the street from the house of* MAJOR BULL-
SHOT-GORGEOUS. *He is a pleasant looking young fellow,
neatly dressed, quick-witted, well-educated—as slaves often
were—and brimming with self-confidence. He is as devoted
to his real master as he finds his present master—the* MAJOR
*—ridiculous. What he most enjoys is organizing people and
events. Now he steps downstage, faces the audience, and
smilingly makes a formal bow.*

DODGER   Mine is the pleasure of unfolding to you this
80      plot; yours to do me the kindness of listening. If anyone
would rather not, I hope he'll get up and go, so leave
a seat for somebody who does.

> [*Waits, while fixing his audience with a gimlet
> eye*]

Well, I'll tell you why you're sitting in this place of

mirth. Here's the title and the plot of the comedy we are
putting on. In Greek it is called "Alazon," which in
Latin we translate as "Gloriosus": "Bullshot-Gorgeous."
    [*Waves a hand backstage*]
    This town is Ephesus. That military Major who just
went off to the forum, is my master: a hard-on swaggering impudent stinker, chock-full of lies and lechery. He      *90*
says all women instinctively run after him; but actually
wherever he goes they all think him quite absurd. In fact,
most of the demoiselles here—as you'll observe—have
crooked mouths through trying to keep a straight face.
    [*Chuckles at his own joke*]
    Now I've not served this man very long and I'd like
you to know how I came to him and left my former
master. So, your attention, please: this is the plot.
    [*Shakes his head sadly*]
    My master was a fine young man in Athens—Athens
in Attica, that is—where he was head-over-heels in love    *100*
with a certain girl[3] and she with him—which is the nicest
way to be in love [*winks*]. Well, he was sent on a govern-
ment mission of public importance to Naupactus. Meanwhile this Major [*grimaces*] comes by chance to Athens
and worms his way into a meeting with my master's
sweetheart. He proceeds with gifts of wine, trinkets, and
extravagant titbits to get round her mother—the old
bawd—and onto the most intimate footing. Then one
day he sees his chance, does this fine military Major:
    [*Gives a little spit into the wings*]
hoodwinks the disgraceful old baggage, this—this      *110*
mother of my master's loved-one: claps the girl on
shipboard without the mother knowing a thing, and
abducts her off to Ephesus much against her will.
    [*Shakes his head at this dastardly action*]
    Naturally, as soon as I hear my master's sweetheart
has been snatched away to Athens, I streak off, book a
passage, and get myself on a ship to bring him the news
at Naupactus. But when we'd put out to sea, the gods
thought fit to let pirates capture the ship, with me on

---

3 Plautus's word is *meretrix*, "prostitute"; but this here, and often
elsewhere, carries far too strong a connotation. There is no outlet
in our social code for a word which says *meretrix* and at the same
time makes you forget it.

board. So there I was, stymied in my voyage to my
master before I'd even started.

[*Sighs, bends toward the audience with the air
and tone of "you won't believe what follows"*]

*120*      The pirate who got hold of me gives me as a present to
this very same soldier, the Major. And when *he* takes
me home to his house whom should I light my eyes on
but my master's girl friend from Athens.

[*Waits for this to sink in*]

As we come face to face she signals me with her eyes
not to recognize her. Later, when the chance arises, she
speaks to me bitterly of her fate and says she longs to
get away from this house and escape to Athens, where,
she says, she is deeply in love with my master. She adds
that there's nobody on earth who so wholeheartedly
abominates this same soldier.

[*Shakes his head*]

When I saw where the girl's feelings really lay, I
*130*      grabbed myself a writing-pad, sealed up a letter and
slipped it to a certain businessman to take to that love-
lorn master of mine in Athens—telling him to come
here.

[*His face lights up*]

Well, he hasn't ignored my message. In fact he's here,
right next door, staying with a friend of his father's: a
delightful old boy who's aiding and abetting his guest in
this affair of the heart. Oh, yes, he's giving us every
possible encouragement in word and deed.

[*With a slow smile*]

As a result, I've fixed up a splendid device inside the
house [*jerks his head toward the* MAJOR's *house*] which
makes it possible for the lovers to meet and spend some
time together . . . You see, the Major gave this girl one
*140*      particular room into which nobody was to set foot but
himself. In the wall of this room, this boudoir, I've
scooped out a hole. It opens up a secret way for the girl
to get from the Major's house to that one [*points toward*
MR. PROLIX's *house*]. The old gentleman knows about
it of course. In fact he suggested it.

[*Leaning forward and taking the audience into
his confidence*]

Now the man the Major's chosen to keep watch on the
girl—a fellow servant of mine—is a pretty worthless sort

of fellow. We're going to give him a very curious disease
of the eyes—oh, so cunningly, so consummate and ambi-
dexterously!—which will make him *not* see what he
really sees.

    [*Does a little dance*]

Just to keep *you* from getting mixed up, however:
this one girl [*indicates the* MAJOR's *house*] is going to   *150*
play the part of two: coming and going from each
house. She's the same girl, of course, but she'll pretend
to be another. That's how we're going to fool her sentry.

    [*His attention is caught*]

Excuse me, there's our neighbor's door. It's the old
gentleman coming out—the nice old boy I told you of.

    [DODGER *steps to one side*]

    [*Enter* MR. PROLIX *from his house. He is a spry
    old body of about seventy, quietly but perfectly
    dressed. His freshly shampooed curly hair and
    beard look as crisp as lamb's wool. Though one
    would expect his lively black eyes to be often
    twinkling, they register at the moment nothing
    but outrage. The old man really seems to be
    worked up: brandishing an embossed silver-
    headed cane, he shouts at the servants standing in
    the doorway*]

PROLIX   And after this, I swear to god,
  If you don't break the legs of any intruder spotted on
    our roof,
  I'm going to rip the rawhide off your backs.
  *Now* all our neighbors know exactly what goes on inside
    my house . . .
  Looking through the skylight . . . Really!
  Can you beat it?
  Well, I'm giving orders here and now,
  To the whole bang lot of you,
  If you see anyone whatsoever
  Getting onto our roof from that soldier's house,
  Unless it be Dodger,
  You're to pitch him headlong into the street.   *160*
  I don't care
  If he says he's chasing a chicken or a pigeon or a pet
    monkey—
  You're all dead men if you don't batter him to bits:

And I want no bones left either.
You'll have to use something else for counters
When they break the Gambling Act at the next party.
            [*Shakes his cane and mutters*]

DODGER [*leaning toward the audience and jerking a finger
        in the direction of the* MAJOR'*s house*]   Strikes *me*
Someone *chez nous* has gone and put his foot in it.
Bones to be broken!
So that's the old codger's edict, eh?
But *I'm* excepted . . . well, that's nice:
I don't give a damn for what he does to the rest.
Let me go up to him.
            [*Takes a step forward*]

PROLIX   Isn't that Dodger coming toward me?

DODGER [*cheerily*]   Mr. Prolix, sir, how are you doing?

PROLIX [*glumly*]   Oh, Dodger, there isn't anyone in the
            world I'd rather see and talk to.

*170*

DODGER   What's going on, sir?
Why are you in such a tizzy about *our* household?

PROLIX [*grimly*]   We're finished.

DODGER   Why, what's up?

PROLIX   The thing's out.

DODGER   What thing's out?

PROLIX [*shaking his cane again*]   Some goddam wretch
            from your house
Has just gone and seen my guest and Goldilocks kissing,
Through the skylight—our skylight.

DODGER   Who did the seeing?

PROLIX   It was one of your colleagues.

DODGER   But which one?

PROLIX [*hopelessly*]  I don't know. He darted off like a
     streak.

DODGER [*coolly*]  I have a suspicion—I'm done for.

PROLIX  I bawled at him as he went.
     "Hey, you there," I says,
     "What are you doing on our roof?"
     "I'm chasing an ape," he says, and disappears.

DODGER [*gritting his teeth*]  God, how it riles me to be
     done for
     Just because of a worthless baboon!                      *180*
     But how's Goldilocks? Is she still inside here?
          [*Nods toward* MR. PROLIX's *house*]

PROLIX  She was when I came out.

DODGER  Then for heaven's sake go and tell her
     To get herself over to our house
     Just about as quickly as she can.
     The whole household's got to see her there, at home . . .
     Unless of course she wants us slaves
     To be martyrs to her love affair
     And all join the Club-of-the-strung-up.

PROLIX [*with new hope*]  As good as told. Anything else?

DODGER  Yes, impress this on her:
     She's not to budge an inch from woman's wiles,
     But apply the book of rules right up to the hilt.

PROLIX  How do you mean?

DODGER  Bamboozle him who said he saw her
     Into seeing that he didn't.
     And even if she's been
     Spotted here a hundred times
     She's still to say she wasn't.
        She's got a mouth and plenty of lip,
     She's full of brass and full of tricks:
     She's shrewd and sure.
     She's got self-confidence and stamina

And she can sham.
    If anyone accuses her

*190*    She turns right round on solemn oath
Outswears him flat.
    She's chockablock with double-think
And double-talk and solemn double-deals.
She's chockablock with stocks of sweet
Seduction and deceit.
Her shelves are stuffed with humbug.
    No woman, sir,
Needs to ask a barrow-boy for deviled apples:[4]
She's got a gardenful at home and all the spices
For concocting every deviled dish there is.

PROLIX [*with a smile*]  All this
    I shall unfold to her if she is here.
But what are you churning over in your mind?

DODGER [*with an admonitory finger*]  Sh-h! Quiet, sir, a
    second.
    I'm calling a committee meeting with my soul
        To consider what's to do,
      What campaign of trickery pursue
    To out-trick that slave who had a view
    Of her kissing through your skylight.
          How make unseen
          A certain sight
      That certainly has been?

PROLIX   Go ahead and think.
*200*    Meanwhile I'll leave you on your own.
        [*The old man steps to one side and with an
        amused quizzical look watches him, while run-
        ning on in an undertone commentary*]
Just look at him now, with a frown on his brow,
    Standing there dreaming up ways out:
With his knuckles he taps his bosom[5], perhaps

---

[4] The play in the Latin is on *mala*, a good word to play with. It
means both "apples" and "something bad." If one wants a Freudian
connotation, it also means a pole or a mast. A fourth meaning, but
possibly not implied here, is "jaw" or "cheek."
[5] In antiquity it was often the heart rather than the head which was
considered the seat of the intelligence.

He intends to summon his brains out.
Now his head's gone awry; left hand on left thigh,
  Right hand is computing on fingers.
Right thigh gets a smack—a terrible whack—
  Oh, he's stuck: his solution malingers.
He's snapping his digits, he's getting the fidgets,
  What a tussle! He's shaking his head:
*That* idea won't work. But he's not going to shirk
  And offer us half-baked bread.

> [DODGER *has been sitting on the curb. Now he*
> *puts his chin on his hand*]

Ah—very solemn![6] He's building a column:
  He's resting his chin upon *that*.
Thanks very much! But I don't care for such
  An erection—oh no, not a scrap.                          *210*
For I happen to know it . . . a foreigner poet[7]
  Was pillaried up on a pillar
While by day and by night
  He was kept pretty tight
By chains that would guard a gorilla.

> [DODGER *shifts again*]

My god, what a pose! As graceful as those
  Which slaves take up sweetly[8] in comedies.
He's not going to rest today till he's guessed
  What he's searching for so, and the remedies.

> [DODGER *jumps up*]

He's got it at last, I believe . . . Oh no, blast!

> [DODGER *has sat down again*]

Now don't go and have a siesta!
Do what you do, or you'll be black and blue
  From mooning around—indeed *yes*, sir!

> [DODGER *seems to have gone into a daydream*]

Dodger, I say! Were you drunk yesterday?
  Hi there! I'm talking to *you*.

---

6 "Solemn" is not in the Latin. My excuse is that it does catch at least
a reflection of the pun between "chin" and "mind" in Plautus's
*mento*.

7 It was said in antiquity of the tragic poet Euripides that his aspect
was that of "a face on a column." The more direct reference here
is to the Roman epic and dramatic poet, Nævius, who was impris-
oned (about 206 B.C.) for lampooning the noble family of the
Metelli. The ambiguity of lines 211–13 has forced me to paraphrase.

8 Plautus's word *dulice*—"in the manner of a slave"—plays with the
word "dulce," "sweetly."

Wake up if you can, break out of it, man:
It's morning I tell you—it's true.

DODGER [*in a trance*]   I know. I heard you.

PROLIX [*executing a little dance in front of him, brandishing
his silver-headed cane*]
                    See the attack?
                        The foe's at your back.
                    Think double-quick,
                        Get help in the nick.
220                 It's high time to sweep
                        On and not sleep.
                    Steal a march round
                        If a way can be found
                    For your army, and then
                        Rally our men.
                    Block off the foe
                        With an ambush and so
                    Cut their supply line;
                        But make sure that our line
                    Is open and lies
                        Intact for supplies.
                    Get on! Go ahead!
                        Be quick or be dead.[9]
                    Just say you'll direct
                        The campaign. I expect
                    We'll certainly win:
                        Do the enemy in.

DODGER [*springing up with melodramatic readiness*]   I do
230      say it: I shall direct.

PROLIX [*shakes him by the hand*]   And I say you'll force
the issue and win.

DODGER [*hands still clasped*]   Jove bless you for that.

9 Paul Nixon in the Loeb Classics, following Leo, omits these lines
(226–228) as doubtful: "Think something up, hit on a plan—
whitehot:/what's been seen's got to be unseen, or what's done'll be
undone./This man is onto something big: building a big barricade."

PROLIX [*still in the stilted phrases of melodrama*]  Pray,
   will you not make me privy to your plan?

DODGER [*imperiously*]  Silence, if you please!
   I shall usher you into the purlieus of my strategy.
   You shall know my plans as well as *I* do.

PROLIX  Plans I'll give you back—intact.

DODGER  [*bending toward* PROLIX *as if he were going to
   impart amazing news to him*]  The soul of my master
   is encompassed
   By the hide of an elephant,
   And he has no more sense than a stone.

PROLIX [*dryly*]  This was not unknown to me.

DODGER  Wait! My purpose—my grand strategy—is this:
   There has arrived from Athens here—or so I'll have it—
   Goldilocks's own twin sister,
   Bringing a lover of hers.
   The girls are as much alike as two drops of milk.
   And the visitors
   Are being lodged and entertained here at your house—   *240*
   Or so I'll say.

PROLIX [*claps him on the back*]  Perfect! Splendid. Con-
   gratulations!

DODGER [*grinning with self-satisfaction*]  Then when that
   slave, my colleague,
   Goes off to the Major to accuse her with what he saw—
   Kissing a strange young man here—
   I'll turn right round and prove to him
   That what he saw was Goldilocks's sister
   Kissing her own young man.

PROLIX  Why, it's terrific!
   That's the story I'll keep to if the Major questions me.

DODGER [*cautiously*]  But be sure to say:
   They're absolutely the dead spit of one another.

> And Goldilocks must be warned about this too—
> Or the Major'll question her and trip her up.

PROLIX   Very neat! . . .
> But what if he wants to see them together—then what?

250   DODGER [*with a wave of the hand*]   Simple. Three hundred
> pretexts can be found:
> "She's not at home, she's gone for a walk,
> She's asleep, she's dressing,
> She's having a bath,
> She's at dinner, at a party,
> Busy . . . not convenient . . . quite impossible."
> Anything you like to put him off:
> Provided only he gets started right
> And believes our lies.

PROLIX [*nodding*]   Seems fine to me.

DODGER   Then go inside and if the girl's there
> Tell her to pop back home *toute de suite*.
> Explain and unfold to her
> This whole concept of the twin sister—
> Then she'll be able to keep to our wonderful plan.

PROLIX [*beaming*]   I'll prepare you a girl fit for a degree.
> Anything else?

DODGER   No. Just go in.

PROLIX   I'm going.

> [MR. PROLIX *enters his house, humming happily to
> himself*]

DODGER [*quietly walking toward the* MAJOR's *house*]
260   I'll go inside as well and advance him by a point
> By discovering craftily what flunky from our joint
> Had a monkey-hunt today; for he surely has let out
> To some buddy on the staff all his news about
> The mistress of my master: how he saw her here next
> door,
> With a fellow, kissing . . . *I* know what they are:
> [*Mimicks*]

"I just can't keep a secret—that's how I am."
If I find the chap who saw her, I'll ready with my ram
And engines of assault—I'm mobilized in full.
I'll take the man by force; oh yes, I will,
And if I *don't* discover him that way,
I'll go sniffing like a hound and track my fox at bay.
          [*His attention is caught*]
Aha! It's our door opening . . . Shh! I mustn't shout.          *270*
Look, it's Goldilocks's guard, my colleague, coming
out.

> [*Enter* POX *from the* MAJOR's *house. He is a small
> weedy fellow, well known for a whiner and
> sucker-up to his master. He can hardly wait to
> find someone to unload his latest gossip onto*]

POX [*muttering as he hurries along*]   Yes . . . yes,
Unless I was sleepwalking on the tiles today,
What I saw next door and no mistake
Was Master's mademoiselle herself—
Goldilocks—but up to no good.

DODGER [*to himself*]   So *he's* the fellow who saw her kissing?
He's given himself away.

POX [*nervously*]   Who's that?

DODGER [*stepping forward*]   Your fellow servant . . . How
are you doing, Pox?

POX [*rubbing his hands*]   Ah! You, Dodger . . . I'm glad.

DODGER   Why? Is something wrong? Out with it.

POX [*wheedling*]   I'm afraid . . .

DODGER   Afraid of what?

POX   That we slaves—oh dear!—today
Are heading for such a slaughtering and stringing up.

DODGER   Head for it on your own, then.

280    That's not the kind of heading-for or heading-from I
       cultivate.

POX [*rubbing his hands again*]   I don't suppose you
    know . . .
    A perfectly frightful piece of news
    That's fallen on our house.

DODGER [*coldly*]   What kind of frightful piece of news?

POX [*clicking*]   Tch! Tch! A disgrace.

DODGER [*turning away*]   Keep it to yourself then.
    Don't tell *me*. I don't want to know.

POX [*following him*]   Well, I can't stop you knowing:
    I chased our monkey today over their roof.

DODGER [*unconcernedly*]   Which simply means, Pox,
    That an idiotic man chased an idiotic animal.

POX [*nettled*]   Damn your eyes!

DODGER [*blandly*]   *You'd* do better . . . to go on with your
    story—
    Now that you've begun.

POX [*sniveling*]   Well, over the house next door, just by
    chance
    I chanced to look down through the skylight,
    And what do I clap eyes on
    But Goldilocks there kissing . . . someone else . . .
    A quite unknown young man.

DODGER [*holding up his hands in pretended horror*]   What,
    Pox? I'm shocked.
    Absolutely shocked!

POX [*gloating*]   Oh, I saw her all right.

DODGER   You? . . . Really?

290 POX   Me. Really . . . with these two eyes of mine.

DODGER [*shaking his head*]   Get along with you! You're
   kidding . . .
   You never saw a thing.

POX [*leering up at him*]   Do you notice anything wrong
   with these two eyes?

DODGER   That's something you'd better ask a doctor.
   But [*wagging a finger at him*]
   For the love of heaven,
   Don't be in a rush to spread that story round,
   Or you'll go crashing into catastrophe—
   Yes, head-over-heels and of your own creating.
   You'd better stop this stupidity at once
   Or you've damned yourself twice over.

POX   Twice? Really! . . . How?

DODGER   Well, just let me tell you.
   In the first place,
   If you accuse Goldilocks falsely—
   That'll finish you;
   And in the second, if it's true,
   You're finished just the same,
   Because *you* were the one put on to guard her.

POX [*shaken but pigheaded*]   I can't vouch for what's in
   store for me,
   But I certainly can for what I saw.

DODGER   Sticking to it, eh? You poor mutt!

POX   Well, what the deuce d'you want me to say       *300*
   Except what I saw?
   As a matter of fact she's there right now:
   Next door.

DODGER [*clapping his hand to his head*]   Hey, d'you mean
   she's not at *home?*

POX [*shrugging*]   Go and see for yourself . . .
   I don't ask anyone to believe what *I* say.

DODGER    That's exactly what I'm going to do.

[*Hurries into the* MAJOR's *house*]

POX [*calling after him*]    I'll wait here for you meanwhile
And keep a crafty watch
To see when that young heifer
Comes back from her pastures to her stall.
[*Placing himself fairly and squarely on the neigh-
boring doorstep—*MR. PROLIX's—POX *begins a se-
ries of gloomy reflections*]
But what shall I do? For the Major
Especially chose me to guard her.
So *if* I let on,
I *am* a dead man;
But if I keep mum
And the facts become known:
I'm a dead man again.
What a cursed affront is a woman!
I go on the roof and she's gone
From her own room:
My god, what a girl! And what gall!
[*Whines and sighs*]
If this gets to the ears of the Major
He'll string us all up—that I wager:
Including yours truly.
By heaven, I'd rather,
Whatever the story,
Keep my mouth shut
*310*                         Than *be* offered up
Oh, so cruelly!
[*Shakes his head glumly*]
No, I simply can't look after a woman who's out for sale.

[DODGER *returns, pretending to be overwhelmed
with apprehension on behalf of* POX]

DODGER
Pox, oh, Pox!
Is there a man on earth who can give and bear
Such appalling shocks?
Is there anyone born
Under a more
Angry and lorn

Star
Than you are?

POX [*nervously*]   What's up?

DODGER   Will you just tell someone to gouge out your eyes,
Because they see the nonexistent.

POX   What's nonexistent?

DODGER   I wouldn't give an empty filbert for your life.

POX [*with a pinched look*]   What's wrong?

DODGER   You ask *me* what's wrong?

POX [*truculently*]   And why shouldn't I ask?

DODGER [*gravely*]   Aren't you going to give instructions
For the clipping of that twaddling tongue?

POX   Why should I give instructions?

DODGER [*at the top of his lungs*]   Because, you nit, Goldi-
locks is at home
And you insisted that you saw her
Kissing and hugging a man next door.                    320

POX [*unmoved*]   Fancy eating bird-seed[10] when wheat is
so cheap!

DODGER   Meaning what?

POX   That you're blear-eyed.

DODGER [*snorting*]   Blear-eyed—you block? You're blind.
She's at home all right.

POX   What d'you mean—at home?

10 Plautus uses the word *lolium*. My dictionary translates this as
"darnel, cockle, tares." At any rate, it was reputed to be bad for
the eyes.

DODGER   I mean, goddammit, *at home.*

POX [*uneasily*]   Go on, Dodger, you're playing with me.

DODGER   Then I've gone and got my hands dirty.

POX   Oh?

DODGER   Yes—playing with filth.

POX   Go to hell!

DODGER   No, that's where you're going to, Pox,
If you don't change your eyesight and your talk.
         [*Listens*]
There's the door. Ours.

> [MAJOR BULLSHOT-GORGEOUS's *front door opens
> and reveals* GOLDILOCKS *standing there. She is an
> exquisitely-shaped young lady, in the latest
> fashion and with her beautiful hair shining in
> ringlets on her shoulders. She flashes* DODGER *an
> exultant smile.* POX, *suspecting a trick, refuses to
> turn around and does not see her*]

POX [*doggedly*]   I'm keeping my eyes glued to this one.
There's no way of getting from this house to the next
Except through this door.
         [*He pats* MR. PROLIX's *front door fondly*]

DODGER [*winking at* GOLDILOCKS]   But look, she's *there!*
You're poxed, Pox.

330  POX [*unmoved*]   I see for myself, I think for myself,
And most of all—I believe for myself.
No man alive's going to bluff me into thinking
She's not in this house.
I'm plumping myself right here:
She hasn't a chance of sneaking past me.

> [*True to his words,* POX *plants himself even more
> fairly and squarely on* MR. PROLIX's *doorstep.*
> GOLDILOCKS, *still standing in the other doorway,*

*exchanges signs—and smiles—with* DODGER, *who*
*signals her back into the* MAJOR's *house*]

DODGER [*jubilantly to himself*]   I've got him.
  Now for hurling him from the ramparts.
  [*sweetly to* POX]   Would you like me to get you to admit
  That you're completely cockeyed?

POX [*defiant*]   Go on, do it.

DODGER   And that you're as brainless as you're blind?

POX   I'd love it.

DODGER [*as if he were in court*]   You say Master's young
  lady is in this house, eh? [*pointing to* PROLIX's *house*]

POX   Yes and I insist I saw her—right there inside—
  Kissing another man.

DODGER   You know there's no connection
  Between this house and ours?

POX   I know that.

DODGER   And not a sundeck, garden, or any communi-
  cation
  Except through the skylight?                           *340*

POX   I know.

DODGER   Well then:
  If she's at home
  And I actually make you see her coming out of the
  house,
  Do you deserve a thorough thrashing?

POX   I do.

DODGER [*sarcastically*]   Watch that door
  So that she doesn't slip from under you
  And cross over to our house.

POX [*fervently*]    My intention exactly.

DODGER [*stepping briskly to the* MAJOR'*s front door*]    I'll
    have her here in a jiffy:
Standing here in the street right in front of you.

POX [*over his shoulders*]    Fine! Go and do it.

> [DODGER *slips into the* MAJOR'*s house, leaving* POX
> *standing where he is, his eyes still glued to the other*
> *front door.*]

POX [*becoming uneasy at* DODGER'*s cocksureness, shifts im-*
        *patiently*]    I am somewhat anxious to know
            If I really saw what I saw,
                And of course also
            If he does what he said he can do:
                Prove her at home. I'm sure
                    I've got eyes in my head
                    And don't need to beg
                For anyone else's instead.
                    [*Grimaces*]
            But this fellow's a terrible fawner.
            He's always forever all over her:
                First to be called for his dinner,
                First to be given his fodder.
            And he's only been about three[11]
                Years in all
            In my master's servants' hall.
            Yet nobody has such a ball—
                As *he*.
                    [*Breaks off*]
        But I'd better mind what I'm doing and watch this door.
        I'll block it off completely—like this.

> [POX *plasters himself against the door with his*
> *arms and legs spread-eagled. The* MAJOR'*s*
> *front door opens quietly and* DODGER *and*
> GOLDILOCKS *stand in the doorway. They can-*
> *not move for laughter. He signals her to*
> *caution*]

*350*

---

[11] Even given the slowness of voyages, this does make the separation
of the lovers happen rather a long time ago. Or has Plautus made a
slip? It is not the kind of slip that would bother him.

DODGER    Sh-h! Don't forget instructions.

GOLDILOCKS [*archly*]    You *do* go on about it.

DODGER    I'm scared stiff you won't be sufficiently subtle.

GOLDILOCKS [*laughing quietly*]    Just give me half a score of
     guileless girls
And I'll make them consummate mistresses of guile
Simply from what I throw away.

DODGER [*pointedly*]    Well, now's the time to work your
     wiles.
I'll drop back a little.
          [*Hangs back and calls out*]
Pox, now what do you say?

POX [*still glued*]    I'm fixed on *this* . . . But I've got a pair
     of ears:
Say what you want.

DODGER    I'd say it won't be long now
Before you're absolutely fixed . . . in that position:
Right outside the town gate—
Arms pronged and all, on a gibbet.

POX    Now what d'you say that for?                              360

DODGER [*snapping his fingers*]    Here, man, look to your
     left.
Who's that young lady?

POX [*forces himself to turn—gasps*]    God in heaven! . . .
     Master's mademoiselle!

DODGER [*with heavy sarcasm*]    I rather think so too . . .
Come on, now—whenever you're ready.

POX [*turning pale*]    For what? What am I going to do?

DODGER    Die—with dispatch.

GOLDILOCKS [*sweeping forward*]    Where is that model
     servant

Who so monstrously slandered
A perfectly innocent woman?

DODGER [*pointing derisively*]    He's all yours, ma'am. There
   he is:
The man who told me all I told you.

GOLDILOCKS [*advancing upon him*]    So, you criminal,
   It was *me* you say you saw, was it,
   Kissing here next door?

DODGER    And with an unknown young man, he said.

POX [*glaring*]    By god, I spoke the truth.

GOLDILOCKS [*louder*]    Me? . . . You saw *me?*

POX    Yes, with these eyes of mine.

GOLDILOCKS [*icily*]    Which I have a feeling you're going
   to lose
   By-and-by:
   They see more than meets the eye.

POX [*shouting*]    I swear I'm not going to be
   Scared out of seeing what I saw.

GOLDILOCKS [*tossing her head*]    It's fatuous and I'm a fool
370    To go on bandying words with this lunatic:
   I've got him by the hair.

POX    Give over threatening me.
   I'm well aware my tomb will be a gibbet.
   It's where my ancestors already lie:
   Father, grandfather, and great-grandfather—
   Yes, and great-great-grandfather . . .
   You won't dig out these eyes of mine with threats.
         [*Clutches hold of* DODGER]
      For love and kisses, tell me:
   Where did she come from?

DODGER [*stiffly*]    Where else but home?

POX  Home?

DODGER [*waving a hand before* POX]   Can you see me?

POX [*indignantly*]   Of course I can see you . . .
[*Thinks aloud*]
But it's sinister, it's queer,
The way she got from here to there.
We have no balcony at all
And no garden anywhere.
All the windows are grated . . . all.
[*Swings his eyes on* GOLDILOCKS]
And yet without a doubt I saw
You—inside—next door.

DODGER   Scum! Still accusing her?
You won't give up, will you?                                    *380*

GOLDILOCKS [*ingenuously*]   Good  heavens!  Then  the
dream I had last night
Has all come true.

DODGER [*with well-prepared excitement*]   Oh! What did
you dream?

GOLDILOCKS [*breathlessly*]   Let me tell you;
And you can both put your minds to it.
Last night I dreamt I saw my own twin sister
Arrive in Ephesus from Athens with her lover.
It seemed they were on a visit here together,
Lodging in the house next door.

DODGER [*with a wink at the audience*]   That's Dodger's
dream . . .
[*as one riveted*]   Go on, go on!

GOLDILOCKS   It seemed I was overjoyed my sister had
come,
But because of her I was caught up, it seemed,
In a ghastly scandal.
For in my dream my own servant charged me—
[*Flashes her eyes at* POX]

Just as you are doing now—
390     With having kissed a strange young man,
When actually it was that twin sister of mine
Kissing her own lover.
And so I dreamt I was wronged: dreadfully slandered.

DODGER [*slapping his thighs*]   Why, this whole dream's be-
    ing worked out in fact.
    Dammit, it all fits! [*with an urgent look at* GOLDILOCKS]
    Get inside, ma'am, and say your prayers.
    I think you ought to tell the Major.

GOLDILOCKS [*moving toward the door*]   Naturally.
    I have no intention of being slandered with impunity.

            [*Throws another look at* POX *as she sweeps off
                        into the* MAJOR's *house*]

POX   I fear I've gone and done it.
    My back's already smarting.

DODGER   I suppose you know you're a goner?

POX [*with a sickly grin*]   Anyway, she's certainly at home
    *now*.
    That's absolutely certain . . .
    And I'm going to keep her fixed:
    I'm going to watch our own front door.
            [POX *shuffles over to the* MAJOR's *front door and
            spread-eagles himself as before*]

DODGER [*sowing further doubt*]   It's extraordinary—isn't
    it, Pox!—
400     The way her dream fitted in
    With your imagining:
    Your belief you saw her kissing.

POX   *Now* I don't know what to believe.
    For what I thought I saw,
    Now I think I didn't see.

DODGER [*mercilessly*]   There isn't a chance, I'd say,
    Of your snapping out of this in time.

Once the thing gets to Master's ears,
You've cooked your goose.

POX [*hopelessly*]    I realize now: a fog befogged my eyes.

DODGER    That's as plain as a pikestaff.
She was in here all the time.

POX [*scratching his head, then immediately remembering he
    is  ᵓread-eagled*]    I don't know what to say for sure:
I didn't see her . . . yet I did.

DODGER    Hell! Your stupidity
Very nearly sent us all to the bottom . . .
Trying to be the boss's blue-eyed boy!
Why, you nearly ruined yourself!
        [*Cocks an ear*]
Excuse me, there goes our neighbor's door.                    *410*

            [GOLDILOCKS, *pretending to be her twin sister,
            comes out of* MR. PROLIX's *house. She has slipped
            on a different dress and put a rose in her hair.
            Using an artificial—somewhat "fruity"—voice,
            she stands giving directions to a slave inside*]

GOLDILOCKS
                Enkindle the fire on the altar:
                I'm full of glory and gladness
                Toward Diana of Ephesus.
            I'll sweeten her nose with the odor
                Of incense grains from Arabia.
            In the places of Neptune she saved me;
                In the boisterous halls of his palace
            When ravaged I was by the waves' race.

POX [*without changing his position, slowly turns his head*]
    Oh Dodger! Dodger!

DODGER [*mimicking*]    Oh Pox! Pox!
    [*switching to severity*]    What do you want?

POX [*gulping and pointing*]    The woman—the one who just
    came out—

It's Master's lady—Goldilocks—
Or isn't it?

DODGER [*rubbing his eyes*]   Damned if it isn't! Looks like
her.
But it's a miracle if she's passed from here to there.

POX [*blinking*]   Can you have the slightest doubt it's her?

DODGER   Seems like it.

POX [*jumping off his doorstep*]   Come on, let's call her.
[*Brazenly walks up to her*]
420     Hi there! What are you doing, Goldilocks?
What business have you here?
I mean, what are you up to in that house?
        [GOLDILOCKS *looks straight past him*]
Got nothing to say? . . . I'm talking to *you.*

DODGER [*grinning*]   You darn well aren't.
You're talking to yourself.
She's not answering.

POX [*at the top of his lungs*]   Hey, you—you stuffed
strumpet,
Wandering abroad among the neighbors—
I'm addressing *you.*

GOLDILOCKS [*giving him a cold, hard look*]   To whom, sir,
are you babbling?

POX [*red in the face*]   To whom? To *you.*

GOLDILOCKS [*unruffled*]   And who *are* you?
What business do you presume with me?

POX [*stammering*]   Y-you ask me who I *am?*

GOLDILOCKS   And why should I not ask what I do not
know?

DODGER [*stepping in front of her with a wink*]   Then who
am *I*, ma'am, if you don't know *him?*

GOLDILOCKS    A great nuisance to me, whoever you are:
    both of you.

POX [*quailing*]    You don't know us?

GOLDILOCKS [*turning her back*]    Certainly not. Neither of
    you.

POX [*nervously to* DODGER]    I'm fearfully afraid . . .

DODGER    Of what?

POX    That we've gone and lost our identities.
    She said she didn't know either one of us.

DODGER [*deadpan*]    My dear Pox,
    This is something I must follow up:
    Are we ourselves or someone else?                430
    Perhaps some neighbor on the sly
    Has gone and swapped us for some others.

POX [*pinching himself*]    Well, I'm all *me*.

DODGER [*tapping himself*]    And so—by god!—am I. [*with
    a sidelong look at* GOLDILOCKS]
    Woman, you're looking for trouble.
        [*She pretends to ignore him*]
    I'm talking to *you* . . . Hi there! Goldilocks!

GOLDILOCKS [*trying not to giggle*]    You must be off your
    head
    To give me such a crazy name.

DODGER    Hoity-toity! . . . By what name, then?

GOLDILOCKS [*pouting*]    Honéstia.

POX    Ha! Ha! Ha! Goldilocks, you little cheat—
    Trying to get yourself another name!
    It's Humbuggia, not Honéstia:
    You cheater of my master!

GOLDILOCKS [*with big wide open eyes*]    *I?*

POX   Yes, you.

GOLDILOCKS   But I only arrived yesterday in Ephesus:
    Last evening from Athens,
*440*    With a young Athenian gentleman, my fiancé.

DODGER [*impressed*]   Well, madam,
    Tell me what your business is here in Ephesus.

GOLDILOCKS [*looking him straight in the eye*]   I heard my
    own twin sister was here,
    And I came to find her.

POX [*between his teeth*]   You're a bad one!

GOLDILOCKS   No, just incredibly silly—
    To be chatting to you two . . . I'm going.
        [*Turns on her heel*]

POX [*grabbing her*]   I won't let you go.

GOLDILOCKS [*struggling*]   Let me loose.

POX   You're caught redhanded, my girl.
    I won't let you loose.

GOLDILOCKS [*in ringing tones*]   If you don't let go of me
    this instant,
    *My* hand and *your* face are coming into collision.

POX [*angrily to* DODGER]   You're just standing by, you
    bastard!
    Why don't you nab her from your side?
        [GOLDILOCKS *swings and catches* POX *a solid blow*
        *on the cheek*]

DODGER [*folding his arms and watching*]   I've no desire to
    get a battering.
    How do I know she's really Goldilocks
    And not someone the dead spit of her?

GOLDILOCKS [*in a wrestler's lock with* POX]   Are you going
    to let me go or not?

POX [*panting*]   Let you go?
  I'm going to drag you home all the way . . .
  Willy-nilly if you don't come willingly.

GOLDILOCKS [*tossing her head toward* MR. PROLIX'*s house*]
  This is where I live, and I'm a guest.                    *450*
  My home's in Athens.
  What *you* call home I want no part of.
  And as to you two men—
  I don't know you and I don't want to.

POX [*snorting*]   Take it to court, then.
  I'm not for the life of me going to let you go:
  Not unless I have your word of honor
  That if I do
  You'll get yourself over into the Major's house here.

GOLDILOCKS [*struggling*]   You're forcing me, you, you—
    who?
        [*After several more seconds of tussle* GOLDI-
        LOCKS *gives way*]
  All right: I give you my word—
  Let me go and I'll disappear
  Into whatever house you say.

POX [*releasing her*]   There! I've let you go.

GOLDILOCKS [*shakes out her tresses and with a mocking
    laugh darts into* PROLIX'*s house*]   Yes, you've let me
    go . . . And I'm gone!
            [*She slams the door in their faces*]

POX [*red with fury*]   Kept her word like a woman!

DODGER [*dryly*]   Pox, you let the quarry slip through your
    fingers.
  She's our master's girl all right.
        [*Bends toward him*]
  Do you want to show real verve?

POX   How?

DODGER [*between his teeth*]   Go into your house and fetch
    me a sword.

POX    What'll you do with it?

460    DODGER [*fiercely*]    I'm going to break into that house
And whomsoever I see inside kissing Goldilocks,
I shall quarter him on the spot.

POX [*hesitant*]    So you think it was she?

DODGER    Good heavens, man! I'm certain.

POX [*wiping his forehead*]    God! What a show she put on.

DODGER    Off with you now and bring me the sword.

POX [*disappearing into the* MAJOR's *house*]    Yes, yes—I'll
have it here in a jiffy.

DODGER [*to the audience, chuckling*]
No one, not even a brigade of dragoons
    Or column of men,
Can match the confident action and cool
    Nerve of a woman.
Oh, the precision with which she has studied
    And acted both parts!
The way she's bamboozled my colleague, that prig
    Of a scrupulous guard . . .
The hole I cut through the wall is a sheer
    Marvel of genius.

POX [*running out of the house*]    Hey, Dodger, we don't
need a sword.

DODGER    Well, what now?

POX [*breathless*]    Master's mistress is here—right at home.

DODGER    At home? . . . N-no?

470    POX    Lying back on her couch.

DODGER [*grimly*]    Then you're predicting your personal
doom.

POX   What do you mean?

DODGER   Well, you've gone and manhandled
The lady from next door.

POX [*going pale*]   O god! I'm afraid I have.

DODGER   And no one on earth can alter the fact
That's she's our girl's twin sister:
Precisely the one you saw kissing through the skylight.

POX [*going weak at the knees*]   Y-yes: it's all obvious
now . . .
She was the one—as you say.
Lord, what a near shave!
What if I'd told the m-master?

DODGER [*stiffly*]   If you've got any sense you'll keep your
mouth shut.
A servant should say much less than he savvies.
In any case I am leaving you now:
I want no part of your maneuvers.
I'm going in here to see my neighbor.
Your muddles upset me. If the master comes
And asks for me, here I'll be—
And here you can come and get me.                          *480*

[DODGER *wanders off, nose in air, into* MR. PRO-
LIX's *house*]

POX [*resentfully*]   So he's gone, has he?
Takes about as much interest in his master
As if he were as free as a goddam freedman.
At any rate, the girl is now inside the house:
I saw her there just now stretched out at home.
I'm going to keep my eye on her—and that's for sure.
[POX *takes up his stance on the* MAJOR's *front
doorstep*]

[*Shouts and recriminations burst from the other
house, and in a moment* MR. PROLIX *stomps out,
brandishing his silver cane and making an excellent
show of rage*]

PROLIX  Hell and damnation! These fellows here next door,
These cursed servants of the soldier,
Take me for a female—not a man at all.
They're simply laughing up their sleeves at me.
Is my invited guest, the lady
Who came from Athens yesterday with her friend,
To be coerced and bandied about like a bauble?
490  And she a full and freeborn citizen!
    [*Marches toward the* MAJOR's *house*]

POX  [*trying to make himself small*]  Lord help me—now I'm done for!
He's making a beeline for me. Oh!
I've landed myself in a mess, I fear.
This old tyke's tirade makes that clear.

PROLIX  [*still advancing*]  I'll show him!
Look here, Pox—
You absolute cesspool, Pox!
Are you the man who made a game of my guest just now—
In front of my house?

POX  [*cringing*]  Dear sweet neighbor, listen.

PROLIX  [*thundering*]  Listen? Me? To *you!*

POX  I—I can explain.

PROLIX  Explain? . . . *That* outrage? *That* irrevocable misconduct?
Do you think you freebooters have the right
500  To do anything you like—you, you ruffian?

POX  [*whining*]  Oh, please, sir.

PROLIX  So help me every god and goddess that there is,
If you're not handed over to me now
For one long-drawn-out and bloody birching
Lasting from the morning till the night.
You smashed my gutters and my tiles,
You chased an ape no better than yourself;

You spied upon my guest from there
As she hugged and kissed her heart's desire.
You had the gall to impute immodesty
To that decent girl next door—
The mistress of your master—
And me with grossest infamy.
Then you trifled with my guest outside my house . . .          510
Oh, if you're not handed to me now
As a holocaust to lash,
I'll heap your master with more shame
Than the sea has combers in a hurricane.
      *[Raises his stick]*

POX [*crumpled before him*]   Oh Mr. Prolix, sir, I'm so
        hard pressed
I've no idea what to tackle first:
Make excuses to you now?
Or if you think it best,
And *that* girl isn't *this*
And this girl isn't that:
Apologize and take the blame . . .
I mean I don't know even now
What I really saw:
That girl of yours is so like ours,
If indeed she's not the same.

PROLIX   Then go inside my house and look:                      520
You'll soon know.

POX   May I?

PROLIX   May you? I *command* you.
Study her at leisure.

POX [*walking backwards and bowing*]   Yes, sir, yes sir! I'll
    do that.

        [*As* POX *disappears into* MR. PROLIX's *house,
        the latter hurries over to the front door of the
             MAJOR and shouts through the grating*]

PROLIX   Hi there, Goldilocks! Quick!
Race over to my house. It's imperative.

Then when Pox has gone, quick,
Race back home again.
> [PROLIX *twiddles his thumbs anxiously on the*
> *doorstep*]

Oh dear!
I'm so afraid she's going to mess it up.
If he doesn't see the girl in there . . . Ah!
The door's opening.

> [POX *staggers out*]

POX   By all the immortal powers! The gods themselves I
      claim
530   Could not make two different women more the same.

PROLIX [*severely*]   And so?

POX [*humbly*]   And so I deserve a clobbering.

PROLIX   And so she isn't this one? [*indicating the* MAJOR's
         *house*]

POX [*still dazed*]   Even if she is, she isn't.

PROLIX   But you saw that one?

POX   That one and her guest:
      Hugging and kissing.

PROLIX   And is that one this one?

POX   I don't know.

PROLIX [*magnanimously*]   Would you like to know—for
         certain?

POX   Very much.

PROLIX   Then go straight into your house and see
         If this one—yours—is there inside.

POX [*full of gratitude*]   Oh yes, sir! It's a wonderful sug-
      gestion.
      I'll come straight back to you outside.

[POX *runs into the* MAJOR's *house*]

PROLIX [*holding his sides with laughter*]    I swear I've never
    seen a human being
More twisted inside out—
More beautifully bamboozled.
[*freezing his laughter*]    But here he is again.

[POX *shuffles out of the* MAJOR's *house and throws
                   himself at* MR. PROLIX's *feet*]

POX    Mr. Prolix, I beseech you,
By all the gods and men, by my own stupidity,                    540
By these your knees . . .

PROLIX [*impatiently*]    Yes, yes—beseech me for what?

POX    To forgive
My senseless insensitivity.
I realize now I've been a stupid, sightless sod.
For Goldilocks is *there*—inside.

PROLIX    So, you've seen them both, you stinker?

POX [*with bowed head*]    I've seen them both, sir.

PROLIX [*tight-lipped*]    Will you please bring your master
    out here.

POX    Oh sir, I do admit
I deserve a dreadful drubbing
And I assert I've deeply wronged
Your lady guest . . .
I thought she really was
My master's woman.
And anyway, my master
Had appointed me to watch her.
But—ah!—two drops of water from one well           550
Could not be as much alike
As that guest of yours is like this girl.
Furthermore I do confess
That through the skylight
I peeped into your house.

PROLIX [*snorting*]   You do confess! I saw you do it.
No doubt you also saw
My two guests kissing there?

POX   Yes, I saw them—why deny it?—
But what I saw was Goldilocks, I thought.

PROLIX   What! You'd rate me with the very scum?
Make me knowingly condoner of an outrage done
560   Against my neighbor in my home?

POX [*pathetically*]   I do realize now at last,
Now that I see the whole thing whole,
That I acted like a blooming fool.
But, sir, I didn't act from spite.

PROLIX [*tartly*]   No, you acted from presumption.
A man in the servant state should aim
To keep his eyes, hands and tongue
Well tamed.

POX [*still kneeling and looking up*]   Sir, if I mutter a word
again
From this day on—
Even what I know for certain—
Have me hamstrung.
I'll hand myself right over to you.
But this time, sir,
Please give your pardon.

PROLIX [*strokes his beard, surveying* POX *with distaste.*
*Finally he growls*:]   I'll force myself to think
You meant no harm;
And for this once, I'll pardon.

570   POX [*still groveling*]   Oh, sir—god bless you!

PROLIX [*gruffly*]   And if you want the gods to bless you too,
You'll damn well hold your tongue in future:
Not know even what you know,
See past even what you see.

POX [*kissing* PROLIX's *feet*]   Oh, that's beautiful advice, sir!

I'll go and do it . . .
But have I apologized enough?

PROLIX   Just go.

POX [*staggers to his feet, bowing*]   Is there nothing else
you'd like?

PROLIX   Yes—not to know you.

POX [*begins to move off, mumbling to himself*]
  He gave me his word *here* . . .
  Nice of him to be so kind
  And stop being angry,
  But *I* know better.
The moment the Major comes in from the forum
I'm to be grabbed—at home.
He and that Dodger are making arrangements
To sell me—I feel it—I've known it some time.   580
Thanks very much! . . . I'll not fall for that.
I'll scuttle away to some little hole
And there lie low for a day or two
Till all this fuss and fury is over.
God knows! I've earned enough retribution
To do for a whole impious nation.

    [POX *slinks off in the direction of the country*]

PROLIX [*gazes after him and chuckles*]
  So the fellow's decamped!
   And I'm darn-well sure
  A stuck pig's sense
   Is a good deal more.
  To be diddled like that—
   Ha ha ha!—
  From seeing what he saw.

  Why his eyes and his ears,
   Even his brain,
  Have collapsed in our favor:
   We're doing fine,
  Oh fine—so far!      590

  The way that girl
   Romped through her part!

> Now I'll return
>     To the parliament,
> For Dodger's back
>     With me at home
> And Pox has gone
>     Off to roam.
> The Senate now
>     Can sit full house,
> So I must go—
>     I mustn't miss
> The sorting out of parts.

[MR. PROLIX, *humming a ditty, goes into his*
*house*]

# ACT III

*Half an hour later. A council of war has been held in* MR.
PROLIX's *house. The time has come for the conspirators to*
*meet outside and clinch their plans.* DODGER *creeps out*
*furtively and calls to the others.*

DODGER [*in a loud whisper, holding up a cautionary hand*]
    Hey! Halcyon, keep the rest of them inside a minute till
    I take a good look around. We don't want our little meet-
    ing to be surprised. We've got to make sure the spot is
    safe from the enemy intelligence . . . Can't risk our
    plans . . .
            [*Mutters to himself as he looks around warily*]
600    A plan's worse than useless if the enemy gets hold of it:[12]
    nothing but a pitfall. Once let the enemy get whiff of
    your strategy and you've bound yourself hand and foot—
    yes, and tongue. They'll do to you exactly what you'd
    planned for *them*. So I'm going to make darn sure there
    isn't a big-ears about—left or right—lying in wait for us.
            [*Tiptoes behind a pillar and gazes down the street*]
610    Good! A strictly vacuous view right to the bottom. I'll
    call them: Hey there! Prolix and Halcyon—come on out!

12 I follow Leo in omitting the following two doubtful (and tauto-
logous) lines: "For a well-planned plan is frequently filched/if the
conference place is carelessly and incautiously chosen."

[*Enter* MR. PROLIX *and* HALCYON. *The latter is a good-looking young man in his early twenties. His carefully tailored clothes of excellent weave show that he comes from the well-to-do professional classes. Though usually of a sunny disposition (and generous to the point of naïveté) his preoccupied look speaks of the problems of love. He is also worried about being a burden to his old friend* PROLIX]

PROLIX    Here we are—at your disposal.

DODGER [*surveying them with approval*]    Good troops are easy to command.
   What I want to know is this:
   Are we to go ahead with the plans we made inside?

PROLIX    Of course! They're perfect for our purposes.

DODGER    And you, Halcyon?

HALCYON    If it pleases you two,
        How could it displease *me?*
            [*Turns to* DODGER]
   What man more than you
        Is mine entirely?

DODGER    Nicely and becomingly said, sir!

PROLIX [*with a twinkle in his eye*]    As well it ought to be!

HALCYON [*turning to* PROLIX *with a sigh*]    Seriously, sir,
        this enterprise
   Makes me miserable as hell:
        Bothers me body and soul.

PROLIX [*putting a hand on his arm*]    Come on! What's bothering you?

HALCYON    That I should thrust on you,
            A man of reverend years,
                These stripling's cares.

They do not suit your soul
            Or character at all.
*620*     That I should see you strain
            Just for love of me
            To further my love affairs,
            And do such things as age
                  Like yours would leave alone . . .
            I blush to cast on you
                  Such worries when you're old.


DODGER [*pretending to be shocked*]    Man,
      What new love is this:
            Blushing for what you do?
      Halcyon, you're no lover,
            You're the shadow
            Of what a lover is.


HALCYON    But to harry
                  Such an elder
                  With a lover's worry!


PROLIX [*with sudden fire*]    What are you saying, my boy?
      Do I seem such a dreary old death's-head to you?
      Such a tottering, terrible old mummy?
      Why, I wasn't born more than fifty-four years ago!
            [*Winks at the audience at this patent untruth*]
*630*    I'm a keen-eyed, quick-handed, neat-footed youngster.


DODGER [*shaking a finger at* HALCYON]
                  His hair is silver perhaps
                        But there isn't the tiniest trace
                  Of age in his heart: the same
                        Beautiful spirit is still
                  Inside him as when he was born.


HALCYON [*promptly*]    Dodger, that's perfectly true;
                  Just as I'm finding out too.
            The way he is kind is the way
                  A very young man might do.


PROLIX [*preening himself*]    What's more, you'll find, my
      boy,
      The harder the task you ask

The more one with you I am
In furthering your lover's aim.

HALCYON   No need to tell me that, sir.

PROLIX   Ah! But I want you to know it direct,
Not at second hand.
For unless one has fallen in love oneself
One can hardly understand
The passionate heart.
And my old body still has
Some love and some juice;                              *640*
And for the finer delights of life
I still have a use:
I can crack a good joke,
I'm a gracious guest.
At table I don't contradict,
At dinners I watch my manners:
I don't talk more than my share,
Shut up when somebody else
Has the floor.
I'm no spitter and hawker—
No sniveling boor. No sir!
My birthplace is Ephesus— not Apulia.
I'm not an animal from Animulia.[13]

DODGER [*to* HALCYON, *tongue-in-cheek*]
What a lovely old man he is
If this inventory is his!
He must have been reared—oh surely!—
In Venus's nursery.                                    *650*

PROLIX [*puffing up with pleasure*]   Oh, you'll find I'm bet-
ter at doing than saying!
I never steal another man's girl at a party.
No! And I don't go grabbing the caviar
Or cornering the cocktails or
Starting a quarrel over the wine.
If anyone gets difficult
I just go home and cut the cackle.

[13] A small town in Apulia (southern Italy) whose inhabitants typified
the country-bumpkin.

>           To be gracious, loving, affable
>           Are what I aim for at the table.

DODGER [*beginning to fidget*]   My dear sir,
>     Everything you do is strictly charming.
>     Show me three such men
>     And I'll pay the weight of them in gold.

HALCYON [*sincerely*]   And *I* say you won't find another
>     Man of his age so delightful
660   Or such a friend to a friend.

PROLIX [*basking in their eulogies*]
>     Well, Halcyon, I'll make you admit
>     I'm still a youngster at heart,
>     Bursting with ways to proffer you help.
>     Do you need a lawyer grave and fierce?
>                 [*Knits his brow and pulls down the corners of
>                                               his mouth*]
>           Here I am! . . . Or one that's suave?
>                 [*Demonstrates with an oily smile*]
>           You'll find me suaver than the sea,
>           More silent and calm, more meltingly
>           Genial than a western breeze.
>     [*with hand to his heart*]   And from this same resource-
>           ful seat
>           I'll produce the liveliest guest for you at dinner,
>           The nicest buddy when you eat,
>           And wizard of a caterer.
>           But when it comes to dancing girls[14]—oh my!—
>           I've got the most curvaceous cutey beat.
>                 [*Executes a little belly-dance*]

DODGER [*stifling a yawn, to* HALCYON]   With such a mass
>           of talent, sir,
>     What would you wish—
>     If a wish could add a single jot?

HALCYON [*earnestly*]   The ability to match
670   His kindnesses with thanks:

[14] The entry of the dancing-girls was an important part of Roman
(and sometimes Greek) banquets. They could be naked and were
chosen for other talents besides dancing.

Yes, and yours—I know how much
Worry I am causing both of you.
Oh, and the expense,
    [*Turns to* PROLIX]
I am putting you to
Bothers me a lot.

PROLIX [*clapping him on the back*]   Foolish boy!
    When one pays out money for a shrewish wife
    Or for an enemy,
    *That* is cost.
    But money spent on an honest guest
    Or on a friend, is money made—
    As money spent on things divine,
    For a wise man, is—sheer gain.
        [DODGER *looks in despair at* HALCYON *but gets no*
        *sympathy from that quarter. Meanwhile* PROLIX
                               *goes on*]
    By the grace of god I have the means
    To entertain you gracefully.
    So eat, drink and enjoy yourself with me:
    Put on the trappings of hilarity.
    It's an open house and I am open too,
    Living the life I wish to do.
    By the grace of god, as I say, I'm rich
    And could have taken a wife of means and parts.    *680*
    But how could I induce
    Myself to introduce
    Into the house a woman that barks?

DODGER [*unable to resist giving* HALCYON *a sharp nudge*]
    Why not, sir? Having children is a very happy business.

PROLIX [*vigorously shaking his head*]   Believe you me:
    having your own freedom[15] is infinitely happier.

DODGER [*with a polite sigh*]   You're an all-round genius,
    sir, at giving good advice.

PROLIX [*off again*]   Oh, I know it's all very nice
    To marry a tractable wife;

[15] The play in Latin is between *liberos,* "children" and *liberum,* a "free person."

But where in the world is she
To be found? . . . Now take me:
Am I really to bring home
A dame who'll never dream
Of saying to me this:
"Buy me some wool, my darling, to weave
You a beautiful soft warm coat to have
For the winter to keep you from cold, and some
Nice thick vests"?
Not on your life!
That's not the sort of thing a wife
Ever suggests.
But before the crow of the cock

690     She'd wake me with a shock
And say:
"Darling, give me some money for Mother's Day[16]
To buy me a present for Mother.
Give me some money to make
Preserves, and some money to take
The woman who predicts
On Minerva's Day, and the priest,
And some for the analyst
Of dreams, and the herbalist.
And wouldn't it be a shame
If we left out the madame
Who tells your future fate
From your eyebrows' state?
Then there's the modiste,
We can't afford to miss.
And the cateress is cross
Because of course
It's been some time
Since she had a dime.
And the midwife's made a fuss
Because she hasn't had enough . . .
And oh! There's nothing worse
Than not to tip the nurse
Who looks after
The young slaves
Under your own rafter."
          [MR. PROLIX *fetches a sigh from the depths*]
This is the kind of expense galore
16 March 1st, held in honor of Mars.

And a great deal more
That stops me taking a wife
Who'd boss me out of my life.                              *700*

DODGER [*distantly*]   Ah, sir: the gods are certainly kind to
you. Once you let go of that liberty of yours, you won't
so easily put it back in its goddam place again.

HALCYON [*somewhat shaken*]   But it *is* an asset, surely, for
a man of great wealth and considerable station to bring
up children to perpetuate his name and family.

PROLIX   What do I want with children when I have so
many relatives? As things are, I lead a peaceful, happy
life: please my fancy as I want to. On my demise my
property gets shared out among my relatives.
     [DODGER *is about to interrupt but* PROLIX *with a
                              sly smile waves him away*]
     Before daylight they're there:                        *709*[17]
Asking if I've passed a peaceful night.
They offer sacrifice—
Give me a bigger part than they give themselves.
I am escorted to the sacrificial banquet.
They ask me home for lunch, and clamor
For me to come to dinner.
The least happy of them
Is the one that's sent me least:
They fight to give me presents.
     Meanwhile I just murmur to myself:
"It's my goods they're gaping after
But it's *me* their competition nurtures and supports."

DODGER [*offhandedly*]   All beautifully thought out, sir!
Your life arranged around you to a tee!
You enjoy yourself—
And that's as good as twins or triplets.

PROLIX [*taking him up*]   By god! If I had children,
Then the troubles would begin.
I'd worry myself silly right away.

17 I omit, with Leo, lines 708 & 710: "They will be at my house, look
after me, come to see how I'm doing, if there's anything I want./
I'll have for children those people who send me presents."

720          My son has a temperature—
             I think he's dying.
             He's fallen down drunk
             Or been chucked off his horse—
             I'm terrified he's broken his legs
             Or snapped his neck.

        DODGER [*with perfunctory politeness as he twiddles his
             thumbs, rocks on his heels with impatience*]    Here's
             a man who's got a right to be rich and have a long
             life:
             He looks after his own and has a good time,
             And he sees to his friends.

        HALCYON [*bursting out with youthful admiration*]    Oh,
             what a lovely man!
             So help me heaven—but I wish the gods
             Didn't lump together all our human lives
             In one indiscriminate lot,
             Instead of doing what a decent salesman does:
             Marking up the price of perfect goods
             To sell as they deserve,
             And cutting down the price
             Of items that are soiled.
730          So should the gods have allotted human life:
             To the man of charming character,
             Sweet longevity;
             To the nasty criminal,
             A quick dispatch.
                  If they'd arranged things so,
             Bad men would be less abundant
             And do their dirty deeds with less abandon.
             What is more:
             The cost of living would—for the good—
             Drop through the floor.

        PROLIX [*holding up his hands in avuncular reproof*]    No,
             it's shallow and it's silly
             To criticize the gods and to abuse them . . .
             But it's time we stopped all this.
             I must do some marketing for you, dear guest,
             To entertain you in my house

As well as you and I could wish
With a slap-up time
And every bang-up special dish.

HALCYON [*with a gesture of reproval*]    But, sir, I'm quite   *740*
    embarrassed
At the cost I've put you to already.
Such hospitality from a friend
No guest can revel in
And not become a nuisance after a three days' stay.
After *ten* days he becomes an Iliad of disasters.
Even if the master
Is not unwilling to put up with it,
The servants grumble.
            [*Meanwhile* DODGER *in a state of restlessness has
            gone and sat down on the doorstep, from where
            during the remainder of this conversation he
            amuses the audience with a series of gestures of
                            impatience and despair*]

PROLIX   Ah! My friend,
    My servants have been trained to serve and not to boss
        me
    Or try to keep me under their thumbs.
    If what *I* want gripes them—well,
    *I'm* the stroke in this rowing outfit:
    They've got to do it just the same
    Even if they hate it, or get a hiding . . .
        Now for that shopping I spoke about.

HALCYON [*as* PROLIX *begins to go* HALCYON *puts a hand on
        his arm*]   If you really must, sir,
    But please don't buy a lot,
    Don't be extravagant:
    Just anything will do for me.                         *750*

PROLIX [*turns on him sharply*]   Oh, stop that now!
    Stop these clichés of such stilted nonsense.
    Now you're pulling that lower-class cant on me
    Which makes guests say the moment they've sat down
    And dinner's on the table:
    "Oh, my host! Was it really necessary

To go to this expense—just for us?
You must have been mad. Why, this
Would do for ten!"
They blame you for what you've bought
But they dig in just the same.

DODGER [*with a combination of admiration and desperate
     irony*]   By god! That's exactly what they do.
How shrewd of him and how observant!

PROLIX [*underlining his remarks with cane in hand*]   And
     none of these same people,
No matter how you pile the food on them,
Ever say:
"Oh, please, stop!
Have this dish removed;
Take away the ham, I'd rather not.
760   This eel, cold, would be superb:
Remove it, to the side with it."
     You won't hear suchlike sentiments
From any one of them.
No, they just tumble and topple across the table, grab-
     bing and guzzling.

DODGER [*with a sigh*]   A good description from a gentle-
     man
Of bad manners, sir!

PROLIX   Oh, I haven't told you the hundredth part.
If only there were time, how I could dissertate!

DODGER [*leaping up from the doorstep*]
               But since there's not, sir,
          Let's get on with the plot, sir.
               I'd like you both to fix
          Your attention on the matter.
          I'll need your service, Mr. Prolix.
               I've hit on an idea
               That's absolutely dapper
          Of shearing our long-haired soldier
          And giving Goldilocks's lover
                    The hope

To elope
And have her.
[DODGER *beckons the other two to his side and clears
his throat. The conversation begins in mock com-
mittee-meeting style*]

PROLIX   I should like to be given the scheme of this idea.   *770*

DODGER   And I should like to be given the ring you wear.

PROLIX   What use will you put it to?

DODGER   When I have it, I'll unfold my scheme to you.

PROLIX   Here you are, sir, use it.
[*Hands over ring*]

DODGER   And here's my grand idea, peruse it . . .

HALCYON   And here are our ears, ready to infuse it.

DODGER [*getting down to brass tacks*]   Now my master is
the most pertinacious pursuer of female flesh that ever
there was, or I believe ever will be.

HALCYON [*vigorously interrupting*]   Hear! Hear! to that!

DODGER   And he asseverates that the beauty of Paris is as
nothing to his; in fact, he says, lays it down on record,
that all the women of Ephesus can't stop from running
after him.

PROLIX [*cynically*]   A good many husbands, *I* can tell you,
heartily wish that what you say were true . . . But I know   *780*
exactly what you mean. So, come to the point, will you,
Dodger!

DODGER   Well, sir, can you find me some perfectly irresistible "femme fatale" whose brains and bosom are equally
replete with wiles and strategies?

PROLIX   Freeborn or freegrown?

DODGER   I don't mind which; but give me one who's on the make—embodies her livelihood in her body—and has some common sense. Intelligence I don't expect. None of them has that.

PROLIX [*doing a little diagram in the air with his cane*]   Do you want her to be sumptuous or only scrumptious?

DODGER [*slightly altering the diagram in the air with a finger*]   You know . . . succulent: just about as young and irresistible a dish as possible.

PROLIX [*after a little more thought*]   Aha! The very thing: one of my own clients—a real swinging doll . . . But what do you want her for?

790 DODGER   You are to take her home to your house, then bring her here all got up like a married woman: hair piled high in a braided coiffure . . . and she's to pretend she's your wife. That's what she'll be told.

HALCYON   *I* don't see where this is getting you.

DODGER [*grinning*]   You *will* . . . Does she have a maid?

PROLIX   A minx of the first water.

DODGER   *She'll* be needed too. This is what you tell the girl and her maid: the chick's to pretend she's your wife but dying for the Major. She gave this ring to her little nymphet—maid—who turned it over to me to pass on to the Major . . . I being the go-between in this affair.
        [DODGER *is getting louder and louder*]

PROLIX [*testily*]   I can hear you, thank you. I'm not deaf. I've got a pair of very good ears.[18]

800 DODGER [*sobered*]   I'll give the ring to him, saying it was sent as a present by your wife through me in order to bring the two of them together . . . That's the sort of man he is: the poor wretch will be simply slavering for her. Whoring is the stinker's only hobby.

18 Leo notes a hopeless gap in the text here.

PROLIX [*beaming*]   If you'd sent the great god Sun to do the searching for you, you'd not uncover two more perfect wenches for this job. Be full of optimism.

DODGER [*waving him on*]   Fine! On with the job. It presses hard.

[*Turns to* HALCYON *as* PROLIX *disappears down the street*]

And now, Halcyon: your turn to listen, please.

HALCYON   At your command.

DODGER   Make quite sure that when the Major comes back home you'll not go calling Goldilocks by her proper name.

HALCYON [*mystified*]   By what name, then?

DODGER [*shocked that he has forgotten it already*] Honéstia.

HALCYON [*apologetic*]   Oh yes, of course! The name we settled on.

DODGER [*with a brisk slap on the back*]   Good! Off with you.

HALCYON [*reluctant to move*]   I'll remember, but what use —I'd like to know—is remembering?

DODGER [*giving him a shove*]   I'll tell you when the time comes. Meanwhile keep your mouth shut. *He's* doing his   *810* stuff now: in due course *you'll* have your part to play.

HALCYON   All right! I go inside.

[HALCYON *enters* MR. PROLIX's *house*]

DODGER   Make sure you keep strictly to what I say.
[DODGER *saunters a few steps toward the* MAJOR's *house, delighted with the intrigue he has set in motion and whistling a little tune*]

What things I'm stirring up!
   Oh, what machines of war
I'm moving forward fast!
   Today I'm going to tear
The Major's girl from him
   When my troops fall in.
But I'll call that fellow, Pox, out here.

   [*Shouts through the* MAJOR'S *door*]
Hey, Pox! If you're not too boxed:
Step outside . . . It's Dodger calling.

> [*Enter* PENNY *from the* MAJOR'S *house.
> He is a fat youth in his middle teens, very
> much at home in the world and well aware
> on which side his bread is buttered. He
> lurches into the street unsteadily*]

PENNY [*thickly*]    Poxsh? . . . He'sh . . . engaged.

DODGER [*eying him with disapproval*]    At what?

PENNY    Absorbing . . . in his sleep.

DODGER    Absorbing?

820    PENNY    Yeah! . . . I mean he's snoring. And snoring is absorbing—of a sorts.

DODGER [*impatiently*]    So Pox is inside asleep, is he?

PENNY [*grinning*]    Asleep? Not his nose. That's snorting—like a trumpet. You see, he looks after the cellar . . . He was just putting some spice into a barrel when he touched a cup and took a nip—privately.

DODGER    Fancy that now! And you were just—helping him. Louse!

PENNY    What are you after?

DODGER    What gave him the nerve to fall asleep?

PENNY [*shrugging*]    His eyes—I presume.

DODGER    That's not what I asked. Tosspot! . . . Come over
here.
[PENNY *crawls toward him*]
You're a dead duck if I don't have the truth.
Did you draw the wine for him?

PENNY [*insolently*]    No, I didn't.

DODGER    You deny it?

PENNY    You're damned right, I do. He said I mustn't say    *830*
I did. So I didn't really draw off eight halfpints into a jug,
and he didn't really gulp the hot stuff off for lunch.

DODGER    And *you* didn't really take a swig either?

PENNY    A swig? So help me heaven! I couldn't swig a
thing.

DODGER    Why not?

PENNY    Because I just sopped it up. The darn stuff was so
peppered it burnt my throat off.

DODGER [*with a deep sigh*]    It is given to some to get gloriously drunk, and to others—to get vinegar and water . . .
A fine cellarer and under-cellarer the cellar's got!

PENNY    You'd damn well do the same if *you* had got it.
You're only jealous because you can't follow suit.    *840*

DODGER    Well well well! . . . Did he ever draw wine be-
fore this?
[*A pause*]
Answer me, you little thief. And, just for your benefit,
I'm telling you, Master Penny, if you let out a lie—I'm
going to murder you.

PENNY [*sticking his tongue out*]    Oh yeah! So *you* can go
and tattle all I've told, and when I get flung out of my
nice cellar stoned, you can get another under-cellarer and
make yourself the cellarer.

DODGER [*holding up his hands in deprecation*]　No no! I wouldn't do that . . . Come along, make a clean breast of it.

PENNY　Honestly, I never saw him draw any. [*grinning slyly*] But it went like this: he'd give *me* orders and then *I'd* draw it.

DODGER　That's why the wine-jars were always standing on their heads?

850　PENNY　God, no, mister! That's not why the wine-jars were always . . . jiggling about. There was a little section of the cellar that was very slippery, and propped up there like this . . .
　　　　[*Gives a demonstration, lolling drunkedly against a pillar*]
was a two-quart jug, and ever so often this two-quart jug would fill itself up . . . Oh, ten times over I've seen it full and empty—mostly full. And when the jug got jolly the wine-jars got jiggling.

DODGER [*with a growl and a shove*]　Off with you—into the house. The jolly jiggling things in the cellar are *you:* holding downright bacchanals there. Wait till I fetch the boss from the forum!

PENNY [*gulping*]　Then I'm finished. If the boss comes home and hears of this, he'll string me up—because I
860　never reported it.
　　　　[*Fixes the audience with a moony look*]
I'm going to get the hell out of here. Put off the reckoning till another day . . . You won't tell him, will you? Promise me!
　　　　[*Begins to stagger away from the house*]

DODGER [*blocking him*]　Where are you off to?

PENNY [*blankly*]　I've been sent . . . somewhere. I'll be right back.

DODGER [*sternly*]　Who sent you?

PENNY   Miss Goldilocks.

DODGER   Go on, then. But come straight back.

PENNY [*darting down the street with an unexpected burst of speed and calling over his shoulder*]   You bet! And in my absence—when the disaster's all divided out—do take my share, will you?

[*Disappears*]

DODGER [*with a slow smile*]   Now I understand what the girl is up to. Pox is taking a nap and she's got rid of her underguard so she can skip across to this house here . . . Fine!

[*His attention is caught by the sight of a striking pair coming down the street*]

Aha! Mr. Prolix with the girl I commissioned him to bring . . . My, what a lovely eyeful! The gods are with us—*I* should say! . . . Holds herself and dresses like a real lady—no mere piece of baggage. What a shapely deal it's shaping into—under *me!*        870

[*Enter* MR. PROLIX *with* MADAM LOVE-A-DUCK *and her maid,* MILPHIDIPPA. LOVE-A-DUCK *is a tall girl in her early twenties, with the body and carriage of a fashion-model, and a deep purring voice.* MILPHIDIPPA *is younger, a mere sixteen: small, dark and lively, with a husky voice and the liquid come-hither look of the genuine sex-kitten*]

PROLIX [*in an expansive gesture*]   And so, Love-a-duck, my dear,
And you too, Milphidippa,
At your house I explained the whole thing to you from A to Z;
But if you haven't grasped our game completely—
Our little gambit, ha ha ha!—
I'm going to give you one more lesson.
If you do understand it on the other hand,
We can talk of something else.

LOVE-A-DUCK [*laughs sarcastically*]   Oh, of course!
        patron,
    I *would* be a witless boob, wouldn't I,
    If I took on work for someone under contract
    And once inside the workshop
880 Let all my tricks of the trade fly out the window!

PROLIX [*apologetically*]   But it's a good thing to caution
        you.

LOVE-A-DUCK [*sarcastically*]   Oh, of course!
    The whole world knows how much it means
    To caution a merry widow.[19]
    In point of fact, my ears had barely begun
    To drink in your dissertation
    When I told you myself exactly
    How the Major could be cut down to size.

PROLIX [*with dogged diplomacy*]   Still, no one on his own
        knows quite enough;
    Though many a time I've seen
    People flee from the territory of good advice
    Long before they'd got there or got any.

LOVE-A-DUCK   Ah! But if a woman
    Has something shocking and spiteful up her sleeve
    She remembers it with a memory
    Irremovable, unremitting and immortal.
    That same woman faced with something honest and
        deserving
    Is oblivious at once:
890 She simply can't remember.

PROLIX [*pointedly*]   That's why I'm afraid of *your* for-
        getting.
    You see, you're going to have the chance—you two—
    Of doing both:
    What you do helps me but hurts the Major.

LOVE-A-DUCK [*winking at* MILPHIDIPPA]   So long as we're
        unaware of doing good,
    You needn't fear.

19 Plautus's actual word is *meretrix*, prostitute. See note 2.

PROLIX [*sighing*]   Oh, what a worthless ware is woman!

LOVE-A-DUCK    Don't worry! Her complement is even worse.

PROLIX   She deserves no better . . . Come along now.
[*They move toward his house*]

DODGER [*adjusting the folds of his tunic, smoothing down his hair, and generally straightening himself*]   Shall I go and meet them?
[*They are upon him before he considers himself ready to be seen by the gorgeous* LOVE-A-DUCK. *He bows*]
Glad to see you safely back, sir.
And so—oh by god!—so stunningly
Decked out for your stroll.
[*Waves a hand delicately toward the two girls*]

PROLIX [*with obvious pride*]   Hm, hm! A good and timely meeting, Dodger.
I present you with the girls you commissioned me to bring:
All suitably bedizened for the business.

DODGER [*his eyes shining*]   Magnificent! You're my man!
[*jauntily toward the girls*]   I'm Dodger. How-do-you-do, Love-a-duck!

LOVE-A-DUCK [*chillingly to* PROLIX]   Who is this character who calls me by my name?          *900*

PROLIX [*chuckling*]   Aha! This is our master-planner.

LOVE-A-DUCK [*unchilling slightly and holding out a hand*]   How-do-you-do, master-planner!

DODGER [*deferentially*]   How-do-you-do, ma'am . . . Please tell me this:
Has he freighted you with full instructions?

PROLIX   The two girls I bring are primed up to the hilt.

DODGER   Let's see how thoroughly.
   I don't want the tiniest slip.

PROLIX   I've added nothing of my own,
   Nothing new, to your instructions.

LOVE-A-DUCK [*cutting in*]   In short, you want your master,
      the Major,
   Made a fool of—don't you?

DODGER   You've said it.

LOVE-A-DUCK   It's all arranged:
   With charm, shrewdness, neatness and finesse.

DODGER   And I want you to pretend
   You're the wife of Mr. Prolix.

LOVE-A-DUCK   His wife I'll be.

DODGER   And pretend you're head-over-heels in love with
      the Major.

LOVE-A-DUCK   I shall be head-over-heels.

DODGER   And that I and your maid are the go-betweens
910   Handling this affair for him.

LOVE-A-DUCK   What a fortuneteller you'd have made!
   Everything you say is coming true.

DODGER   And that little minx of a maid of yours
   Passed on this ring from you to me for him with love.

LOVE-A-DUCK   Completely correct!

PROLIX [*with resentment*]   What's the earthly use of all this
      repetition
   Of things they know by heart?

LOVE-A-DUCK [*laying a hand on his arm*]
                  No, it's better.
            Think, dear sugar-daddy,

>How a decent shipwright
>Lays the keel down true and straight,
>Then the ship comes easy
>Once the framework's ready.
>So this keel of ours
>Is straight and set and steady.
>And our master-builder
>Has workmen not unskilled, sir;
>So if our timber-dealer
>Doesn't dilly-dally—                                   *920*
>I know that willy-nilly.
>Our ship will soon be ready.

DODGER   No doubt you also know the boss, my Major?

LOVE-A-DUCK [*throwing up her hands*]   What a question!
  How could I escape knowing
  Such a public nuisance:
  With his pomades and his permanent waves,
  And his scent-drenched, wench-bent, lecherous ways?

DODGER [*anxiously*]   But he doesn't know *you*, does he?

LOVE-A-DUCK [*impatiently*]   How could he know me,
    never having seen me?

DODGER [*rubbing his hands*]   How prettily you talk!
  When we've finished with him
  He won't be sitting pretty.

LOVE-A-DUCK [*a little tartly*]   Why don't you leave the man
    to me
  And stop your worrying?
  If *I* don't make a pretty ass of him
  You can blame me for everything.

DODGER   Go on, then, go inside:
  And get to work with all your wits.

LOVE-A-DUCK [*with a reassuring smile*]   Leave it to us.

DODGER   Come, Prolix, get the girls inside, sir.        *930*
  I'll meet the Major in the forum,

Give him this ring and tell him
It comes to me by your wife,
Who's sighing away her life for him.
When he and I get back from the forum
Send Milphidippa to us—the moment we're back—
As though she comes on a secret mission.

PROLIX [*ushering the girls to the front door*]   We will.
Don't give it a thought.

DODGER   If you'll look after that,
I'll see to it he comes here—ha ha!—
With his goose already stuffed.

[*Goes off in the direction of the forum*]

PROLIX [*calling after him*]   A pleasant walk and pleasant
work!
Let me tell you: if I make a real success of this
And my young guest gets the Major's girl today
And carries her away to Athens—
If we pull this off, I say,
I've got something—something special—for you.
[*The sound of* DODGER'*s jubilant shout in the
distance*]

LOVE-A-DUCK [*with a nod toward the* MAJOR'*s house*]   Is
940       the girl lending a hand?

PROLIX   Oh, in the neatest, prettiest way!

LOVE-A-DUCK   Then the future is secure.
With all our talents for subversion added up,
I feel quite sure
We'll never be outclassed in gamesmanship.

PROLIX [*lending an arm to* LOVE-A-DUCK]   Very well, then,
let's go in and there review
Our parts, so when the Major comes we'll carry them
through
With precision and finesse,
And do
The job without a mess.

LOVE-A-DUCK [*taking his arm with a laugh*]
                    Yes,
            We wait for *you!*

                              [*The three of them go into* MR.
                              PROLIX's *house*]


# ACT IV

MAJOR BULLSHOT-GORGEOUS *and* DODGER *walk slowly down
the street on their way back from the forum. The* MAJOR
*seems to swell as he walks, sniffing with self-satisfaction.*

MAJOR    It gives one such a rosy feeling
    To have things going so rosily—all according to plan.
    Today I sent my agent to King Seleucus
    With the recruits I've mustered for him.
    *They'll* police his kingdom for him
    While *I* take a rest.                                   *950*

DODGER    Ha ha ha ha ha!
    Stop worrying about King Seleucus.
    I've got something much nearer at home.
        [*Winks*]
    She's new, she's dazzling . . .
    There's a proposition which I'm authorized to bring.

MAJOR [*halting in his tracks*]    Aha! Then everything takes
        second place.
    I'm with you, speak—
    I'm all ears, and all yours.

DODGER [*drawing him into the shadows*]    Shh! Look round
        and see
    There's no one about to overhear us.
    I'm under strictest orders—shhh!—
    To handle this with secrecy.

MAJOR [*majestically surveying the neighborhood*]    There's
        no one about.

DODGER [*feverishly undoing a knot in his handkerchief and*

*taking out* PROLIX's *ring*]   Here . . . the first install-
ment, sir . . . of her passion.

MAJOR [*reaching out a trembling palm*]   What is it?
Where's it from?

DODGER [*holding up the ring*]   From a dazzling and de-
lectable lady
Who is in love with you and pines
After your excruciatingly handsome—mm, mm—
Handsomeness.
And now her maid has brought this ring
960      From her to me to give you.

MAJOR [*snatching the ring*]   And she?
Is she freeborn or a slave set free?

DODGER [*shocked*]   Tut tut, sir!
Do you think I'd have the nerve
To act as go-between
For you and a woman once a slave—
When you can't even take care of
All the freeborn ladies after you?

MAJOR [*smugly*]   Married or unmarried?

DODGER [*archly*]   Married *and* unmarried.

MAJOR [*ponderously*]   One and the same woman!
Married and unmarried—how?

DODGER   Girl bride—groom a granddad.

MAJOR   Haaa! . . . Great!

DODGER   Oh, she's lovely! Every inch a lady.

MAJOR [*swinging his eyes on him*]   I warn you—no lies!

DODGER   The only girl in the world to touch you.

MAJOR [*with an incredulous whistle*]   Go on? . . . She *must*
be a beauty.
Who is she?

DODGER  The wife of old Prolix here—
Right next door.
She's simply dying for you, sir:
Wants to get away from him—
Can't stand the old geezer any more.                                        *970*
She's sent me to you begging and beseeching
You'd let her have the permit and the privilege
Of being yours.

MAJOR  *Her* wish? By God, *I'm* willing.
    [*Slips on the ring*]

DODGER [*whistling*]  And is *she!*

MAJOR [*clutches* DODGER *by the shoulder*]  What are we
    going to do with the other one—
The bird inside the house?

DODGER [*shrugging*]  Oh, just go and tell her to buzz off—
Wherever she wants to.
As a matter of fact, her twin sister's here,
*And* the mother:
They want to fetch her.

MAJOR [*panting with excitement*]  Eh, d'you mean it?
    Her mother's come to Ephesus?

DODGER [*casually*]  That's what they say: those who ought
    to know.

MAJOR [*slapping his thighs*]  God, what a chance to get
    the girl out of the house!
It's perfect.

DODGER [*lowering his voice*]  And of course you want to
    do it—er—*perfectly?*

MAJOR  Of course! Just you tell me how.

DODGER  Well, you'd like to shift her straight away,
    Wouldn't you?
But you'd also like her to go—gratefully, yes?

MAJOR [*nodding vigorously*]  That's what I'd like.

DODGER    Then this is what you do.

980    You're pretty rich ...
Tell her to keep all the jewels and trinketry you fitted
    her out with,
Keep them as a present—and go ...
Remove herself to wherever she wants to.

MAJOR [*slowly*]    An excellent suggestion—y-yes,
But make darn sure
I don't go and lose *her*
And then have the other one change her mind.

DODGER    Pooh! Such scruples!
*She* adores you. You're the apple of her eye.

MAJOR [*puffing himself up*]    Venus—adores me.

DODGER [*cocking his head*]    Sh-h, quiet! It's the door.
Over here, sir. Out of sight.
    [*He pulls him into deeper shadow as* MILPHIDIPPA
    *steps into the street out of* MR. PROLIX's *front
    door*]
It's her packet-boat coming out: her go-between,[20]
The one who brought me the ring I handed you.

MAJOR [*looking her up and down with a subdued wolf-
    whistle*]    Hm! A pretty little baggage.

DODGER [*with a wave of his hand*]    Why man, compared to
    her mistress
She's nothing but a baby baboon—
The chick of a pterodactyl.[21]
    [*They watch* MILPHIDIPPA *darting her head about*]
    Just look at the way
She chases about with her eyes
990    And bird-catches with her ears!

---

20 I omit, with Leo, line 987: "Packet-boat? What d'you mean?"/
"It's her little maid coming out."
21 A nice problem in anachronisms: Plautus's *spinturnix* ($\sigma\pi\iota\nu\theta\alpha\epsilon\iota\varsigma$)
—a small ugly extinct bird—is as unknown to *us* as the pterodactyl
was (probably) to the ancients.

MILPHIDIPPA [*to herself as she spots them*]   So here's the
    circus—in front of the house—
  Where I do my tricks.
  I shall pretend I do not see them
  Or even know they've got here.

MAJOR [*cocking his head*]   Quiet!
  We'll strain our ears and see if she mentions *me*.

MILPHIDIPPA [*looking about in every direction except where
    they are*]   I hope there's no one lurking near
  Minding someone else's business,
    Not his own . . . and spying:
  Somebody who never
  Has to sing for supper.
  They're the sort I'm most afraid of.
  Such could block me, such could balk me
    Somehow, somewhere,
  As my mistress leaves the house
    On her way here
  Full of passion for this hero
  Who's so dashing, who's so darling . . .
    Oh, the handsome Major!

MAJOR [*digging* DODGER *in the ribs*]   So this one's dying
    for me too?
  Lauds my looks . . . I'll be damned!
  Her admiration needs no elbow grease.                  *1000*

DODGER [*distractedly*]   I don't follow.

MAJOR [*smothering guffaws at his own joke*]   It's already
    scoured, highly polished.

DODGER [*pulling himself together*]   Can you wonder when
    it's focused all on you:
  Such a highly polished subject!

MAJOR   Ah yes! And her mistress herself
  Is pretty well groomed—pretty elegant.
  I swear to you, Dodger,
  I begin to fancy her a bit already.

DODGER   What! Before you've even clapped eyes on her?

MAJOR [*thumping him on the back*]   Believing you is good
     as seeing.
     Besides, this little packet-boat
     Sets me on a course of loving—
     Even *in absentia*.

DODGER   Oh not her, sir!
     Not for love and kisses!
     She's engaged to *me*.
     If the mistress marries you today,
     The packet-boat and I get spliced at once.

MAJOR [*with a grunt of satisfaction*]   Then what are you
     waiting for?
     Go up and speak to her.

DODGER [*preparing to step forward*]   Just you follow me,
     sir.

MAJOR   I'm right behind you.

MILPHIDIPPA [*sighing*]   Oh, how I wish I could meet the
     man
*1010*      I came out here to see!

DODGER [*pushes the* MAJOR *back into the shadows and, out
     of sight, addresses* MILPHIDIPPA]   So you shall.
     Your wish will be fulfilled.
     Be full of confidence and have no fear:
     There is a certain man who knows
     Where the man you're searching is.

MILPHIDIPPA [*pretending to be mystified*]   Whom do I hear
     so close?

DODGER [*mysteriously*]   A comrade in your councils
     And a partner in your plans.

MILPHIDIPPA [*clapping her hand to her mouth*]   Good
     heavens, then!
     What I'm hiding is not hid.

DODGER   Is not hidden, yet is hid.

MILPHIDIPPA   How can *that* be?

DODGER   Hidden from the falsely friendly
Safely with your faithful friend.

MILPHIDIPPA   What's the watchword—
If you're one of our Bacchantes?

DODGER   A certain woman is in love with . . .
A certain man.

MILPHIDIPPA [*giggling*]   Silly!
Quite a lot of women are.

DODGER   Are, but don't send presents from their fingers.

MILPHIDIPPA   Ah! Now I understand you:
The rough places you make plain . . .
But is anyone about?

DODGER [*shoving the* MAJOR *further into the shadows and
stepping out*]   Yes and no . . . if you want him.
[*Bows*]

MILPHIDIPPA [*fluttering her eyes*]   Oh! . . . Can I have you
to myself?

DODGER   For a short or long—
Intercourse?

MILPHIDIPPA   Just a sentence.

DODGER [*to the* MAJOR]   I'll be back.                    *1020*

MAJOR [*peevishly*]   What about *me?*
Have I got to stand about
So dashing and damn handsome all for nothing?

DODGER   Stand by, sir, and be patient:
It's your affair I'm working on.

MAJOR [*agonized*]   Hurry! I'm on tenterhooks.

DODGER    One must tread carefully—don't you know?—
    Handling merchandise like this.

MAJOR [*sinking back into the shadows*]    All right! All
    right!
    Whatever you think'll get results.

DODGER [*to* MILPHIDIPPA]    The man's as stupid as a
    stone . . .
    I'm with you again—what would you like?

MILPHIDIPPA    Some advice.
    How's this Troy to be attacked?

DODGER    Pretend she's dying for him.

MILPHIDIPPA    I know that.

DODGER    Go into raptures
    Over his face and figure—
    His fantastic actions.

MILPHIDIPPA [*pouting*]    That's all organized—
    I showed you just a while ago.

DODGER [*lamely*]    For the rest then, keep alert:
    Take your cue from me.

MAJOR [*with a hiss from the shadows*]    Hey, there!
    Suppose *I* could have a share
    In what's going on?
            [DODGER *slips back to him*]
1030    Good! Back at last!

DODGER    Right here, sir. At your service.

MAJOR [*jealously*]    What's the woman telling you?

DODGER [*pulling a long face*]    Her poor mistress, she says,
    Is moaning and groaning—completely distraught:
    Worn out with weeping;
    Because she needs you,

Because she doesn't have you,
So she's sent her maid to you.

MAJOR [*smugly*]    Tell the girl to come here.

DODGER [*holding up an admonitory finger*]    Now you know
    what you're about, sir?
Be superior.
You don't care for the idea.
Bawl me out for making you so vulgar.

MAJOR [*with a knowing grin*]    Yes, I've got it.
I'll keep to that exactly.

DODGER [*loud and peremptorily*]    So you want me to call
    The woman who wants you?

MAJOR [*working his face into a picture of disdain*]    If she's
    got anything to ask—
Let her approach.

DODGER    Approach, woman—
If you've got anything to ask.

MILPHIDIPPA [*fluttering with awe as she steps forward and
    curtsies*]
O-oh!—Oh! Prince Charming!

MAJOR    So she knows my surname!
Heaven grant your wishes, woman.

MILPHIDIPPA [*almost incoherent with palpitation*]
T-the permission t-to—to
Pass a lifetime with you, sir.

MAJOR [*looking down his nose*]    You ask too much.

MILPHIDIPPA    Oh, it's not for *me*, sir!
For my mistress—she's languishing.

MAJOR [*distantly*]    Many another woman,
To whom it is not given,                                    *1040*
Craves precisely *that*.

MILPHIDIPPA [*her eyes swimming with admiration*]   And
    no wonder!
No wonder you're so dear, sir:
A man so handsome, such a hero,
Such a priceless specimen
Of bravery and beauty.
Was there ever man
So fit for deity?

DODGER [*hand on his heart*]   By Hercules! In point of fact,
He's hardly human.
     [*between his teeth*]   I bet there's more humanity
In a goddam vulture!

MAJOR [*apologetically to* DODGER]   She's in such raptures
I must extol myself a little.
     [*Puffs himself up and begins to stride about*]

DODGER [*to* MILPHIDIPPA, *who can hardly contain herself*]
Just look at how the jackass struts!
     [*to the* MAJOR]   Sir, won't you answer her?
She's the woman from the woman I just mentioned.

MAJOR [*managing to yawn*]   Which one?
I recall so many.
I really can't remember.

MILPHIDIPPA [*pathetically*]   From her who plunders
Her own fingers
Just to robe
Yours with riches. [*pointing to the ring on the* MAJOR'S
    hand*]
Yes, that's the ring I brought to Dodger.
He passed it on to *you*, sir,
From the lady who so loves you.

MAJOR   Well, what now, girl?
Why don't you tell me?

MILPHIDIPPA [*melodramatically, as she wrings her hands*]
*1050*        Spurn not the heart that craves you:
        And has no life except in yours.

> To be or not to be hence onwards
> Lies in him that she adores.

MAJOR [*striking a pose of magnanimous sternness*]   Well,
what does she want?

MILPHIDIPPA   To address you, to embrace you,
> Oh, sir, to caress you.
>> Yes, yes, yes! ʸᵒᵘ
>> For unless you
> Bring her help, her heart is broken.
> [*Snatches his hand*]
>> Great Achilles, grant my prayer.
>> Handsome hero help a lady.
>> Show your noble nature—
>> Oh, king-killer! Oh town-taker!
> [DODGER, *on the point of collapsing, shakes his
> head at the* MAJOR *in signal to stand firm*]

MAJOR [*pushing her away*]   God, how tedious all this is!
[*with mock sternness at* DODGER]   I've told you often
enough, you bum,
Not to commit me to the common run.

DODGER                Woman, do you hear?
> I've told you before and I tell you now:
>> Without a fee commensurate
>>> This prize boar
>>> Does not inseminate
>>> Every little sow.                    *1060*

MILPHIDIPPA [*on her knees*]   He can have any sum he asks.

DODGER   Three hundred golden sovereigns, then.
He won't take less from anyone.

MILPHIDIPPA   Good gracious! That's scandalously cheap.

MAJOR   Greed never was a vice of mine.
I'm rich enough and I've got more—
A whole bushelful of golden sovereigns.

DODGER [*making absurd gestures behind the* MAJOR'*s back*]

Not to mention treasure . . . Oh, and silver!
Not just mounds of it, but mountains.
Why, not even Aetna's higher.

MILPHIDIPPA [*with huge eyes*]   O-oh, how exciting!
[*under her breath*]   What a liar!

DODGER [*in an undertone to* MILPHIDIPPA]   Good sport, eh?

MILPHIDIPPA   How'm I doing?
Playing up to you all right?
        [*Returns to the* MAJOR]
For the love of mercy, sir,
Send me back to her.

DODGER [*nudging him*]   Why don't you give her an answer?
Either you will or you won't.

MILPHIDIPPA [*dabbing her eyes*]   Yes, why would you torture
A poor desperate soul
Who's never done you any harm?

MAJOR [*melting*]   Tell her to come out to us herself.
Say I'll do all she asks.
        [*He begins to strut again*]

MILPHIDIPPA   Oh sir!
1070   Now you're acting as you ought to:
She wants you and you want her.

DODGER [*to himself*]   No flies on that girl, by Jove!

MILPHIDIPPA   And you haven't spurned my prayer
But granted what I asked for.
[*aside to* DODGER]   Doing all right, eh?

DODGER [*exploding*]   Lord! I just can't keep from laughing.

MILPHIDIPPA [*almost doubled up*]   That's why I had to
turn my back on you.

MAJOR [*striding into their orbit again*]   My girl, you
    haven't an inkling
What an honor I'm paying your mistress.

MILPHIDIPPA   Oh sir, I do have an inkling—
And I'll tell her so.

DODGER   He could sell this service to another woman
For his weight in gold.

MILPHIDIPPA [*struggling to keep a straight face*]   Good
    heavens, yes! I believe you.

DODGER   Great warriors—nothing but—
Are born from the women he makes pregnant.
His sons live eight hundred years.

MILPHIDIPPA [*to* DODGER *under her breath*]   Get on with
    you—you liar!

MAJOR [*striking a monumental pose*]   As a matter of fact,
They live a good straight thousand:
From epoch to epoch.

DODGER [*apologetically*]   I kept the figures down, sir,
In case she thought I might be lying.

MILPHIDIPPA [*hand on mouth to simulate wonder—and
    hide her laughs*]   God have mercy!
How many years will he live himself
If his sons live so long?                                    *1080*

MAJOR   My girl, I was born on the day after
Jove was born to Ops.[22]

DODGER   If he'd only been born the day before Jove
It's *he* who'd now be reigning in heaven.

MILPHIDIPPA [*almost hysterical*]   Enough, enough, I en-
    treat you!

22 The wife of Saturn and eventually identified with Rhea, the mother
of Jupiter. She was the old Italian goddess of fertility.

Let me leave you alive—
If it's still possible.

DODGER   Why don't you go, then,
Now that you've got your answer?

MILPHIDIPPA [*hanging back, entranced*]   Y-yes . . . I shall
go and bring the lady, sir,
On whose behalf I am acting . . .
Is there . . . anything else . . . you wish?

MAJOR   Just not to be more handsome than I am:
My looks are such a bore to me.

DODGER [*to* MILPHIDIPPA, *sharply*]   Well, what are you
waiting for?
Aren't you going?

MILPHIDIPPA [*tearing her eyes away*]   Yes . . . going.

DODGER [*behind her as she goes to the door*]   And there's
this, too—are you listening?—
Tell her with consummate art
And give her a galloping heart.
[*Lowers his voice*]
Tell Goldilocks, if she's there,
To cross to us over here—
The Major's waiting.

MILPHIDIPPA [*to* DODGER, *whispering*]   She's here with my
mistress:
[*Nods toward* PROLIX's *house*]
1090   They've been listening to our talk.

DODGER [*whispering back*]   Splendid!
Our little chat'll help them
Steer a cleverer course.

MILPHIDIPPA [*loudly*]   You're holding me—I'm off.

DODGER   I'm not even touching you,
Let alone . . . I'd better not say!
[MILPHIDIPPA, *with an encouraging glance at*

DODGER *over her shoulder, goes into* PROLIX's
house]

MAJOR [*shouts after her*]  Tell her to get a move on and
  come out.
  We'll make this matter a priority.
          [*Turns to* DODGER]
  And now, Dodger, what am I going to do?
  We can't let this girl in
  Till we get the other out.

DODGER [*assuming indifference*]  Why ask *me?*
  I've already told you the way to do it:
  The jewelry and the costumes you equipped her with—
  Let her have them . . .
  Let her snaffle the lot.                                    *1100*
  Tell her it's time she went back home.
  Say her twin sister's here with her mother
  And it's a very good thing for her
  To go back home with them.

MAJOR  How do you know they're here?

DODGER  Because I saw that sister of hers
  With my very own eyes.

MAJOR  Have they met, those two?

DODGER  They have.

MAJOR [*suddenly leering*]  A fine strapping lass, eh what?

DODGER [*with disgust*]  Oh, *you* want to corner everything!

MAJOR [*still leering*]  And where did the sister say the
  *mother* was?

DODGER [*coolly*]  Lying on board ship with sore and swol-
  len eyes.
  *So* the captain says who brought them here . . .
  This captain's staying with our next door neighbor.      *1110*

MAJOR  And *he?* A lovely lusty lad, eh?

DODGER [*with a curl of the lip*]   Come off it, sir!
A fine stallion for the mares you are:
Running after everything—male and female . . .
Let's get down to business.

MAJOR [*beginning to fidget*]   Now about that advice you
    were giving me—
I'd like *you* to talk it over with her.
You and she get along so well together.

DODGER   Oh, no no, sir! Surely you, sir,
Must do that little job yourself?
Say you've simply *got* to have a wife:
Relatives are pushing, friends are pressing.

MAJOR [*nervously*]   You really think that?

*1120* DODGER   How could I *not*?

MAJOR [*bracing himself*]   Very well, I go inside.
Meanwhile, you keep watch before the house
And call me when the other one comes out.

DODGER   Just look after your own performance, sir.

MAJOR [*attempting a swagger*]   I'll look after it all right.
If she won't go quietly, I'll—I'll
Kick her out.

DODGER [*with force*]   Oh, don't do that, sir:
Much better have her leave
Happily and grateful.
Give her those things I told you to.
Let her carry away
All that jewelry and stuff you fixed her up with.

MAJOR   God, I hope she does!

DODGER   You'll persuade her quite easily, I think.
But go on in. Don't keep standing here.

MAJOR [*dithering*]   I'm yours to command.

[*Walks uncertainly into his house*]

DODGER [*grinning at the audience*]
        Ha! Ha!
    This womanizing Major,
    Does he differ in one jot
    From the picture that I gave you—       *1130*
        Eh what?
    Now for Love-a-duck to join me here
    Or her minx of a maid or Halcyon . . .
        [*As the door of* PROLIX'*s house opens*]
    Jumping Jupiter! What timing everywhere!
        The very ones I wanted here,
          Coming out *en bloc*
        Next door.

[MADAM LOVE-A-DUCK, MILPHIDIPPA *and* HALCYON,
*with the air of conspirators, step cautiously into the
street*]

LOVE-A-DUCK [*beckoning her accomplices*]    Come on, look
    about and be alert:
There may be someone watching us.

MILPHIDIPPA    No one around that I can see
    Except the very one we want.

DODGER [*stepping forward*]    As I do you.

MILPHIDIPPA    Hi! Master-planner—what are you doing?

DODGER    *I* master-planner? Bah!

MILPHIDIPPA    What on earth?

DODGER    Next to you I'm hardly fit
    To plug a peg in a wall.           *1140*

MILPHIDIPPA [*coyly*]    Oh go on!

DODGER    Yes, you're the smoothest little vixen ever.
    [*turning to* LOVE-A-DUCK]    The way she trimmed down
        the Major—
    It was a treat!

MILPHIDIPPA [*pleased*]    I'd hardly started.

DODGER   Never mind! The whole thing's shaping nicely.
Just go on as you are—you're wonderful.
The Major, if you please,
Has gone to beg his mistress to abandon him
And—ha ha ha!—depart with mother and sister for
Athens.

HALCYON [*throwing his cap into the air*]   Hip hip! . . .
Magnificent!

DODGER   What's more,
All the dress and jewelry he heaped on her—
He's giving her the lot . . . a present—
Just to get rid of her.
I told him to.

HALCYON [*beaming*]   Then the thing's a dead certainty:
She wants to go and he wants to have her gone.

DODGER [*wagging a finger gravely*]   Ah ah! Don't you
know
1150   That when one's almost out of a steep well,
Right at the top,
That's when the danger's at its height—
Of falling right to the bottom again?
We've got our little operation to the top,
But one whiff of suspicion from the Major
And we don't get it out.
Now is the moment for the greatest guile.
        [*Surveys them all grandly*]
    I see we have enough material for the purpose:
Three women, you for a fourth, me fifth,
And the old gentleman making six.
With all our chicanery lumped together—
The whole six of us—
I'm pretty sure we could undermine and take by storm
Any goddam city on this earth . . .
So go and put your minds to it.

LOVE-A-DUCK [*pointedly*]
    That's why we're here—
    Entirely at your disposition.

DODGER   Charming of you.
These, then, are your instructions, madam.

LOVE-A-DUCK   Thank you, General.
I'll follow them to the letter—
As far as in me lies.                                    *1160*

DODGER   I want the Major sunk—
Hook, line and sinker.

LOVE-A-DUCK   An order, sir, which is to me
Sheer self-indulgence.

DODGER   And you know how, don't you?

LOVE-A-DUCK [*clasping her bosom*]   Oh yes!
I pretend I'm torn in two by my passion.

DODGER   Right.

LOVE-A-DUCK   And because of this passion
I've divorced my husband—
            [*Tosses her head in the direction of* PROLIX's
            *house*]
Just to marry *him*.

DODGER   Correct.
But there's one thing more:
Say that this house [*jerking a thumb at* PROLIX's *house*]
Is part of your own dowry
And that after you divorced him
The old man left you here . . .
We can't have the Major
Scared to enter another man's house later.

LOVE-A-DUCK [*nodding*]   A sound precaution.

DODGER   And when he comes out of his house
I want you to stand a little way off,
Pretending you're no match for his crushing good looks: *1170*
You're overwhelmed by the sheer style of him,
And of course in ecstasy

    Over his figure, his face, his charm, his beauty . . .
    Got it straight?

LOVE-A-DUCK [*laughing*]   Completely.
Will you be satisfied with a performance so finished
That it's flawless?

DODGER   Absolutely.
    [*Turns to* HALCYON]
Your turn for instructions now, sir.
The moment all this is done
And Love-a-duck's gone inside—
*You* hurry over to us here in a sea captain's togs.
You'll wear a broad-brimmed hat—navy blue[23]—a
woolen eye-patch, and a navy-blue cloak (that's the sea-
man's color you know) fastened at the left shoulder with
1180  a free arm dangling. You're all tackle-and-trim: hell
yes! You're a skipper . . . The old man, by the way, has all
the props you need—some of his slaves are fishermen.

HALCYON [*scratching his head*]   Fine! I'm all togged up
But you don't tell me what to do.

DODGER   You come here to fetch Goldilocks in her
    mother's name, saying that if she's going to Athens she
    must hurry with you to the harbor and give instructions
    for the things she wants on board, to be carried to the
    ship. If she's not coming, you say you're going to cast
    off immediately since there's a fair wind.

HALCYON   A pretty pleasing picture! Proceed.

DODGER   The Major'll promptly urge her to get a move on
    and go, so as not to keep her mother waiting.

1190 HALCYON   Ha! You're a crafty one!

DODGER [*with a broad grin*]   And I'll tell her to ask for me
    as her assistant in carrying her luggage down to the har-

---

23 Plautus says: *ferrugineaus,* "the color of iron rust." Or does he
mean a sort of gunmetal-blue, or even dark green? We can't be sure.
Lucretius, using the word some 129 years later, distinguishes it from
green and red.

bor . . . Ha ha! To the harbor, naturally, he'll order me
to go with her . . . And after that, I don't need to tell
you, sir: I'm off to Athens with you, straight.[24]

HALCYON [*grasping his hand*]    And when you get there,
I shan't let you be a slave three days
Before I set you free.

DODGER [*spontaneously embraces* HALCYON. *Then, briskly:*]
Off with you now, sir,
And put on your togs.

HALCYON [*beginning to go*]    Anything else?

DODGER [*winking*]    Yes. Remember everything.

HALCYON [*blithely*]    I'm off.

> [*He disappears into* PROLIX's *house*]

DODGER [*turning to the two girls*]    And you get going in-
side too.
I'm pretty sure the Major's
On the point of coming out.

LOVE-A-DUCK [*dropping him an ironic curtsy*]    Your commands, my Commandant,
Are posted in our hearts.

DODGER    In which case, away with you, scram!
Look, the door's opening. Perfect timing!

> [*The two girls scuttle away into* PROLIX's *house*]

DODGER [*smiling to himself*]    Out he comes in fine fettle:
he's got his wish—
Gaping, poor fool, in his paradise.

> [*The* MAJOR *strides out and straight up to*
> DODGER. *He bursts out exultingly*]

MAJOR    She's agreed.

[24] By now it seems obvious that there really will be a ship waiting,
bound for Athens.

Goldilocks has agreed . . .
*1200*    My heart's desires—just what I wanted—
And all nice and friendly.

DODGER    What on earth kept you in there so long?

MAJOR [*smugly*]    I'd no idea till this moment
How much that woman loved me.

DODGER    You mean it?

MAJOR [*wiping his brow*]    Why, I had to argue and
    argue—
She's as stubborn as a log—
But finally I got what I wanted.
And I granted her, handed her,
Everything she wished for, everything she asked for:
I even handed her *you.*

DODGER [*leaping to attention*]    Even me? . . . What!
        [*Quickly pulls a long face*]
How can I live without you?

MAJOR [*patting him on the back*]    Come, man, don't be
    downcast!
I'll see you're freed from her.
I tried every way I could
To make her agree to go without you,
But she kept right on.

DODGER [*in a small crushed voice*]    Ah well!
I'll leave it to the gods—and you.
*1210*    It's a bitter pill . . . losing such a wonderful master,
But at least I'll have the happiness of knowing
That *your* beauty and *my* efforts
Landed you the girl next door:
Whom now I bring you.

MAJOR [*moved*]    Say no more.
I'll give you liberty and riches
If you bring it off.

DODGER    Bring it off! It's done.

MAJOR [*holding his side*]   Oh, how I ache for her!

DODGER [*in his best bedside manner*]   Gently does it, sir.
  Relax; not so eager . . .
  But here she is, coming out.

> [DODGER *and the* MAJOR *step to the side as*
> MADAM LOVE-A-DUCK *and* MILPHIDIPPA *emerge*]

MILPHIDIPPA [*in a whisper, as she catches sight of them*]
  There's the Major, ma'am,
  All ready for you.

LOVE-A-DUCK [*also whispering*]   Where?

MILPHIDIPPA   On the left.

LOVE-A-DUCK [*making a grimace*]   I see him.

MILPHIDIPPA   Look at him sideways
  So he won't know we see him.

LOVE-A-DUCK   Yes, I see him.
  Ah! Milphidippa—
  Now's the time for two bad girls
  To become much worse.

MILPHIDIPPA [*giggling*]   You begin.

LOVE-A-DUCK [*gathering herself together and launching her-
    self melodramatically*]   No-o?
  You don't mean you actually met him?
  [*aside to* MILPHIDIPPA]   Don't spare your voice: make
    him hear.

MILPHIDIPPA [*cockily*]   Why, I spoke to him face to face—   *1220*
  Calmly—took my own time—
  Quite at home—just as I felt like.

MAJOR [*aside to* DODGER]   D'you hear what she says?

DODGER [*nodding*]   I do.
  The girl's in transports because she met you.

LOVE-A-DUCK    O you fortunate girl!

MAJOR [*aside*]    How they seem to fall for me!

DODGER    Naturally!

LOVE-A-DUCK    But it's a miracle, what you tell me.
    You actually went up to him and asked?
    Why, they say he has to be approached
    By letters and ambassadors—
    Just like a king.

MILPHIDIPPA    I dare say.
    I had a terrible time getting near him
    And winning him over.

DODGER [*nudging the* MAJOR]    What glory, sir, you have
    among the ladies!

MAJOR [*shrugging*]    I put up with it—since Venus wishes.

LOVE-A-DUCK [*piously lifting up her hands*]
                    I offer the Lady Venus thanks
                        Exceedingly,
                    And pray and beseech her
                        Pleadingly:
                        To let me have
                        The man I love
                        The man I yearn for.
                    Make him kind to me,
                    Not turn from me:
1230                For whom I burn.

MILPHIDIPPA    I piously hope so, madam,
    Though lots of women yearn for him
    And he scorns them—spurns them all—
    You're the exception, madam.

LOVE-A-DUCK [*wringing her hands*]    That's what so worries
    me: his disdain.
    His eyes may change his mind for him
    Once he sees me.

His superior taste will turn him away
From the very sight of me.

MILPHIDIPPA [*laying a hand on her arm*]   No, it won't. Be
more cheerful, ma'am.

MAJOR [*aside*]   She doesn't think much of herself, eh
what!

LOVE-A-DUCK [*sorrowfully*]   I fear you painted me in too
glowing colors.

MILPHIDIPPA   Not at all,
I made you out less pretty than you are.

LOVE-A-DUCK [*almost hysterical*]   But if . . . if
He will not marry me . . .
I'll hug him by the knees, I'll—I'll
Beg him to—or else . . .
Or else if I fail to win him,                                        *1240*
I'll commit suicide.
I can't live without him. I realize *that*.

MAJOR [*starting forward*]   I've got to stop her committing
suicide, surely?
Shall I go to her?

DODGER [*holding him back*]   Far from it.
You'll make yourself cheap
Lavishing yourself like that.
Let her come to *you:*
Let *her* do the seeking and pining and waiting.
You don't want to go and ruin your reputation, do you?
Then, for god's sake be careful.
It's never been given to mortal man—
I shouldn't think—except to two:
You and Sappho's Phaon,[25]
To be so blessed by love of woman.

---

[25] Phaon was the young sailor—according to legend—with whom
the poetess, Sappho, fell in love in middle age and for whose sake
she threw herself off the Leucadian cliff when he went to Sicily.

LOVE-A-DUCK [*as if throwing reserve to the winds*]   I'm going to him if you don't call him out:
   Please—my little Milphidippa!

MILPHIDIPPA [*holding her back*]   No no!
   Let's wait till somebody comes out.

LOVE-A-DUCK [*tossing from left to right*]   I can't stand it.
   I'm going in to him.

MILPHIDIPPA   The doors are shut.

LOVE-A-DUCK   I'll break them open.

1250 MILPHIDIPPA   You're out of your senses.

LOVE-A-DUCK [*blindly advancing*]   If he has ever been in
   love,
   If his wisdom match his beauty,
   Whatever I may do in passion—
      He will forgive me.

DODGER [*holding the* MAJOR *in check*]   Fancy that, sir!
   She's gone quite dotty over you, poor thing.

MAJOR [*at breaking point*]   It's—it's . . . mutual.

DODGER [*shocked*]   Sh-h! You don't want her to hear.

MILPHIDIPPA [*making a sign of encouragement to her mistress*]   Why do you stand there, in a trance?
   Why don't you knock?

LOVE-A-DUCK   Because the desire of my heart is not within.

MILPHIDIPPA   How do you know?

LOVE-A-DUCK [*sniffing wildly*]   Oh, I know it! Without a
   doubt,
   If he were inside—
   My nose would smell him out.

DODGER [*with a hiss in the* MAJOR's *ear*]   She's a crystal-
   sniffer, sir.

MAJOR [*sublimely*]   Venus rewards her for being in love
 with me
With preternatural powers.

LOVE-A-DUCK [*sniffing her way along*]   Somewhere . . .
 quite near,
Is the one I desire . . .
I smell him—yes—I swear.

MAJOR   Strike me,
If she doesn't see better with her nose than her eyes!

DODGER   Blinded with love, sir.

LOVE-A-DUCK [*finally decides to see the* MAJOR *and is about
 to swoon*]   A-ah! Hold me up . . . please.

MILPHIDIPPA [*supporting her*]   What is it?

LOVE-A-DUCK   Keep me . . . from falling.

MILPHIDIPPA   Whatever for?

LOVE-A-DUCK   Because I can't stand.                    *1260*
My spirit swoons . . . at the vision.

MILPHIDIPPA [*with ponderous alertness*]   Oh, I get it:
 You've spotted the soldier?

LOVE-A-DUCK [*tragically*]   Ye-es.

MILPHIDIPPA [*playing dumb*]   I don't see him. Where is
 he?

LOVE-A-DUCK [*clutching her bosom*]
You would see him, you *would*
If you loved him.

MILPHIDIPPA [*pertly*]   I'd love him all right—
Not a whit less than you—
With your permission, ma'am.

DODGER [*nudging the* MAJOR]   You see, sir, how the ladies

Fall for you to a woman—
At first sight!

MAJOR [*dryly*]   Perhaps I never told you:
I'm the grandson of Venus.

LOVE-A-DUCK [*pushing* MILPHIDIPPA *toward them with
    trembling hands*]   My little Milphidippa, please,
Go up to him and speak.

MAJOR [*fervently*]   How she adores me!

DODGER [*with a sign to the* MAJOR]   The maid's making
    for us.

MILPHIDIPPA [*curtsying and pretending to fumble*]   S-sirs,
    I want you to . . .

MAJOR [*ogling her*]   And *we* want you.

MILPHIDIPPA [*panting*]   Sir . . . I've brought my mistress
    out—
As you told me.

MAJOR [*coldly, as he controls himself*]
So I see.

MILPHIDIPPA   Then do tell her to approach.

MAJOR   I've persuaded myself . . .
        [*Long pause*]
*Not* to detest her like the others—
Seeing you've begged me.

MILPHIDIPPA [*with a gesture toward the tottering* LOVE-A-
        DUCK]
But she won't be able to find words
1270   If she comes near you.
Her eyes have popped out of her head
And lopped off her tongue.

MAJOR [*pompously*]   Something's got to be done,

It seems to me,
About this woman's malady.

MILPHIDIPPA [*doing her eye-flutter*] The moment she
spotted you
She was taken with quivering and quaking.

MAJOR [*sublimely*] Even armed soldiers do the same;
Don't be surprised at a mere woman . . .
But what does she want me to do?

MILPHIDIPPA Go to her house, sir.
She wants to live with you—
Spend her life with you.

MAJOR [*alarmed*] What! *I* go to her house—
A married woman's?
Her husband would catch me there.

MILPHIDIPPA Her husband? She's thrown him out—
*And* because of you.

MAJOR But how could she do that?

DODGER [*quickly*] Because the house belongs to *her*—
Her dowry.

MAJOR [*pricking up his ears*] Is that so?

DODGER It certainly is.

MAJOR [*decisively*] Tell her to go home.
I'll join her there.

MILPHIDIPPA [*her eyes liquid with solicitation*] *Please*
don't keep her waiting.
Her whole soul's on tenterhooks.

MAJOR [*with ill-suppressed excitement*] No no, I won't.
Off with you.

MILPHIDIPPA [*taking the dazed* LOVE-A-DUCK *by the hand*]
We're going, sir.                                    *1280*

[MILPHIDIPPA *leads* LOVE-A-DUCK *into* PROLIX's
*house, her eyes riveted on the* MAJOR *in a state
of shock*]

MAJOR [*his attention caught by someone coming down the
street*]   But what do I see?

DODGER   What *do* you see?

MAJOR [*pointing*]   Look: all got up like a sea-green sailor.

DODGER   And making for our house too:
Wants you, that's plain . . .
Why, it's the skipper.

MAJOR   Coming to fetch the girl, I expect.

DODGER   Oh yes, of course!
[*They step back and watch, as* HALCYON, *thinking
he is alone, stands poised to knock on the* MAJOR's
*front door*]

HALCYON
If I weren't so well aware
That love has had a share
In every kind of dirty trick—
I'd certainly think again
Before my own campaign
For loving let me sally forth like this.
But since I know it's true
That men have done and do
For love a lot of shabby things
And things which are not nice
From Achilles'[26] sacrifice
Of friends without a twinge
For slaughtering (a binge!)
And . . .
[*Breaks off as he sees* DODGER *and the* MAJOR]
Oh-oh! There's Dodger,
Standing with the Major.
1290    I've got to change my tune.

26 Achilles, at Troy, withdrew his forces from the battle to punish
Agamemnon for having taken the girl, Briseis, from him.

*[Loudly and impatiently]*
Damn it all! I say
The daughter of delay
   Is surely woman.
And when she makes you wait,
The time it seems to take
   Is twice as long
As any time the same.
I really think their game
   Is one of habit.
Here I've come to get
Goldilocks, and yet . . .
   *[Strides to the door disgustedly]*
Oh, I'll bang on the door.
   *[Does so]*
Hullo, hullo! Is anyone there?

DODGER *[stepping up to him]*   What is it, young man?
What do you want? Why are you knocking?

HALCYON *[brusquely]*   I'm looking for Goldilocks.
I come from her mother. If she's going
She's got to go. She's holding us up.
We want to sail.                                           *1300*

MAJOR *[bustles forward]*   It's all ready.
Eh! . . . Dodger . . . the trinkets and clothes,
All her baubles and valuables—
Get someone to help you carry the lot
Down to the ship.
It's all packed—everything I gave her.
Let her remove it.

DODGER   Right, sir.

   *[DODGER goes out, winking at HALCYON as he passes]*

HALCYON *[with a voice like a ship's megaphone]*   Hell's
   bells, get a move on!

MAJOR   He won't keep you.
   *[Surveys HALCYON's eye-patch with curiosity]*
What's it for? What have you done to your eye?

HALCYON [*curtly*]   Dammit—I've got one good eye!

MAJOR   I mean the left one.

HALCYON [*spitting*]   If you want to know, it's because of
    the sea.
    That's why I don't see so well in that one . . .
    The sea and love.[27] Oh, it's bitter!
    If I'd kept away from the sea and love
    I'd be seeing with it as well as the other . . .
        [*Stamps impatiently*]
    They're late. They're holding me back.

1310 MAJOR   Look, here they come.

        [DODGER *appears in the doorway of the* MAJOR'*s
        house, leading and supporting* GOLDILOCKS *who dabs
        her eyes with a handkerchief*]

DODGER [*severely*]   For love and kisses, ma'am,
    Aren't you *ever* going to stop crying?

GOLDILOCKS [*bursting out again*]   H-how can I help c-cry-
    ing?
    I've had such a lovely life here . . .
    And n-now I'm leaving.

DODGER [*giving her arm a secret squeeze*]   See? Your man
    there . . .
    He's come from your mother and sister.

GOLDILOCKS [*glowing but managing a glance of supreme
    indifference*]   I see him.

MAJOR [*fussily*]   Hey there, Dodger!

DODGER [*hurrying over*]   What, sir?

MAJOR [*with a knowing look*]   Why aren't you giving
    orders

27 This is the best I can do with Plautus's play on: *Eloquar/maris* . . .
*abstinuissem/amare*. A translator desperately throws in his own pun
where there is no way out for the author's.

For all that stuff I gave her
To be carried out?
          [DODGER *goes to the door and shouts to the porters
inside*]

HALCYON  [*stomping up to* GOLDILOCKS]  Goldilocks,
    ma'am, good morning.

GOLDILOCKS  [*almost collapsing with mirth at the sight of
    him, but managing a sob*]  A-and good morning to
    you, s-sir.

HALCYON  [*hardly able to keep from flinging his arms
    around her*]
    Your mother and sister asked me
    To give you their best wishes.

GOLDILOCKS  And they have mine.

HALCYON  They're waiting to sail.
    They beg you to come while the wind's still fair.
    Of course they would have come along with me
    If your mother's eyes had been a little better.

GOLDILOCKS  [*after a pause, fixing her eyes on the* MAJOR
    *as if she is about to be torn in two*]
    I'm going . . . I must force myself . . .
    It would be wrong not to go.

HALCYON  I understand.

MAJOR  She'd still be a little simpleton
    If she hadn't lived with me.                              1320

GOLDILOCKS  [*between sobs*]  That's what's so p-painful . . .
    To be wrenched away from such a man.
          [*Turns a tear-stained face to the* MAJOR]
    You could make anyone—just anyone—
    Brim with culture.
    My being with you gave me character.
    And now I see I've got to . . . t-to give it all up . . .
    The distinction and the . . .
          [*Breaks down completely*]

MAJOR   Don't cry.

GOLDILOCKS   I can't help it . . . when I look at you.

MAJOR   Come, my dear, bear up.

GOLDILOCKS   Only *I* know how much it hurts.

DODGER [*pulling a long face*]   I know, Goldilocks,
  I'm not surprised you were so happy here with him;
  I'm not surprised his bravery and beauty
  And all his winning ways
  Hold your heart back here.
  I'm only a slave
  But when I look at him
        [*Takes out a handkerchief*]
  I too begin to cry . . . at being torn away.
        [*Turns away his face to hide his laughter*]

GOLDILOCKS [*flinging out her arms*]   One last embrace,
    please—
  Oh may I?—before I go.

MAJOR   You may.

GOLDILOCKS [*throwing herself against him*]   O light of my
    eyes! Life of my soul!

DODGER [*draws her away and directs her tottering steps to*
1330     HALCYON]   For god's sake hold the woman up
  Or she'll dash herself to pieces.
        [*She faints into* HALCYON's *too-eager arms*]

MAJOR [*eying them*]   Hey, hey! What's going on?

DODGER   The poor girl!
  It's given her a turn, sir:
  The thought of leaving you.

MAJOR   Run inside and fetch some water.

DODGER [*glancing apprehensively at* HALCYON]   Don't
  waste your time on water.

All she needs, I'd say, is quiet.
[*in alarm as the* MAJOR *goes toward her*]   Oh, no no,
    sir! Don't interfere:
She's coming to.

MAJOR [*eying* HALCYON *and* GOLDILOCKS *doubtfully*]
    Their two heads are too darn close:
    I don't like it.
            [HALCYON, *unable to restrain himself, gives her
                what looks very much like a kiss*]
    [*shouting*]   Hey, sailor, unlip your lips:
    You're asking for trouble.

HALCYON [*coming to his senses*]   I was only trying to
    see . . .
    If she was breathing.

MAJOR   Then you should have used your ear.

HALCYON [*shrugging*]   If you'd rather—I'll let her go.

MAJOR [*dithering*]   No no! Hang on to her.

DODGER [*as a hint to the lovers*]   I'm a little uneasy.

MAJOR [*trying to speed up the departure, to the porters*]
    Hurry out with all that stuff of hers:
    The stuff I gave her.

                [*Porters emerge, carrying trunks and cases*]

DODGER [*attempting to distract the* MAJOR *from the lovers*]
                And now before I go,
                Dear household god,
                    One last goodbye!
        And you, my fellow slaves, goodbye!
            God bless you men and women.                    1340
                In your conversations, please,
                    Speak well of me,
                Though I'll be far away.
                            [*Sobs up his sleeve*]

MAJOR [*patting him on the shoulder*]   Come, come,
    Dodger, cheer up!

DODGER [*breaking into sobs*]   B-b-but I can't help w-w-
   weeping
Because I'm leaving you.

MAJOR   There, there! Bear up.

DODGER [*still sobbing*]   Only *I* know th-the p-pain.

GOLDILOCKS [*opening her eyes*]   A-ah! What's this?
   What's happening?
What do I see? . . . Good morning, Morning!

DODGER [*to her between his teeth*]   So you've come to?

GOLDILOCKS [*horrified*]   Good heavens!
   Who's this strange man I've embraced?
I'm ruined . . . Oh, am I sane?
      [*Sinks back into* HALCYON'*s arms*]

HALCYON [*whispering into her ear*]   Have no fear, my
   heart's desire.

MAJOR [*hearing something*]   What was that?

DODGER [*hurriedly*]   She's lost consciousness again, sir.
   [*into the lovers' ears, with a hiss*]   I'm afraid, I'm terri-
      fied
The whole thing's going to burst wide open.
      [GOLDILOCKS *quickly revives*]

MAJOR [*overhearing*]   What did you say?

DODGER [*wildly extemporizing*]   Just that all that stuff, sir,
      [*Jerks a finger at* GOLDILOCKS'*s luggage*]
   Carted along behind us through the town,
Won't it tend to make certain people
Turn against you?

1350 MAJOR [*snorting*]   I gave away what's mine, not theirs.
   I don't care a rap for "certain people" . . .
God speed you now—get going.

DODGER   I only say it for your sake, sir.

MAJOR [*waving them on impatiently*]   And I believe you.

DODGER [*with a wan smile*]   So it's goodbye, sir.

MAJOR [*holding out his hand*]   All the best to you, my
    man.

DODGER [*bustling the others off*]   Get a move on, quick!
    I'll follow in a minute.
    I want a last word with my master.

> [*The procession of* GOLDILOCKS, HALCYON *(hold-
> ing her up) and porters moves away down the
> street in the direction of the harbor.* GOLDILOCKS
> throws back long wistful glances]

DODGER [*choking out the words*]   Sir, you've always
        thought your other
    Servants much more loyal than *I* was;
    But now I want to thank you deeply
    For everything. And if you wished it
    I'd rather be a slave of yours
    Than someone else's freedman.
        [*Gives a sob*]

MAJOR   Tut tut, my man! Cheer up!

DODGER [*gulping*]   And when I think of how I've got to
    Change my ways to ways of women—
    Forget about the ways of soldiers . . .

MAJOR   Come on, be a man!

DODGER   I can't, sir, I've lost all inclination.            *1360*

MAJOR   Go, follow them, don't hang back.

DODGER [*making a supreme effort*]   Then . . . goodbye, sir.

MAJOR   Goodbye, my man.

DODGER [*stopping*]   And please remember, sir,
    If ever I can free myself

I'll send you a message . . .
You won't abandon me?

MAJOR   That's not in me.

DODGER [*looking him straight in the face*]   Ponder some-
          times on how loyal to you
I always was. And if you do, sir,
One day you'll discover who
Your friends and enemies really are.

MAJOR   Oh, I do know.
Many a time I've pondered it.

DODGER   Even so, sir, though you've known it,
Today you'll know it thoroughly.
Indeed, you'll even go so far as
Say I've proved my worth today.

MAJOR [*touched*]   I can hardly keep from telling you to
          stay.

DODGER [*in panic*]   Oh, don't do that, sir!
People'll say that you're a liar:
Untruthful, break your promises,
That of all your servants here
1370   I'm the only faithful one . . .
Oh, if I thought it could be done
Decently, I'd press you to it.
But no, it can't be . . . so don't do it.

MAJOR   Well then, off with you.

DODGER   I'll put up with . . . the future.

MAJOR   So, it's goodbye.

DODGER [*abruptly turning away to prevent a collapse*]   I'd
          better just . . . break away.

                    [*Shaking with emotion, he dashes off in the
                              direction of the port*]

MAJOR [*fondly calling after him*]   Once more, goodbye.

[*reflectively stroking his chin*]   Before this affair I
    always thought him
The very worst of servants. Now I find him
Quite devoted to me . . .
When I come to think of it,
I was a fool to let him go.
       [*Turns toward* PROLIX's *front door*]
Now to announce myself to my heart's desire.
But wait—there goes the door.

    [*He steps back as a* SMALL BOY *of about twelve
    skips out of the front door, shouting to those inside*]

BOY    Oh, don't go on so! I know my job.
I'll discover him, wherever on earth he is.
Yes, I'll follow him up . . .
Nothing'll be too much trouble.                            *1380*

MAJOR [*to himself*]    He's obviously looking for *me*.
I'll approach the lad.
      [*Goes up to the* BOY *and strikes a noble pose*]
Ahem!

BOY [*with exaggerated excitement*]    Oh, sir, I was looking
    for you:
Most magnificent, most champion,
Most manly man—
Looked after amongst men
By two deities.

MAJOR [*avuncularly*]    Which two?

BOY    Mars and Venus.

MAJOR    Clever boy!

BOY [*breathlessly*]    The lady . . . she begs you to go inside,
    sir.
She wants you, asks for you, waits for you:
She's full of yearns, sir.
Do help the lovesick lady.
    [*A pause*]
Why do you stand there?
Why don't you go inside, sir?

MAJOR [*taking a deep breath*]   I go.

> [*The* MAJOR *pushes through* PROLIX's *front door*]

BOY [*grinning from ear to ear*]
>He's in the meshes good and proper:
>The trap is set, the old man ready
>To jump on him—this ruttish, cocky,
>Ribald, coxcomb, strutting rotter:
>Who thinks that every lady can
>Fall at sight for such a man—
>>When really
>They think he's awful—everybody—
>Women just as much as men . . .
>But now to leap into the riot:
>Inside I hear them . . . far from quiet.

1390

> [*The* SMALL BOY *is swept aside when, to the sound of pandemonium, the door opens and* MR. PROLIX *bursts out, brandishing his silver cane and shouting to the slaves, who drag out the struggling* MAJOR. *The cook,* CARIO—*a big fat man with a one-tooth grin—stands over him with a carving-knife*]

PROLIX
>Haul him along
>And if he won't come
>Pick him up bodily:
>Chuck him out high
>Anywhere under
>The earth and sky:
>Rend him asunder.

MAJOR [*shorn of sword and cloak, and in his underwear*]
Oh, for the love of heaven, Prolix, please!

PROLIX [*mimicking him*]   Oh, for the love of heaven . . .
you're wasting your breath!
> [*to* CARIO *grimly*]   Cario, see your knife's good and
sharp.

CARIO [*grinning as he tests it on one of his own hairs*]   Lor'
bless you sir, it's just champing

To be let loose to lop him—ahem! ahem!—
In the randy region of his lower parts,
And string his trinkets round his neck,
Ahem! ahem! Like a baby's rattle.
        [*Pretends to take a swipe at the* MAJOR]

MAJOR [*with a shriek*]   It's murder!

PROLIX   Not quite . . . it's premature.

CARIO [*with a flourish of his knife*]   Shall I let fly now, sir?   *1400*

PROLIX [*casually*]   I think I'd like him clobbered first.

CARIO   *We'll* let him have it.[28]
        [*Several people close in on the* MAJOR]

PROLIX [*an inch from his face*]   What gave you the nerve
    to seduce another man's wife?
You dirty swine!

MAJOR [*rolling his eyes to heaven*]   For the love of all the
    gods, sir,
She came to me on her own.

PROLIX [*snapping his fingers at a couple of slaves*]   That's
    a lie . . . Beat him.
        [*They raise their cudgels*]

MAJOR   Wait. I'll explain.

PROLIX [*testily to the slaves*]   What's keeping you?

MAJOR [*shaking all over*]   Won't you let me speak?

PROLIX   Speak.

MAJOR   I was implored to go to her.

PROLIX   But how did you dare?
    Take that.
            [*Strikes him with his cane, and the slaves join in*]
28 Leo notes a lacuna here.

MAJOR    Ow! Oi! Ow! Please!
I've been clobbered enough.

CARIO [*running his thumb down the knife*]    Sir, how soon
can I cut?

PROLIX    Whenever you like.
[*to the slaves who hold him*]    Spread the brute apart—
stretch him out.
[*The* MAJOR *is pushed onto his back.* CARIO,
*still grinning, stands over him with the carving-
knife*]

MAJOR [*in a white panic*]    No! No! Please! Listen
Before he cuts.

PROLIX [*grimly*]    Speak out.

MAJOR [*hoarse with fright*]    I didn't want to . . . and I
didn't
Do anything . . . God! I thought she was a widow.
1410    That's what that little bawd of a maid let on.

PROLIX [*after a long pause, during which the* MAJOR *sweats,
pants and whimpers*]    Swear.
Swear you won't hurt a living soul
Because of this thrashing you've been given here today,
Or because of any future thrashing—
If we let you go alive from here . . .
You horny little grandson of Venus!
[*A burst of laughter from all around*]

MAJOR [*abjectly*]    I swear by Jupiter and Mars
That I won't hurt a living soul
For the slugging that I've suffered here today.
Moreover, if I go away from here intact,
Still with my manly testi . . . monials,[29]
I've been let off lightly for my act.

PROLIX    What if you break your word?

[29] This is the nearest I can get to Plautus's play with the word
*intestabilis:* someone without the power to bear witness in court and
someone without the genital gland. Castration was, of course, a
punishment inflicted by an injured husband.

MAJOR  Then let me live without
Those, er, testimonials—forever marred.

CARIO [*judicially*]  I move we give him one more clobbering
And let him go.

MAJOR [*in ringing tones*]  Oh, god bless you always
For coming to my rescue!

CARIO [*quickly*]  And *you* give us
A hundred pieces of gold.

MAJOR  What for?

CARIO  In evidence of the signal fact                    *1420*
That today we let loose from here,
Together with—ahem—"testimonials" intact,
The darling little grandson of Venus . . .
Otherwise—and don't imagine you deceive us—
You shall not leave us.

MAJOR [*immediately*]  You'll get it.

CARIO  That's more sensible.
But your uniform, your soldier's cloak, your sword—
Give up all hope of these—you won't get them back.
          [*Sees the look of protest in the* MAJOR's *eyes*]
Shall I clobber him again, sir,
Or will you now undo him?

MAJOR [*with a sickly smile*]  Have a heart:
I'm so battered I'm undone already.

PROLIX [*stiffly*]  Let him loose.
          [*The servants untie him*]

MAJOR [*staggering to his feet*]  I'm so grateful to you.

PROLIX  If ever I catch you here again,
You'll lose those testimonials.
          [*Another guffaw from the servants*]

MAJOR [*humbly*]    I don't contest it.

PROLIX    Cario, let's go in.

> [MR. PROLIX, *followed by* CARIO *with his knife, and
> the other servants, make a solemn procession back
> to the house*]

MAJOR [*sits rubbing his bruises, but suddenly brightens at
the sound of voices coming down the street*]    Ah, my
own servants!
Look, I see them.

> [*His slaves, headed by* POX,[30] *gather round him—
> in his underwear as he still is*]

MAJOR [*urgently*]    Goldilocks—has she gone yet, tell me?

POX    Oh, ages ago!

MAJOR [*crushed*]    What a catastrophe!

POX [*surveying him with interest*]    You'd say something a
good deal stronger
If you knew what I know, sir:
That fellow with the woolen eye-patch
Over his left eye—huh!—
1430    Was no sailor.

MAJOR [*clutching him*]    Who was he, then?

POX [*smugly*]    Goldilocks's lover.

MAJOR [*jumping up and shaking him*]    How do you know?

POX [*freeing himself*]    I just know.
Right from the time they were outside the city gates
They never stopped kissing and embracing.

MAJOR [*sinking back onto the curbstone*]    What a sorry
fool I am!
Now I see it:

---

[30] Some editors, worried by the fact that POX had said he was going
to disappear for a few days, give this part to a slave.

Led along the garden path . . .
So Dodger was the lousy rat
Who got me tangled in this trap!

[*After a pause, the* MAJOR *pulls himself together,
rises with dignity, and faces the audience with a
faint smile*]

If other lechers could so fare,
Fewer lechers would be here.
Their nerves would be on keener edge
And they less keen on carnal knowledge.

[*Beckons his company of slaves*]

Let's go back now to my house.
And, Audience, will you clap for us?                *1437*

# THE
# PRISONERS
(CAPTIVI)

for Margaret Tanner:
loved grandmummie of Pandora
Martin
Vanessa
and Cordelia

# THE CHARACTERS

**ERGASILUS**
*A parasite*

**HEGIO**
*An old gentleman of Aetolia*

**FOREMAN OF PRISONERS**
*A servant of Hegio*

**PHILOCRATES**
*A young prisoner from Elis, captured by the Aetolians*

**TYNDARUS**
*His servant, captured with him*

**ARISTOPHONTES**
*Another young prisoner from Elis*

**A BOY**
*Servant of Hegio*

**PHILOPOLEMUS**
*Hegio's son, prisoner in Elis*

**STALAGMUS**

**OTHER PRISONERS**
*Bought by Hegio*

**SERVANTS**[1]

---

[1] Sometimes I translate the Latin *servus* as "servant," sometimes as "slave." Neither English word is an exact synonym of the Latin. My reluctance to use the word "slave" is because the word has overtones and connotations that go beyond the servility or the severity of the Latin *servus*.

## TIME AND SETTING

Early morning in a street in Aetolia, central Greece. TYNDARUS dressed as a freeman, and PHILOCRATES dressed as a slave, are chained to a pillar outside HEGIO's house. The exit at stage left leads into town, that at stage right to the harbor. An actor walks downstage and addresses the audience.

# PROLOGUE

PROLOGUE   See these two prisoners standing here,
Standing by on their own two feet as it were?
Well, they're *standing* on them, not sitting—ha ha ha! . . .
      [*His laugh trails away at the conspicuous lack of response*]
At least you can see I'm not lying.
      [*Resumes briskly*]
Hegio, the old man who lives here, is the father of *that* one.
      [*Jerks a thumb toward* TYNDARUS. *Frowns*]
What! Father's son a slave? How come?
Listen and I'll tell you.
      [*Takes a step toward the audience*]
The old gentleman had two sons.
One of them when four years old was stolen by a slave,
Who took to his heels and sold him;
Yes, sold him in the country of Elis[2] to the father of *that* one.
      [*Indicates* PHILOCRATES]
Get me? . . . Fine . . . Oh, dear!                                    10
There's a man at the back shaking his head.
      [*Waves to him*]
Come nearer, sir.
      [*Waits, but there is apparently no move*]
Take a seat, for god's sake, or take a stroll.

2 The most western district of the Peloponnese, with a capital of the same name.

You're reducing an honest actor to a beggar.
          [*Still no move. He grits his teeth*]
I'm not going to blow my lungs out just for you . . .
As for the rest of you—you solid ratepayers—
I'll discharge this—er—plot . . . I mean debt,
I'm not a dawdler when it comes to paying up.
As I was saying:
The slave skidaddled with his young master
And sold him to this man's father, [*pointing to* PHI-
          LOCRATES]
Who bought the boy and gave him to his son
(They were about the same age) to be his own.
Well, here he is back at home, his father's slave.
The father doesn't know, of course.
          [*Shakes his head*]
Ah, we poor humans!
Aren't we just the footballs of the gods!
So he lost one son—you understand.
Then war broke out between the Aetolians and the
          Elians,
And he lost the other. Which in war is no surprise.
The boy was bought by a doctor in this selfsame Elis.
Meanwhile Hegio begins to trade in prisoners of war,
Hoping to find one he can exchange for his missing son.
He hasn't an inkling there's a son at home.
Then yesterday, when he heard an Elian cavalier of the
          highest rank and family had been captured,
He wouldn't spare a nickel if it could save his son
And to increase his chances of bringing him home
He bought both these prisoners [*with a toss of the head
          toward* PHILOCRATES *and* TYNDARUS]    from the com-
          missioners at the sale of spoil.
However, [*winking at the audience*]
These same two prisoners came to a private arrangement
          of their own,
Whereby Tyndarus, the slave, could get his master home:
They changed clothes and names.
So, that one [*pointing to* TYNDARUS] is calling himself
          Philocrates,
And this one [*pointing to* PHILOCRATES], Tyndarus:
He's him and him's he—just for today.
Yes, today, right here, Tyndarus is going to carry off his
          trick and set his master free;

20

30

40

And by the same token, unwittingly,
He's going to come to the rescue of his brother
And help him to return a free man to his fatherland and
    father.
[*with a wry smile*]    Ah, that's so like life!
We often do more good by chance than by design.
These two, without knowing it,
Have so plotted and contrived, so put their heads together
    and fixed it,
That Tyndarus stays here as his father's servant.
Yes, here he is slaving away to his own father—                 50
And has no idea of it.
      [*Strokes his chin reflectively*]
Well, well, when I come to think of it,
What little mannikins we are! . . .
Never mind: it's life we put before you,
Though we put it in a story.
      [*Picks up briskly*]
There's one other thing I'd like to underline:
It'll pay you to pay attention to this play,
It really will.
This play isn't written to the usual formula,
It's not like other plays at all:
There aren't any smutty lines you can't repeat;
There's no perjured pimp or meretricious tart,
No overblown, swaggering major . . .
And don't be dismayed if I said
The Aetolians and Elians were at loggerheads:
All the battles are offstage. [*grinning*]                      60
It would be tantamount to cheating—wouldn't it?—
If we, this company, all togged-up like funnymen,
Suddenly switched to tragedy.
So if anybody wants a fight,
He can go and get himself embroiled at law with a good
    tough antagonist,
And I warrant him a battle scene
He won't ever want to see again.
      [*Bows to the audience*]
Well, I'm off. Goodbye.
You kind hearthside critics here
And you wonderful warriors at war.

              [*Leads the two prisoners out*]

# ACT I

ERGASILUS *minces in from the direction of the forum. He is dressed up in frayed elegance, with more than a suspicion of rouge and pomade on his rather haggard face, and reeks of cheap perfume. Carefully arranging a lock of hair over his forehead, he accosts the audience with forced brightness—and a lisp.*

ERGASILUS    Fairy Tartlet's what the young blades call me here,
    La-di-da! . . .
70    Because I turn up willy-nilly at their junketings.
        [*Picks up the edge of his toga*]
    Oh, it's absurd, I know,
    But they think it's awfully funny.
    Actually it *is* quite accurate.
    You see, at parties when the gambling starts,
      A young lover calls on his fairy tartlet—
    His own fairy tartlet—
    To be with him as he makes a throw.
    [*simpering*]    And does fairy-tartlet feel the call?
    I'll say she does! . . . So do we all:
    We poor parasites who never ever [*with a little petulant stamp*]
    Get a call to a ball, at all.
    We're like mice:
    Nibble, nibble all the time
    At other people's provender.
    And at the recess
    When *they* go off to their rural areas,
    You can guess
    What kind of recession our molars get.
        [*Wiggles two fingers at the side of his head*]
80    We're like snails in a heatwave
    When no dew falls,
    Sucking their own juices up:
    Yes, that's us.
    During the holidays we poor parasites just crawl
    Into our own shells:

Live on our own juice for eats
While the juicy people
Live on their country seats.
[*suddenly fierce*]   Wuff wuff wuff!
We're like a pack of raging hounds
While vacation lasts,
But when it's past [*stroking himself*]
We're Golden Receivers, Peck-in-ease and Great Banes.
     [*Corners of his mouth dropping*]
What's more, by god,
In this goddam city,
A parasite who can't take punches on the nose
Or let a vase
Be smashed to pieces on his head,
Had better go and take himself—yes, he ought!—
To the station of Three Arches with a sack    *90*
And be a porter. [*with a grim smile*]
*My* precious fate precisely—
Or most likely.
[*confidentially*]   It's like this, you see:
When my lord and master
Fell into the hands of the enemy—
Oh yes, the Aetolians and Elians are at war—
Aetolia being here
And Elis over there,
Where my Philopolemus is a prisoner:
He being the son of old Hegio here
Who lives in that house over there . . .
My my, what a stricken house it is!
Every time I look at it I cry . . .
   [*Pulls out a handkerchief*]
Oh dear! . . . Where was I?
Yes, of course:
For the sake of his son,
This poor man's taken on
A rather dirty job—not up his street at all.
He's gone into the slave trade: buys up men,   *100*
Hoping that some day he'll exchange someone
For his son.
   [*Pats his paunch with a hollow look*]
God! How I want him to succeed.
If Hegio doesn't get him back—I'm a wreck.
There's not a thing for me with these young stinkers:

They're devoted to themselves, the lot.
But Philopolemus,
He's a young gentleman of the old school, that one.
I've never ironed out the creases from his frown
And not got a handsome handout.
His father's the same: a proper gentleman.
That's whom I'm off to see.
Ah, his door's opening!
    [*Chuckles*]
The times I've—ahem—passed out . . . he he he! . . . of
    that door, loaded!
       [*Stands to one side and waits*]

[HEGIO *comes out of the house. He is a brisk, pleasant-looking old man, neatly dressed and carrying a walking stick. He is followed by his* FOREMAN OF PRISONERS: *large, robust, with a whip in his hands*]

*110* HEGIO   Now about those two prisoners I bought from
    the war-commissioners yesterday,
Please take note:
Put the light irons on them
And strike off those heavy ones they're coupled with.
Let them walk about at will, indoors or out;
But keep an eye on them . . .
A captive at large is a pretty flighty bird:
You won't catch him twice.
Give him a chance to flit—
And that's it.

FOREMAN [*dryly*]   Naturally, sir, we all prefer
Our liberty to slavery.

HEGIO [*pointing with his walking stick*]   All except you,
    it would appear.

*120* FOREMAN [*smiling*]   Well, without the price of a fee[3]
Would you rather I showed a pair of heels to make me
    free?

HEGIO [*pretending to be shocked*]   You'd better not.

3 Meaning: he is without the money to buy his liberty.

For the price of that
I'll pay you tit for tat.

FOREMAN [*airily*]  Oh, I'll just imitate
That flighty bird of yours you said would fly.

HEGIO [*shaking his stick*]  Just you try
And I'll clap you in a cage by and by.
            [*They both laugh*]
But let this nonsense stop.
Just mark my orders and be on your way.
I'm off to my brother's to ascertain
If my other prisoners are all right
And weren't too restive in the night.
Then I'll come straight home again.
            [*The* FOREMAN *bows and goes into the house*]

ERGASILUS [*with a loud sigh*]  A pity this old gentleman
      has to be a jailer
To save his pitiable son!                              *130*
Ah well, if it gets him back here
I can stand it . . .
He can even be an executioner.

HEGIO [*turning*]  Who spoke there?

ERGASILUS [*thrusting forward*]  I did. I am ill:
Sick with worry for your sorrow.
I'm dwindling, aging, wasting, sinking
Downhill.
I'm all skin and bones, I feel so deeply for you.
Not a thing I eat does me any good at home.
Only the merest smidge of something does,
If I roam.

HEGIO  Ah, good morning, Ergasilus!

ERGASILUS [*seizing his hand*]  All the gods bless you,
      Hegio—bounteously.
            [*Bursts into tears*]

HEGIO [*pretending to be taken aback*]  Please, no tears.

ERGASILUS   W-w-what—no tears! N-n-no cataracts for
such a youth?

140   HEGIO [*putting an arm around him*]   There, there! I al-
ways knew
You were a good friend to my son
And he to you.

ERGASILUS [*sobbing*]   It's only when we've lost what we've
got
That we poor mortals realize what we've not.
It wasn't till your son was taken prisoner
That I saw how much he meant to me,
And now I miss him desperately.

HEGIO [*patting him on the back*]   Come come! If you a
merè outsider so take on,
Think what *I* must feel about the boy's catastrophe,
And he my only son.

ERGASILUS [*tearing himself away*]   *Me* an outsider . . . to
*him*?
[*choking*]   A-a-ah! Hegio, don't say such a thing.
Don't let it enter your head.
He was your only son;
To me he was everything:
150   The one and only one.   [*sobbing again*]

HEGIO   I think it's fine of you
To make your friend's mishap your own.

ERGASILUS [*cries out, clutching his stomach*]   Aah! Here's
where it hurts.
All my forage troops have been dispersed.

HEGIO [*hiding a smile*]   And meanwhile there's no one to
take on
This forage army for you, which you say is gone.

ERGASILUS [*dismally*]   Would you believe it,
Ever since your dear Philopolemus was lost
Everybody runs a mile from the post!

HEGIO [*laughing*]    Everybody runs a mile from the post?
   Goodness me, I'm not surprised:
   Your forage army has to be
   So wide and so diverse.
   First, you want some Turkey[4] . . . yes?         *160*
   Many kinds of Turkey, naturally;
   And Greece of course.
   You're Hungary too for Hamburgers and for Finns,
   For Frankfurters absolutely and Sardines . . .
   Or is it Sardinians?

ERGASILUS [*with stunned admiration*]    Oh, the talent that
   the world can miss!
   What a general this mere private is!

HEGIO
   Cheer up a little then.
   In a few days I'm sure we'll have him back again.
   I've got an Elian prisoner in there,
   A young man from the topmost drawer . . .       *170*
   Oodles of money—a millionaire.
   There's no question I can change him for my son.

ERGASILUS    Let's hope to heaven you can.
   Meanwhile, ahem . . . are you asked to dinner anywhere?

HEGIO [*off his guard*]    Nowhere I can think of.
   What's that to you?

ERGASILUS [*polishing his nails*]    Oh . . . it's just my birth-
   day.
   I thought I'd invite you home to dinner—chez vous.

HEGIO [*with a burst of laughter*]    How nicely put!
   It'll be very frugal. Do you mind?

ERGASILUS [*puckering his face*]    Not too awfully awfully
   frugal . . .
   Not what I'm used to at home?

4 In order to capture some of the effect of the puns in the original,
I have had to tamper with geography.

HEGIO   Come on, accept my bid.

ERGASILUS [*assuming the stance of an auctioneer*]   Going,
       going, gone—to you, sir.
       Since no one's making me a better offer
180     (Something really favorable to me and all my friends)
       I'll knock it down—my whole estate—to you, sir;
       But on my terms.

HEGIO   Your whole estate—ha ha!
       You mean your hole-y empty state.
       All right then, but come early.

ERGASILUS [*tucking his handkerchief around his neck*]
       Fine! I'm ready now.

HEGIO   Are you really?
       Then go and hunt a hare.
       You've only got a weasel so far.
       My board is stony fare.

ERGASILUS [*blithely*]   Then I'll come with my teeth
       shod . . .
       You can't put me off that way, Hegio.

HEGIO [*teasingly*]   The fodder's rough.

ERGASILUS [*screwing up his face*]   What, is it brambles?

HEGIO   Well, things that root in the earth.

ERGASILUS   Like pork?

HEGIO   No, like green stuff.

190 ERGASILUS   Open a home for health . . .
       Anything else?

HEGIO   Yes, come in good time.

ERGASILUS [*skipping away*]   You're telling *me!*

               [*Exits cheerfully in the direction of the forum*]

HEGIO [*with a sigh*]    Now I'll go inside and do some sums:
   Find out just how broke I am;
   Then, as I said, to my brother's home.

[*Goes into his house*]

# ACT II

*The* FOREMAN OF PRISONERS *comes out from a side door
of* HEGIO's *house, leading a group of slaves in which* PHILO-
CRATES *and* TYNDARUS *are conspicuous for their looks and
bearing. The latter is dressed in the remnants of his master's military uniform, and* PHILOCRATES *himself wears
slave's clothes. All the prisoners have identity discs round
their necks. They chatter and grumble. The* FOREMAN
*lines them up outside the house fussily and gestures for
silence.*

FOREMAN    Well, it's the will of heaven, boys,
   This little spot of trouble of yours.
   Take it in your stride,
   Then it won't seem so hard.
   Back at home you were free men, I surmise.
   Well, now you're slaves.
   Better get used to the idea.
   Better do what your master tells you to.
   Whatever he does is right,
   Even when it's wrong . . . clear?                    *200*

PRISONERS [*drawling it out*]    O-o-h n-no!

FOREMAN [*fatuously*]    Now then,
   No need for a hullabaloo and hubub.
   No use letting your eyes get wet, men.
   Chins up in time of trouble!

TYNDARUS [*nudged by* PHILOCRATES, *assumes a ridicu-
      lously affected accent*]    I say, we're in chains, we
      feel such fools.

FOREMAN    How d'yer think your boss would feel,

How'd he get his money's worth
If he took off those chains and let you loose?

TYNDARUS [*innocently*]  Oh, doesn't he trust us?
We'd know how to behave if he set us free—
Wouldn't we?

PRISONERS [*with a derisive groan*]   Y-e-s.

FOREMAN [*heavily*]   Yes, you'd run for it.
*I* know what you're up to.

PHILOCRATES [*shocked*]   Us—run?
Where would we run to?

FOREMAN
Home.

PHILOCRATES   The idea of it!
Acting like runaway slaves!

FOREMAN
Absolutely!
210   And I wouldn't blame you if you got the chance.

TYNDARUS [*grandly indicating* PHILOCRATES *and himself*]
Allow us to ask you one favor.
        [*Takes out a coin and plays with it*]

FOREMAN   Well . . . what may that be?

TYNDARUS   Can he and I talk alone somewhere:
Apart from you and the rest?

FOREMAN [*his eyes on the coin*]   I think it can be arranged.
        [*Takes the coin, bites it and pockets it*]
Scatter, the rest of you.
        [*Waves them out*]
I'll retire in there . . .
But mind you make it short.

TYNDARUS
That's what I intended.   [*with a sign to* PHILOCRATES]
Hey, Philocrates—over here.

FOREMAN [*to the slaves still hanging about*]  Go on.
 Leave them to themselves.

> [*The prisoners filter back into the house through
> the side door, murmuring*]

TYNDARUS [*with exaggerated politeness*]  We deeply ap-
 preciate this, both of us . . .
 Having the privilege of doing what we please.
 And we owe it to you; we really do.

> [*The* FOREMAN *grins sheepishly and goes out of sight*]

PHILOCRATES [*reassuming his role as master*]  Pst! Tyn-
 darus—over here, please.
 We don't want anyone listening in,                        220
 And leaving us with a leaky plot.
 A plot's no plot but a disaster
 If it isn't watertight.
> [*They edge farther away*]
 If I'm your slave and you're my master
 We've got to keep our eyes and ears alert:
 Take damn good care, if no one's to suspect.
 We've got to be shrewd and thorough
 And keep a cool head.
 It's a big job we have got on hand,
 And we can't afford to go to sleep on it.

TYNDARUS [*solemnly*]  I shall be everything you want, sir.

PHILOCRATES  I hope you will.

TYNDARUS
 Yes! My own life's cheap
 To make yours dear.                                        230

PHILOCRATES [*putting a hand on his shoulder*]  I know,
 I'm well aware.

TYNDARUS [*looking him straight in the eyes*]  When what
 you wanted, you have got,
 *Then* be aware of it and don't forget.
 Most people tend—
 Yes, almost more than not—

To be the soul of affability,
While they're on the make,
But, when they've made it,
To lose all faith
And all integrity.
[*smiling*]   Now I am telling *you*
How you are to act with *me*.
And what I say, I'd say to my own father.[5]

PHILOCRATES
You're being a second father to me too ...
Oh, I could go so far
As call you father.

TYNDARUS [*shyly*]   I know it.

PHILOCRATES   For that very reason I must impress on you
240         once more:
I'm *not* your master—I'm your slave.
Please, please hang on to *that*.
The immortal gods have made it clear,
Have willed that I the master
Should now become your fellow prisoner.
So, by all my former right to give an order,
I beg you by our sad unsettled state,
By my father's lenience toward you,
By our slavery,
By all the vicissitudes of war:
Pay as much attention to me now
As when you served me.
And remember this—oh, do remember!—
Who you were and who you are.

TYNDARUS [*with a wry smile*]   Yes, now I am you
And you are me.

PHILOCRATES   Fine! If you can keep it up
250         Our little machination has some hope.

> [*The front door opens and* HEGIO *is seen
> giving instructions on the threshold*]

5 *Quod tibi suadeam, suadeam meo patri.* (237) Leo brackets this
line as doubtful.

HEGIO    I shall be back in a minute
    After I've found out what I want from these . . .
    But where are they—the ones
    I ordered to be brought out?

PHILOCRATES [*advancing with a cocksure grin*]   You've
    fixed it, mister, as far as I can see, in such a way
    You needn't go looking very far:
    We're absolutely stiff with chains and jailers.

HEGIO [*shrugging apologetically*]   I know it,
    But anyone who guards against deception
    Really has to see he's on his guard;
    Otherwise, when he thinks he's guarding—
    He's being gulled.
    Anyway, don't you think it's hardly rash
    Of me to keep an eye on you?
    You cost me quite a lot
    Of plain hard cash.

PHILOCRATES
    Bless you, sir,
    We've no more right to make a fuss
    Because you try to keep us
    Than *you* have with *us*
    If we seize the chance to scatter.                    *260*

HEGIO [*sadly*]   My own son is in your country.
    My own son is kept a prisoner there
    Just as you are here.

PHILOCRATES   A prisoner of war?

HEGIO   Yes.

PHILOCRATES [*wryly*]   So we are not the only ones to
    make a mess of it!

HEGIO [*signaling* PHILOCRATES *to a marble bench*]   Come
    over here, young man.
    I want to ask you something personal . . .
    I trust you'll hand me out no lies.

PHILOCRATES [*ingenuously*]    None that I know, sir,
And none that I don't know either.

TYNDARUS [*looking on and chuckling to himself*]
Now the old man's in the barber's chair
Now the clippers are in the air
He's got no towel around him,
To save his clothes.
Which is it?
Crew-cut or only trim?
Who knows!
But if the barber does his stuff
He'll have off every bit of fluff.

HEGIO [*looking intently at* PHILOCRATES]    Well now, Tyndarus, tell me about yourself.
*270*    Would you rather be a slave or free?

PHILOCRATES [*diplomatically*]    *I* go for the nearest thing
to happiness
And the furthest thing from misery,
But if you want to know, sir,
It wasn't a bad life in slave's livery.
I was treated as a son of the house, no less.

TYNDARUS [*in a murmur*]    Brilliant, my boy!
Talk of intelligence, I wouldn't give a thousand pounds
for Thales!6
Next to Philocrates, the man from Miletus
Is the merest amateur . . .
How beautifully he's trimmed his tongue to loss of
grandeur!

HEGIO    And who were Philocrates's people over there—
In Elis?

PHILOCRATES [*in an awed whisper*]    The Goldfingers, sir:
Easily the richest—
The most important family there.

HEGIO    And the young man himself: how grand is *he*?

6 The celebrated Greek philosopher and scientist, born about 640
B.C. in the city of Miletus, in Asia Minor.

PHILOCRATES   Oh, very grand: in top circles.                    *2797*

HEGIO [*beaming*]
    And rich? Well covered?

PHILOCRATES   You're telling *me*!
    The old man's simply rolling.

HEGIO   His father's alive, is he?

PHILOCRATES   Was when we left him.
    Whether he is now or not,
    You'd have to go down to Hades and ask there.

TYNDARUS [*grinning to himself*]   Playing safe for sure!
    Not only can he dish out lies,
    He can also moralize.

HEGIO   What was his name?

PHILOCRATES [*looking him straight in the eye*]   Oh . . .
    Giltedgedsecurityatsixpercentson.[8]

HEGIO [*nodding approval*]   Because of his money, I
    suppose?

PHILOCRATES [*innocently*]   Oh no! Because of his nerve
    and his insatiable rapacity.
    His real name was Praisedbegodforbullion.[9]

HEGIO [*slightly worried*]   You mean, the old man's rather
    close?

PHILOCRATES [*throwing up his hands*]   Close? He's ad-
    hesive.
    Why, to give you some idea:
    When he sacrifices to his own tutelary spirit              *290*

[7] Leo brackets as doubtful line 280: "You mean in Elis he's considered really *something*?"
[8] The Latin (or rather the Greek) is: Thensaurochrysonicochrysides,
"Son of gilded riches surpassing treasures of gold."
[9] Line 288, bracketed by Leo as doubtful: *Nam ille quidem Theo-
doromedes fuit germano nomine.*

He uses ten-cent altar-ware from Samos,[10]
Just in case the deity goes off with it.
You can tell from that
How much faith he has in "human" nature.

HEGIO [*rising from the marble bench*]   I see . . .
Now, Tyndarus, come with me:
I'm going to pump your master.
      [*Goes over to another bench and sits down near
      the real* TYNDARUS]
Philocrates, your man's behaved with tact;
Like any decent man, in fact.
I know about your family—
He's told me that.
If you'll just see fit to confirm . . . ahem! . . .
It won't do you any harm.
Anyway, I know already.

TYNDARUS [*looking out over the audience with distant and
      melancholy dignity*]   He did his duty, sir,
Telling you the truth,
Although I'd much prefer
He'd kept from you
My breeding, rank and wealth.
Never mind,
300    Now that I've lost my native land and liberty
I suppose I must expect to find
Him giving more respect to you than me.
War has ground us down together.
But I can remember a time
When he hardly opened his mouth.
Now, if the fancy takes him,
He can actually hurt me.   [*shaking his head ponder-
      ously*]
How Fate molds and twists us to her whims!
Look at me: a slave
Who once was free,
Tossed to the bottom from the top—
Who once held sway:

10 An island in the Aegean off the coast of Asia Minor. No doubt
the Japan of the period when it came to cheap pottery. Samos also
produced large quantities of wine.

Yes, at another's beck and call.
    [*Gazes at* HEGIO *with solemn assurance*]
Nevertheless, I still can say:
If I've got a master like *I* was
When I was the headman of the house,
I shall not fear his being unfair or harsh.
    [*After a pause, and a quick glance at* PHILO-
    CRATES *for approval*]
There's something, Hegio, I must ask,
If it isn't utterly repugnant to your wish.

HEGIO   Not at all. Speak up.

TYNDARUS [*solemnly*]   Like your son, I once had liberty.   *310*
Like him too, by force of war,
I had it snatched from me;
And now like him (slaving for us over there)
I am here and slave for you.
There is a Providence I'm sure
That hears and sees everything we do,
And it will treat him there
As kindly as you treat me here.
Kindness always reaps in kind,
Maltreatment draws exactly such.
The way you miss your son,
My father misses me as much.

HEGIO [*impressed but not to be put off*]   Of that I'm well
   aware,
But are you willing to confirm
What this fellow said of you?

TYNDARUS [*winking at* PHILOCRATES]   I confirm the fact
   my father's rich,
(My home is too)
And that my family's of the best . . .
But, Hegio, I implore of you
Not to let your soul become obsessed
With what I'm worth.                   *320*
Otherwise my father,
Even though I'm son-and-heir,
May decide there's much more sense
In leaving me to be a servant in this place

(Well-fed and clothed at your expense)
Rather than become a beggar over there
And in disgrace.

HEGIO [*apologetically*]   You must not imagine I am one
Who thinks that every particle of profit is sheer gain.
I know too well how money has unmade
Many a man,
That there are times
When men by making money, lose.
No: gold is something I despise.
Innumerable are those that gold has led astray.
Therefore listen carefully
To what I now propose:

330
You Elians hold my son, a captured slave.
Get him back for me
And without your giving up a single penny
I'll set you free—this man too.
Otherwise I shall not let you go.

TYNDARUS [*trying to hide his rapture*]   A most reasonable
     and fair request,
You most reasonable of gentlemen, of men the best . . .
But—does your son belong to someone private
Or the state?

HEGIO   To someone private:
To a doctor with the name of Menarchus.

TYNDARUS [*in astonishment, to himself*]   Good heavens!
He's a client of my master's.
          [*Turns enthusiastically to* HEGIO]
The thing's as easy as raindrops rolling off the roof.

HEGIO [*tears welling up*]   Just get him back.

TYNDARUS   I will . . .
But there's something, Hegio, I must ask.

HEGIO   Anything—just anything
That does not hinder *that*.

TYNDARUS   Listen, then you'll tell.

I'm not asking to go scot-free myself,
Not until my slave's return.
What I want
Is that you let me use him as a forfeit:
Dispatch him to my father as a ransom for your son.    *340*

HEGIO [*hesitating*]  To be quite frank, I'd rather send
    another,
As soon as there's a lull.
He'll see your father
And carry out your mission just as well.

TYNDARUS [*taken aback*]  But it's useless—
A complete waste of time—
To send a total stranger to him:
Send Tyndarus.  [*points to* PHILOCRATES]
He'll bring it off the moment he arrives.
You couldn't send a better man.
He's honest and reliable,
A servant after your own heart:
Just the one
To whom a person might entrust his son.
You need have no anxiety;
I'll guarantee his loyalty.
I know his character,
And he's conscious of my kindness to him, sir.         *350*

HEGIO [*looking from* TYNDARUS *to* PHILOCRATES]  Very
    well, I'll take your word for it.
Send him, if you want to, as the forfeit.

TYNDARUS
I want to all right, and quickly too.
I want to see this enterprise a fact.

HEGIO
Have you any objection then
To paying me a hundred pounds:
In case he doesn't turn up again?

TYNDARUS
Not in the least . . . It's a fair bargain.

HEGIO [*claps his hands and the* FOREMAN *appears*]
Free that man, will you . . .
No, both of them.

TYNDARUS [*as the* FOREMAN *begins to unlock his chains*]
God bless you for your kindness, sir,
And for this riddance of my fetters.  [*as the chains fall
off*]
Phew! What a relief to shed one's collar!

HEGIO [*smiling indulgently*]   A good deed done to a de-
cent human being
Wins a reward beyond the doing.
[*Waves away* TYNDARUS's *further thanks*]
Now if you're willing
To send that fellow on his way,
Tell me exactly and in detail
(When he's reached your father)
What he has to say . . .
360      Shall I call him for you?

TYNDARUS   If you will.

HEGIO [*as he rises and goes toward* PHILOCRATES]   Let's
hope the whole thing turns out beautifully
For you, for my son, for me.
[*standing before* PHILOCRATES]   Well, young fellow,
your new master
Has a job for you to do:
Something special for your old one.
So I've let him have you
Under forfeit of a hundred pounds.
He says he wants to send you to his father
As a ransom for my boy in Elis.
He and I are going to barter sons.

PHILOCRATES [*with a rough-and-ready humor*]   Suits me
fine to do a good turn
To either of you gentlemen:
You or him.
You can use me like a blooming wheel:
Round and round I'll whiz,
370      Whichever way you like: yours or his.

HEGIO [*patting him on the back*]  Bravo, my man! You
    give yourself a tip
When you bear your slavery without a gripe.
Come.
        [*Leads him to* TYNDARUS]
Your man, Philocrates!

TYNDARUS [*as if making an after-dinner speech*]  Sir, I'm
    filled with thanks
For your giving me the chance
Of making him a messenger
And sending him to see my parents.
Now he can give my father a full account
Of how I'm doing here
And what I want.
        [*Turns to* PHILOCRATES, *trying not to bat an
        eyelid*]
Tyndarus,
This gentleman and I have just made plans:
I'm sending you to Elis,
Under forfeit, to my father.
Should you not return here
I'll owe on your behalf one hundred pounds.                380

PHILOCRATES  Strikes me as very fair.
    In any case his father
    Is expecting me or someone
    With news from here.

TYNDARUS [*to* PHILOCRATES, *with a glint in his eye*]  Pay
    attention please
To what I wish you to announce to him.

PHILOCRATES [*suppressing a smile*]  Yes, Philocrates:
    I've always done my best for you
    And shall go on
    Working the hardest that I can
    In anything to do with you.
    I'll go to every length
    To follow up and push things through—
    Oh, with all my heart and soul and strength!

TYNDARUS  Very fitting, to be sure!
    Now will you listen, please.

Salute Mother and Father first,
Then my relatives,
Then anyone you see
Who bears goodwill to me.
*390*    Say that I am here, and well,
A servant to this gentleman of sterling worth,
Who has accorded me and accords me still
The utmost kindness he could treat me with.

PHILOCRATES    I need no injunctions on that matter, sir.
It is graven on my memory.

TYNDARUS    If I didn't have a sentry guarding me
I might imagine I was free.
Tell my father of the bargain
We've struck on Hegio's son.

PHILOCRATES    Oh, I've got it pat.
Don't waste time telling me.

TYNDARUS [*ignoring him*]    He is to ransom and remit the
    lad
In exchange for *both* of us.

PHILOCRATES [*impatiently*]    I'll remember *that*.

HEGIO
But as soon as possible:
It's vital to each side.

PHILOCRATES [*laying a hand on* HEGIO's *arm*]    You long
    to see your son
No sooner, I assure you, sir,
Than he to welcome his.

HEGIO    Yes, mine to me's as dear
As his to any man's.

PHILOCRATES [*nudging* TYNDARUS]    Is there nothing else
*400*    you'd like to tell your father?

TYNDARUS [*casting about*]    Say that I'm well and . . .
    and . . .
Oh, Tyndarus, launch out on your own!

Say that you and I have never had a quarrel,
That you've never misbehaved
Or I been disagreeable,
And that you've served your master well
In spite of every trouble.
Say that you've never let me down,
Never doubted, never been disloyal
Even in the blackest moment.
Once my father hears this, Tyndarus,
And sees the spirit that you've shown
Not only to his son but him,
He'll never be so mean
As not to buy your liberty outright.
Once I'm there, to foster *that*
And make him readier to do it,
Will be the object of my every effort.

     [PHILOCRATES *tries to interrupt but is brushed*
       *aside*]

For don't I owe it
To your devotion, friendship, wisdom, care,       *410*
That I've been given the chance
Of seeing once again my parents?
You were the one
Who relayed to this gentleman
My substance and my birth.
Yours was the forethought
That got an owner's fetters stricken off.

PHILOCRATES   Yes, as you say:
I did all this.
It warms my heart that you remember it.
You deserved it anyway.
Ah, dear Philocrates,
If *I* should also start to tell
The million ways you treated me so well,
Night would crowd on day.
For had you been a slave
Your sweet concern for me
Could not have shown more constantly.

HEGIO [*clapping his hands rhapsodically*]   Gods above!
What loyalty!
What nobility of natures!

It moves to tears.
How they love . . . each other.
How it appears!
420     The way that splendid slave
Heaps his praise
On his master!

PHILOCRATES[11]   I assure you, mister,
The praise he heaps on me
Is only a fraction
Of what I ought to heap on *him*.

HEGIO   Here's your chance then
Of crowning all you've done,
And discharging this for him with scrupulous dispatch.

PHILOCRATES [*in ringing tones*]   Oh, my eagerness to go
and do it
Is only matched
By will to see it done.
Which to prove, I hereby swear:
Philocrates—by almighty Zeus!—
I'll never let you down.

HEGIO   You're an honest fellow, sir.

PHILOCRATES   And I'll never do a thing to you
I wouldn't to myself.

TYNDARUS [*with a searching look at* PHILOCRATES]   It's in
the achievement, the finished act,
430     I look to see you prove your word.
And if I've said far less of you
Than I should have liked,
Please be impressed by what I'm saying now
And do not be annoyed.
[*Takes a step toward* PHILOCRATES *and puts a
hand on his shoulder*]
I'm asking you to bear in mind just this:
You're being sent home on trust and under forfeit.
*My* life meanwhile remains in pawn.

11 Nixon and others give this line (less aptly I think) to Tyndarus.

So don't forget me the moment you are out of sight.
I shall be slaving here:
A slave instead of you, and left behind.
Do not consider you are free,
And do not leave me in the lurch.
Don't shirk the task of bringing home
This man's son.
Remember you have cost a hundred pounds.[12]
*I* was faithful; *you* keep faith;
All faithlessness be far from you.
My father, I can guarantee, will do his part.                    *440*
Be my everlasting friend,
And keep the new friendship you have found.[13]
    [*He points to* HEGIO]
There, shake on it!
My hand in yours . . .
Never be less true
Than I am now to you.
    [*They shake hands in silence*]
And so to work.
You are my master now,
My protector and my father.
In your hands are all my hopes,
And all my health and wealth.

PHILOCRATES    Quite enough injunctions! Won't it be
    enough
Just to deal with these and change them into facts?

TYNDARUS    Quite!

PHILOCRATES    Then I'll return replete with all you want,
And with what you want too, sir. [*with a nod to* HEGIO]
Anything else?

TYNDARUS    Only that you come back soon.

PHILOCRATES    It points that way.

HEGIO [*Takes a step forward and addresses* PHILOCRATES]
Well, Tyndarus, come along with me.

12 Leo brackets this line (438) as doubtful.
13 Some read *hunc iuventum inveni* as "obtain this youth."

I have to get you traveling money from the bank,
And a passport for you from the prætor.

450 TYNDARUS [*apprehensive*]   What passport?

HEGIO   One to take with him and show the army,
To get from here to home.
Now will you please go in.

TYNDARUS [*from the doorstep*]   Bon voyage, Tyndarus!

PHILOCRATES [*grinning all over*]   Goodbye, goodbye!

[TYNDARUS *turns and goes into the house*]

HEGIO [*chuckling to himself*]   Well, well!
I struck a bargain when I bought those men:
Saved my son from servitude (so god will!);
Yet the fuss I made before I purchased them!

[*Claps his hands and the* FOREMAN OF PRISONERS
*emerges with a couple of slaves*]

HEGIO   Keep him safe inside, m'lads.
Don't let him set a foot outside without a guard.
I'll soon be home . . .
Must see my other prisoners at my brother's house
And find out what is known of *this* young man.
[*Nods to* PHILOCRATES]
Come along, Tyndarus, please:
I must see to your dispatch—
460    Yes, that's the first thing to be attended to.

[*Exits down the street, with* PHILOCRATES *following*]

# ACT III

ERGASILUS *shuffles in from the forum, looking more tired
and hungry than ever.*

ERGASILUS   It's damned hard on a man
When he's got to go and look for his food
And has the damnedest time finding any.

It's even harder when he has the damnedest time
Looking for it and then not finding it.
[*with a deep sigh from the belly*]　But it's hardest of all
When he's ravenous and there *is* no food to find.
God! I'd like to gouge the living daylights out of this
　miserable day:
It's loaded with meanness—
Every human being is mean to me.
I've never seen a leaner, hollower, more hunger-bloated
　day:
A day when not a thing goes right.
My stomach, my palate, my gullet
Are having a goddam gala—on nothing.
　　　　[*Pats his belly with a groan*]
To hell with being a parasite!
The young fellows these days
Fence themselves around
From us poor broke buffoons,　　　　　　　　　　　*470*
Us punchdrunk sods from Sparta:[14]
We're not wanted now—
Not even below the salt as bottom-benchers.
We're twaddle mongers without meat or money.
The ones that get invited now
Are strictly those that can return the invite.
　　　　[*Spits into the street*]
They do their own shopping too—
Province once of parasites—
And their own blasted pimping
(Solemn as judges) just off the forum.
For us jokers they wouldn't give a fig;
They're all egoists.
[*leaning toward the audience confidentially*]　Why, soon
　after I had left you
I accosted a group of young gentry in the forum.
"Hullo" says I, "where are we having lunch today?"
Not a syllable in reply!
"Don't all shout at once," says I.
They're dumb as mutes. Not a smile.　　　　　　*480*
"Where's dinner then?"
They shake their heads.
So I tell a story:

14 The Spartans were famous both for their abstemiousness and
their ability to take punishment.

One of the ripest from my repertoire—
It used to get me dinners for a month—
Not a soul laughs.
The whole thing's fixed, I saw at once.
No one even had the grace to bare his teeth,
Like a disagreeable pup, even if he couldn't roar.
            [*Shrugs his shoulders*]
Well, I left them,
(I was only being ridiculous),
And went up to some others,
Then some others, then finally—
Some others.
It was all the same:
They're in cohoots the lot of them,
Like the oil-sellers in the Velabrum.[15]
[*smiling dismally*]    So here I am back again.
There's no point being ridiculous.
The place was stiff with parasites
All on the prowl.
            [*Makes a petulant little flap of the hands*]
There's a law in foreign parts,
In Rome to be precise,[16]
Against clubbing-up on parasites
And depriving them of victuals and vitality.
I'm going to have that law on them—I *am*.
I'll set a day, fix a fine:
Ten dinners given me at my convenience . . .
Just when prices soar.
I'm going to—for sure!
            [*Doggedly collects himself and begins to go*]
Now for the harbor:
My last gastronomic hope today.
If that falls flat there's nothing for it
But come back to the old man's iron rations.

            [*Looking about for a possible host,* ERGASILUS
                *hurries off in the direction of the harbor*]

[*Meanwhile* HEGIO *appears in the street, returning from his*

15 A market district off the Tiber. Plautus enjoyed mixing his scenes:
Rome with Greece.
16 A line I have interpolated to make clear that Plautus (once again)
though pretending to be in Greece, is really in Rome.

*brother's. He has a couple of servants with him, and* ARISTO-
PHONTES: *another of his young prisoners from Elis*]

HEGIO     [*humming happily to himself*]

> When things are going well
>> There's nothing nicer surely.
> I did the world some good
>> Yesterday by merely
> Purchasing those men.
>> Now when people see me                          *500*
> They come right up and say:
>> "Congratulations!" to me.
> I'm back, but oh so limp!
>> They stopped so much to tell me,
> And trying to get away
>> Was quite enough to kill me.
>> [*Sits down and mops his brow*]

Yes, at last I escaped to the prætor's office,
And still out of breath asked for the passport.
I got it on the spot,
Gave it to Tyndarus and off he went.
That done, I hurry home;
Then straightaway to my brother's
Where the rest of my prisoners are.
"Does any of you know Philocrates of Elis?" I ask.
Finally this fellow here calls out: [*indicates* ARISTO-
     PHONTES]
"Yes, he is a friend of mine."                     *510*
"Well, he's at my house," I say.
The man's all over me at once and begs to come and
     see him.
So I have the chains struck off and then . . .
[*turning to* ARISTOPHONTES] Here you are, young man:
Follow me and see your friend.

> [*As* HEGIO *and his party enter the house,* TYN-
> DARUS *rushes out with a terrified glance at* ARIS-
> TOPHONTES]

TYNDARUS   Oh now's the hour I'd so much rather
> Be something past than something present.
> Health, wealth and hope have fled: are absent.
> My day has come, my life is over.
>
> No chance of safety or survival,

No departure or arrival,
No hope of turning back the crisis,
520    No cloak to drape my crafty lies with.

No excuses for backsliding,
No loophole for my sins, and neither
Room for bluff, nor bolthole either
For trickery to go and hide in.

It's popped, it's open, broken, gaping:
Everything I kept clandéstine.
Nothing's left but to invest in
The death my master is escaping.

That fellow who has just gone in
Puts the final touches to me,
He knows my master and he knew me,
He's Philocrates's cousin.

No god of safety now can save me
Just a brilliant visitation
530    Of some special machination.
Dammit, surely nature gave me

Something subtle, something fertile
For this silly situation.
Or am I absolutely stricken,
    Stuck and futile?

[HEGIO *comes out with* ARISTOPHONTES *and*
*servants*]


HEGIO [*looking around*]    Well, where is he, I want to know:
    The fellow who just bolted from the house?

TYNDARUS [*from behind a pillar*]
            I'm done for now, the game is over:
            Tyndarus, they've got you collared.

            What to say? Make up what story?
            What admit and what say 'no' to?

            It's dicky, dicey, shaky business.
            Nothing's left to put my faith in.

            I wish before you'd left your homeland
            You'd gone to hell, oh Aristophontes!

            All my plans you've made a mess of,

>                    The campaign's over now unless I
>                    Get a bright idea from somewhere.

HEGIO [*seeing him and calling* ARISTOPHONTES]   Come
>        along: here's your man.
>        Go and speak to him.

TYNDARUS [*shrinking away*]   Lord! I'm in the darnedest   *540*
>        pickle.

ARISTOPHONTES [*as* TYNDARUS *turns away*]   Come off it,
>        Tyndarus.
>        What d'you mean avoiding my eye?
>        Yes, actually trying to cut me
>        As if I were a perfect stranger!
>        I know I'm just a slave—like you—
>        But I, at home, at least was free.
>        You've been slaving it in Elis
>        Ever since your boyhood.

HEGIO   Good gracious, d'you expect him *not* to avoid
>        your eye
>        And treat you like dirt
>        When you call him Tyndarus and not Philocrates?

TYNDARUS [*pulling* HEGIO *aside and inventing wildly*]
>        Hegio, this man in Elis
>        Was known to be a raving lunatic.
>        Don't let him fill your ears with fables.
>        Why, at home he went sprinting after
>        His mum and dad with a javelin,
>        And sometimes he'd have a fit of—
>        You know what—
>        The disease people spit on.[17]                      *550*
>        Keep well away from him.

HEGIO [*horrified*]   Fend him off! Fend him . . .

ARISTOPHONTES [*dumfounded*]   What the hell! . . . A
>        raving lunatic, am I?
>        And went sprinting after my own father with a javelin?
>        And I've got the disease people spit on—have I?

[17] Epilepsy.

HEGIO    There there! Never mind.
It's quite a common malady
And spitting often cures it.

ARISTOPHONTES [*gulping*]    What, you too? You actually
believe him?

HEGIO    Tut tut! What is there to believe?

ARISTOPHONTES [*at the top of his lungs*]    That I'm a mad-
man.

TYNDARUS [*in a quick whisper*]    Do you see him now?
That savage look?
It's as I said. A fit's coming on.
You'd better look out.

HEGIO [*moving away*]    I knew he was mad the moment he
called you Tyndarus.

TYNDARUS [*in a low voice*]    Sometimes he doesn't even
560         know his own name
Or who he is.

HEGIO [*eying him nervously*]    And there he was, giving
out that you and he were bosom cronies!

TYNDARUS    I've never heard the like.
Might as well claim that Alcmæon and Orestes
Were cronies too,
Yes, and Lycurgus into the bargain.[18]

ARISTOPHONTES [*shaking his fist*]    Why, you cheap little
convict!
You've got a nerve . . .
Don't I know you through and through?

HEGIO    My dear sir, the one plain fact

[18] Three famous madmen in Greek mythology: Alcmæon and
Orestes were pursued by the Furies after killing their mothers (they
subsequently recovered). Lycurgus was punished by Dionysus for
having forbidden the cult of Bacchus to his subjects. He went mad
and cut off his son's limbs imagining he was slashing at a vine.

Is that you do not . . .
Tsch tsch! Calling him Tyndarus instead of Philocrates!
You don't know the man you see
And you name the man you don't see.

ARISTOPHONTES [*throwing up his hands*]   But, sir, he says
    he's him: the one he's not
And says he's not the one he really *is*.

TYNDARUS [*with a curl of the lip*]   So you produce yourself
    from nowhere
To undo the word of Philocrates?

ARISTOPHONTES   I like that!
    You're the one that's been produced, I'd say,
    And to undo the truth . . .
    Come on: look me in the eye.

TYNDARUS [*standing well back and surveying him*]   Well?

ARISTOPHONTES   Now are you going to tell me you're not
    Tyndarus?                                              570

TYNDARUS [*coolly*]   Now I tell you: I certainly am not.

ARISTOPHONTES [*incredulous*]   Are you going to say you're
    Philocrates?

TYNDARUS   I most certainly say I am.

ARISTOPHONTES [*hopelessly to* HEGIO]   And you believe
    him?

HEGIO   Naturally: more even than you or me.
    For the man your memory tells you is this man,
    This very morning went away to Elis:
    To this fellow's father.

ARISTOPHONTES [*snorting*]   Father, my foot!
    The fellow is a slave.

TYNDARUS [*quietly*]   And so are you, free though once you
    were,

As free *I* hope to be someday
When I've brought his son home to liberty.

ARISTOPHONTES [*exploding*]   What, you charlatan!
You actually call yourself freeborn?

TYNDARUS [*smugly*]   No, not Freeborn: Philocrates.

ARISTOPHONTES [*struggling for composure*]   What! . . .
Hegio, this nasty little swindler
Is making a fool of you.
He's a slave himself:
580      In fact the first slave that his master had.

TYNDARUS [*with a toss of the head*]   Just because you your-
     self
In your own home and country
Didn't possess a thing and not a bite to eat,
You want to make everybody else the same.
I'm not surprised:
That's what you wretched have-nots do—
Curse and begrudge everyone who *has*.

ARISTOPHONTES   Hegio, please!
Don't go on giving credence to this crazy rascal.
You've pulled a real booboo once already,
If I'm not mistaken . . .
He says he'll get your son back, does he?
I don't like the sound of that at all.

TYNDARUS   Of course you don't!
*You* don't want it to happen.
     [*Raises his eyes to heaven*]
But with the help of the gods I'll make it happen:
*I'll* restore his son,
And he'll restore me home to Elis and my father;
That's why I sent my father Tyndarus.

ARISTOPHONTES [*roaring*]   But you *are* Tyndarus.
590      You're the only slave called that in Elis.

TYNDARUS [*on his dignity*]   Still taunting me with being a
     slave, eh?
Just because we got the worst of it in battle.

ARISTOPHONTES [*clutching his head*]   I can't contain myself another second.

TYNDARUS [*tugging* HEGIO *by the sleeve*]   D'you hear *that*,
      sir?
   Shall we make a run for it?
   If you don't have him seized
   He's going to start heaving bricks at us.

ARISTOPHONTES [*seething*]   I'm choking.

TYNDARUS [*in* HEGIO's *ear*]   Look: his eyes have caught
      fire:
   It's a fit, Hegio.
   Do you see the spots coming out all over him?
   Aren't they lurid?
   It's a black attack all right.

ARISTOPHONTES [*waving his arms*]   Black? Hell and dam-
      nation!
   If this old man had any sense
   He'd see you tarred from head to foot
   And made a torch of.

TYNDARUS [*springing behind* HEGIO *for protection*]   Ha!
      It's downright delirium now: possession.
   It would be a damn lot safer, Hegio,
   To have him seized.

ARISTOPHONTES [*looking round for a weapon*]   I'm suffo-
      cating.
   God! If I only had a rock                                    600
   I'd bash the brains out of this addlepated blackguard.
   He's driving me to frenzy.

TYNDARUS [*gritting his teeth*]   D'you hear? He wants a
      rock.

ARISTOPHONTES [*desperately*]   Hegio—please—a word
   with you alone.

HEGIO [*guardedly*]   Say it from there, then, if you must.
   I can hear.

TYNDARUS [*in a hoarse whisper*]   I should just think so!
   Go any closer and he'll bite your nose off.

ARISTOPHONTES   For the love of god, Hegio,
   Don't believe I'm mad or ever was,
   Or suffer in the least from the disease this creature men-
      tioned.
   If you're the least bit afraid, have me tied.
   *I'm* ready . . . provided *he* is too. [*with a killing glance at*
   TYNDARUS]

TYNDARUS [*alarmed*]   Good grief, Hegio!
   Tie up the one that wants it.

ARISTOPHONTES   And *you* keep quiet, you false Philocra-
      tes.
610   In a moment I'll have you exposed as the true Tyndarus:
   Yes, as large as life.
            [TYNDARUS *is making frantic gestures to him from
            behind* HEGIO's *back*]
   What are you shaking your head at me for?

TYNDARUS [*innocently*]   *I* shake my head at you?

ARISTOPHONTES [*to* HEGIO]   What would he do, sir, if *you*
   came nearer?

HEGIO [*hesitating*]   What do you say, Tyndarus:
   Shall I go right up to this lunatic?

TYNDARUS [*vigorously*]   Pointless, sir.
   He'll only reduce you to ridicule.
   He'll froth with verbiage
   And you won't know head from tail.
   Believe me, except for camouflage and dress,
   You've got a real Ajax[19] here.

HEGIO [*after a pause*]   Never mind. I'm going up to him all
   the same.
            [*Takes a few hesitant steps toward* ARISTOPHONTES]

19 Next to Achilles the bravest of the Greeks in the Trojan War.
When the armor of Achilles was awarded to Odysseus rather than
to him, he went mad with rage and ran out slaughtering sheep—
thinking them to be his enemies.

TYNDARUS [*no longer in the shelter of* HEGIO]   Now I'm
      done for . . .
   Stand between the axe and altar;
   Haven't a notion what to do.

HEGIO [*mastering his nerves*]   I'm at your disposal, Aristo-
      phontes.
   What can I do for you?

ARISTOPHONTES [*folding his arms*]   You're going to hear
      the truth, Hegio:
   The opposite of what you think is false.
   But first of all, I mean to make quite clear:                620
   I am *not* mad;
   And I'm not in the least sick,
   Except of slavery.
         [*Solemnly lifts up his hands*]
   So help me the king of gods and men
   And return me to my native land again:
   This fellow's no more Philocrates than you or I.

HEGIO [*with a look of apprehension*]   Will you kindly tell
      me then who he is.

ARISTOPHONTES   The very one I told you from the start.
   If you find this isn't true,
   I willingly forfeit my parents and my liberty
   To you.

HEGIO [*with a hard look at* TYNDARUS]   What have *you* got
      to say to that?

TYNDARUS [*stalling for time*]   Simply that—hm—I'm your
      slave and you're my master.

HEGIO [*testily*]   That's not what I'm asking . . .
   Were you once a freeman?

TYNDARUS [*with a shifty glance at* ARISTOPHONTES]   I was.

ARISTOPHONTES [*impassioned*]   You were not. It's ridicu-
      lous.

TYNDARUS   How do *you* know?

Were you my mother's midwife . . .
You're so sure about it.

ARISTOPHONTES    We were both small boys when we first
630      met.

TYNDARUS [*acidly*]    And now we meet again, both grown
        up. So what?
If you had any decency at all
You wouldn't meddle with my affairs.
Do *I* meddle with *yours*?

HEGIO [*to* ARISTOPHONTES *apprehensively*]    Wasn't his
        father called
"Giltedgedsecurityatsixpercentson"?

ARISTOPHONTES [*with a guffaw*]    Nothing of the kind.
In all my born days I've never heard the like.
Philocrates's father's called "Praisedbegodforbullion."

TYNDARUS [*to himself*]    That does it!
        [*Clutches his heart melodramatically*]
Stop it, Heart. Stop thumping.
Keep still, damn you! . . .
Jittering up and down when I can hardly stand—
God! I'm in a dither.

HEGIO    Am I to take it as beyond all doubt, then,
That this man was a slave in Elis
And isn't Philocrates at all?

ARISTOPHONTES [*grimly*]    Further beyond doubt than
        you'll ever be again.
640      But where is he now: Philocrates?

HEGIO [*with a forlorn sigh*]    In a place I by no means wish:
The land of his heart's desire.
But do, please, look into this.

ARISTOPHONTES    I assure you, I already have.
I've given you the evidence.

HEGIO    Are you sure?

ARISTOPHONTES   As I said:
  It's further beyond all doubt than you'll ever be again.
  We've been friends, Philocrates and I,
  Since our boyhood days.

HEGIO [*bitterly*]   Unlucky sucker that I am!
  I've been duped, nipped, torn
  Limb from limb by this . . . this
  Confidence-trickster.
  He's twiddled me round his little finger.
          [*Clutches at* ARISTOPHONTES *with a desperate
          hope*]
  But your friend, Philocrates,
  What does he look like?

ARISTOPHONTES   I'll tell you:
  Thinnish face, sharp nose,
  Fair skin, dark eyes,
  Reddish hair curled and close.

HEGIO [*with a groan*]   It all adds up.

TYNDARUS [*to himself*]   Adds up to the fact that I've
    stepped
  Into a first-class disaster.
          [*Begins to rub himself*]
  Goodbye, you unhappy birches destined to die
  On my poor tail today!                                    650

HEGIO [*shaking his head sadly*]   I see: I've been hood-
    winked.

TYNDARUS [*to himself, burlesquing grand opera*]   O fet-
    ters, fetters, fly to me
                  Clasp my ankles lovingly
                  And I will now look after ye.

HEGIO [*in a doleful monotone*]   They've played fast and
    loose with me today,
  Those chisel-twisting convicts—haven't they?
  The first one made himself a goddam slave,
  *This* stinker is a man of liberty.
  I've kept the shell and thrown away the nut.

A proper painted fool:
That's what they've made of me.
          [*Swings his stick ominously*]
Well, this one at least will never get away.
          [*Claps his hands*]
Boxer, Browser, Biffim, come on out,
And bring your whips.

                    [*Three enormous slaves emerge with cudgels and rawhides*]

BOXER [*with a moronic grin*]   It's not for sawing logs, sir, is it?

HEGIO [*pointing to* TYNDARUS]   Clap the handcuffs on that wretched man.

TYNDARUS [*gulping*]   Why, what's going on?
Wh-h-at have I done?

660   HEGIO [*seething*]   You ask *that*?
You sin sower, crime hoer,
Double-trouble reaper!

TYNDARUS [*with sudden impertinence*]   And harrower.
You can't leave that out.
Farmers always harrow before they hoe, sir.

HEGIO [*throwing up his arms*]   You see?
The downright nerve of the man!

TYNDARUS [*with mock meekness*]   An innocent and harm-less slave, sir,
Needs no nerves;
Especially dealing with his master.

HEGIO [*to the slaves*]   Fasten his hands—and see they're tight.

TYNDARUS   I am all yours, sir.
Have them amputated if you like.
But what's it all about?
What makes you so upset?

670   HEGIO [*smoldering*]   Because, singlehanded, you,

With your dirty doubledealing
And deft chicanery,
Have torn to tatters, brought to ruin,
Me and mine,
Have obliterated my every prospect, hope and purpose,
By hoaxing Philocrates away from home . . .
I really thought he *was* a slave and you were free.
Yes, you said so—both of you—
And swapped your names accordingly.

TYNDARUS [*attempting casualness*]    Y-yes, I admit it;
Everything is as you say:
You were diddled out of him
By my arrangement, my sagacity.
But good grief, good sir!
Is that really why you're so annoyed with me?                     680

HEGIO [*his voice rising*]    You'll pay for it, by Jupiter:
The maximum penalty.

TYNDARUS

                I don't care if I die
                    if it's not for doing wrong.
                And even if he fails
                    to keep his word and come
                And *I* die here alone,
                    this at least will be
                Remembered when I'm gone:
                That I set a master free
                    from foes and slavery;
                Restored him to his own
                    Father and his home.
                And, for his head,
                    risked mine instead.

HEGIO [*acidly*]    Oh fine!
It'll make a glorious splash in Hades, that.

TYNDARUS [*solemnly*]    Who dies with glory, is not wholly
    dead.                                                          690

HEGIO [*rapping the pavement with his stick*]    When *I've*
    given a good and lively exhibition
Of you, Tyndarus, on torture,

And sent you packing to perdition for your lies,
Whether you are half or wholly dead
Can be an object for surmise.
You can be described for all I care
As "alive and kicking,"
So long as you are dead as mutton.

TYNDARUS   Do that, sir, and I can swear,
If *he* comes back—as I am confident he will—
It will cost you dear.

ARISTOPHONTES [*to himself, clapping his forehead*]   Good
        heavens! . . . I get it now:
At last I see what it's all about.
My pal, Philocrates, is safe at home.
And magnificent news it is:
700    I couldn't wish for better for a friend;
But . . . oh dear! . . .   [*biting his lip*]
What have I gone and done to Tyndarus here:
In irons because of me and what I said?

HEGIO [*to* TYNDARUS]   Didn't I warn you earlier
    Not to mislead me on the slightest point?

TYNDARUS   You did.

HEGIO   Then why did you tell me lies?

TYNDARUS   Because the truth would have undone
    The person I was trying to help.
    As it is, untruth has done him very well.

HEGIO   And undone *you*.

TYNDARUS   But saved my master.
    I am happy to have saved a son
    Entrusted to me by his father.
    You think that wicked, do you?

HEGIO [*with a snarl*]   Monstrous.

TYNDARUS   There I differ, sir.
710    In my opinion it is right.

Imagine for a moment that a slave of yours
Had done the selfsame service to *your* son:
What sort of feelings would *you* have then?
Wouldn't you give that slave his liberty?
Surely he would be your favorite slave?
Answer me.

HEGIO [*reluctantly, with a shrug*]    I suppose so.

TYNDARUS [*promptly*]    Then why are you in such a rage
    with me?

HEGIO    Because you showed more loyalty to him than me.

TYNDARUS [*flabbergasted*]    What! Did you really think
In a single night and day
To teach a man just captured,
Fresh to your service,
To prefer your interests to a man's
He's been reared with since a boy?                        *720*

HEGIO [*icily*]    In that case, go to *him* for sympathy.
    [*with a nod to the slaves*]    Take him off—
Off to where some fine fat fetters wait,
Heavy as lead.
    [*with a peremptory wave of the hand*]    Straight to the
    stone quarries with you then:
There while the other men
Chip away their eight blocks of stone a day,
You shall do half as much again,
Or Mister Twice-three-hundred-stripes will be your
    name.

ARISTOPHONTES [*stepping forward*]    Hegio, for the love
    of god and man,
You can't just lose this human being.

HEGIO [*with a raw laugh*]    Lose? We'll see to that.
At night I'll have him shackled, under guard;
By day he'll lever stones out underground.              *730*
A good long torture's what I plan:
Not just twelve hours of it for this man.

ARISTOPHONTES [*shocked*]    Sir, is this your fixed design?

HEGIO [*grimly*]   Fixed as death.
  [*turns to the slaves*]   March him off to Hippolytus the
    smith
  And have the heftiest fetters forged on him:
  Then to the quarry outside the gates,
  Where my freedman, Cordalus, is;
  And tell Cordalus this:
  I want him treated at least as well
  As the man that's getting—hell.

TYNDARUS [*with dignity*]   Why should I ask for mercy
  When mercy you don't give?
740   I risk my life, but so do you.
  And when I am dead,
  Then death shall have no bite.
  But if I live—
  Even to a great old age—
  That is still but short a time
  To suffer what I'm threatened with.
          [*Raises his hand*]
  Goodbye and good luck to you,
  Though I should wish you something less.
  [*turning*]   And Aristophontes:
  I hope you get what you deserve.
  I owe it to you that I am suffering this.

HEGIO [*with a toss of the head*]   Take him away.

TYNDARUS [*not making a move*]   I ask this only:
  If Philocrates returns,
  Let me see him please.

HEGIO [*roaring*]   Get him out of my sight,
  Or I'll damn the lot of you.

TYNDARUS [*smiling bravely as he is hauled away*]
  Sheer horsepower, by Jiminy,
750   They push *and* pull!

                          [TYNDARUS *is bundled out of sight*]

HEGIO [*still growling*]   Straight to the lockup with him,
    and a good thing too.
  I'll show the rest of them—these captives—what I
    mean.

I'll scotch behavior of this kind.
Why, if this fellow   [*indicating* ARISTOPHONTES] hadn't let on,
They would have led me down the garden path till the end of time.
From now onwards I'm not trusting anyone, not I.
That's certain:
Once bitten, twice shy.
            [*Wipes a tear from his face*]
Poor fool!
I imagined I was buying back a captured son.
*That* hope has quite collapsed.
One son I lost, a boy of four years old,
Stolen by a slave;
Since when there's been no trace of slave or son.                    760
And now my elder boy a prisoner of war . . .
What kind of curse is this, what doom,
To have children in a vacuum?
[*to* ARISTOPHONTES, *with a new harshness*]   Come on, you:
Back to where you came from.
I'm not showing clemency to anyone
Since none is shown to me.

            [HEGIO *stomps off in the direction of his broth-
            er's house, with* ARISTOPHONTES *following*]

ARISTOPHONTES [*dryly*]   Charmed out of chains—now I see—
I am to be charmed back again.
            [*The party proceeds down the street*]


# ACT IV

*Some hours later.* ERGASILUS *hurries in. He is elated and
executes a little jig, singing*

            Jupiter Almighty
            How you have preserved me,
            Pampered me, increased me!

            With boundless abundance,
            Wealth unto redundance
            You have heaped me!

770     Praises, profits, pleasure, playing,
     Feasts and holidays and toastings;
     Loads of food and endless drinking,
     No more sucking-up and fawning.
     I can curse and I can bless.
     O happy day that has amassed
     On me such happy happiness:
     I've got a pension—what a plum!—
     Without a goddam string attached.
     Hurry, hurry, run and tell him:
     Hegio, old man, I come
     With better news—ah richer, richer!—
     Than even you could ask the gods for.
    [*Throws his cloak around him*]
     I'll clinch the matter like the slaves
     Clinch it in the comic plays:
     Fling a cloak round, race to tell
     Him first the thing that's gone so well.
    [*Winks at the audience*]
     I hope this news will do me good
780     And get me everlasting food.

[HEGIO *enters with a hangdog look, muttering to himself*]

HEGIO  The more I think about it
   The bitterer it makes me:
   The way those two completely duped me.
   And never once did I see through it!
     [*Shakes his head*]
   When these tidings get around
   I'll be the laughingstock of town.
   In the forum when they see me
   Everyone will whisper: "Eeh!
   There's that brilliant senile dotard
   Who was made a perfect fool of."
     [*Notices* ERGASILUS *and stops*]
   Isn't that Ergasilus over there:
   All trussed up for a flying dash?
   What on earth can he be up to?
     [*Goes up some steps onto a balcony and watches*]

ERGASILUS [*rushing about in a solo charade*]  On with it,
790  Ergasilus, on: no dallying.
     [*Draws himself up on the step*]

I hereby admonish and declare:
That if any human being should dare
Stand in my way,
He has by his own decision
Lived too long a day.
And in that case,
He falls where he stands—flat on his face.

[*The rest of the dialogue between* HEGIO *and* ERGASILUS
*is in the form of asides*]

HEGIO [*from the balcony, bemused*]   Thinks he's in the
    boxing ring, does this one?

ERGASILUS   Yes, that I can guarantee.
    So, all of you make damned sure
    You keep to where you are
    And don't bring your business up my street.
    For my punches come like catapults,
    My elbow is a sling,
    My shoulder is a battering ram; what's more,
    One wallop from my knee
    Will make you bite the dust,
    And one encounter
    Have you looking for your teeth—
    Oh yes, sir!

HEGIO [*with a quizzical grin*]   What's all this blather for?
    I'm absolutely fascinated.

ERGASILUS [*throwing a succession of puny punches*]   I'll
    make it memorable, by gad!
    Time, place and *me*.                                    800
    Who stands in my way
    Blocks his own existence off
    Immediately.[20]

HEGIO   Memorable for what, I wonder? Such bravado!

ERGASILUS   I've given you due notice.
    Wherefore, if you come to grief you can't claim ignor-
    ance:
    Stay at home. Don't court my violence.

[20] Leo brackets this verse (801): *Qui mihi in cursu opstiterit, faxo
vitae extemplo opstiterit suae.*

HEGIO [*chuckling*]   By Jupiter, he certainly has restocked
    his cockiness with fodder!
    I pity the poor mutt that had to lend a larder.

ERGASILUS [*swiping at his shadow*]   That goes for millers,
    too,
    Who keep their pigs on bran
    And make the place so smelly, nobody can pass.
    Just let me catch a sow
    On the public thoroughfare,
    And I'll knock the stuffing out of them—
810    I mean their owners—right there.

HEGIO   Royal commands, eh? The imperial ukase?
    He's had a square meal all right:
    He's stuffed himself with brass.

ERGASILUS [*holding his nose*]   Not to mention those jerks
    the fishmongers,
    Jogging round their stinking fish on jolting nags,
    And sending people packing into the forum
    From the arcades with the stench.
    I'll sling a fish-creel in their faces
    And give them an inkling
    Of what other noses think.
    [*raising his voice*]   Yes, and the butchers
    Who bereave mother sheep of little ones,
    And gather lambkins for the slaughter,
    Then sell you tough old mutton
    At twice the price,
820    Passing off an octogenarian ram for prime wether.
    Just let me catch a ram coming down the street:
    I'll damn that ram and blast his master.

HEGIO   Issuing his decrees, eh!
    A minister of agriculture, if you please!

ERGASILUS [*beginning to dance and sing again*]
        I'm no parasite, not now:
        More like royalty—
        Yes, royal . . . and how!

        Down at the harbor

I've got me a larder
For tummy and me . . .
          [*Breaks off*]
Oh, I'm dawdling. Stop it, Ergasilus!
Go and load old Hegio with happiness:
          Luckier than a lucky
          Man can be.

HEGIO [*raising his eyebrows*]   Hm! What's this euphoria
     this most euphoric man
Wants to burst on me?

ERGASILUS [*pounding on the door*]   Hullo there! Where
     are you?
Is anyone at home?
Is no one going to open up?                               *830*

HEGIO [*dryly*]   He's come for dinner.

ERGASILUS   Hey! Open both doors,
     Or I'll bash them down and pound them into sawdust.

HEGIO [*with a sly glance at the audience*]   It'll amuse me
     to have a word with him.
          [*Shouts from the balcony*]
     Ergasilus!

ERGASILUS   Who called "Ergasilus"?

HEGIO   Here, look this way.

ERGASILUS [*looking everywhere except the balcony*]   A
     command that Fortune never gave me.
Who is it?

HEGIO [*loudly*]   Look up at me, it's Hegio.

ERGASILUS [*in a rush of words*]   O you ecstatically ecstatic
     man!
You've made contact with me in the nick of time.

HEGIO [*tartly*]   And you're so pert,
     I wonder whom you got to give you luncheon at the
     port.

ERGASILUS [*wreathed in smiles*]   Give me your hand.

HEGIO   My hand?

ERGASILUS [*coming up the balcony*]   Your hand, I say.
Immediately.

HEGIO   Take it.

ERGASILUS [*peremptorily*]   Be happy.

HEGIO   What for?

ERGASILUS   Because I tell you.

HEGIO [*hopelessly*]   Look, mister,
840    In my case grief and joy got turned around.

ERGASILUS [*in a wide gesture*]   I'll wipe away every speck
of grief.
Come on: a big bang of joy!

HEGIO   Oh, all right.
[*dismally, with a wan smile*]   Ha ha! I rejoice . . .
But what for?

ERGASILUS   You're doing fine . . . Now command . . .

HEGIO   Command what?

ERGASILUS [*rubbing his hands*]
A fire to be lit—a tremendous fire.

HEGIO   A tremendous fire?

ERGASILUS   Exactly. As big as possible.

HEGIO [*snorting*]   Indeed!
Do you think I'm going to burn my house down
Just for you—vulture!

ERGASILUS [*flapping his hand*]   Aha! . . . Don't be peevish.
Will you or will you not

Give the order for the pots
To be set on the stove and the dishes washed,
The fats all sizzling, the tidbits broiled,
And the coals redhot? . . .
Oh, and someone to go and buy the fish?

HEGIO  He's sleepwalking.

ERGASILUS  And someone else to go for pork . . . then the
lamb . . .
And fine fat pullets.

HEGIO  Do yourself proud, don't you, given the chance!

ERGASILUS [*excitedly*]  Mussels and oysters and mackerel,  *850*
Tunny and turbot and trout . . .
Oh, and some nice cream cheese.

ERGASILUS [*sourly*]  It's easier to name these things than
eat them,
In my house, Ergasilus.

ERGASILUS [*hurt*]  You don't suppose I'm saying all this
Just to please myself, do you?

HEGIO  Don't fool yourself:
What you'll get to eat here
Will be something between a naught and zero.
So, come with room for a hole . . .

ERGASILUS [*vigorously shaking his head*]
Blowout—
One that even *I* can't stop you having.

HEGIO  What, *me*?

ERGASILUS  Yes, you.

HEGIO [*with a hollow laugh*]  Then you *are* my master.

ERGASILUS [*smugly*]  No, just a benefactor.
Would you like me to make you happy?

HEGIO [*wearily*]   I'd prefer it to being unhappy.

ERGASILUS [*smirking*]   Your hand, then.

HEGIO [*holding it out*]   All right: my hand.

ERGASILUS [*squeezing it*]   The gods are with you.

HEGIO   I don't feel anything.

ERGASILUS   Of course you don't:
860        You're out of the briar patch[21] now
           And your troubles are scratched, ha! ha!
           Just lay the table for the service
           And have a nice plump lamb brought in.

HEGIO   Why?

ERGASILUS   To sacrifice.

HEGIO   Who to?

ERGASILUS
           Me, of course.
           I'm your Jove almighty now.
           I'm Salvation, Fortune,
           Lightheartedness and Joy:
           All rolled into one.
           So you'd better put this deity into a good mood
           With lots of damned good food.

HEGIO [*sarcastically*]   Strikes me you're hungry.

ERGASILUS [*pinching-in his middle*]   No—it strikes *me*.

HEGIO [*in a tired voice*]   Have it your own way . . . I don't
       mind crawling.

ERGASILUS [*merrily*]   Don't I know it!
       It's a habit you fell into as a boy.

21 The Latin is: *Non enim es in senticeto, eo non sentis.* Paul Nixon
cleverly captures the pun with: ". . . you're out of the wood, that's
why you don't twig it."

HEGIO
   Oh, go to hell!

ERGASILUS   No, you, sir . . . hm, ought to thank me for
   my news . . .
   The exciting report
   I'm now reporting from the port.
   [*with a sidelong grin*]   He-he-he! . . . Going to pamper
   me a bit?

HEGIO   Get along with you, you clown.                   *870*
   You've come too late.

ERGASILUS [*slyly*]   That might have been a valid point
   before:
   Had I come too early. He! he! he!
           [*Braces himself*]
   Get ready now for the ecstasy I bring.
           [*A pause, then very quietly*]
   I've just seen your son,
   Your own son Philopolemus,
   Down at the port:
   Alive, safe, well.
           [*Another pause*]
   I saw him in the packet boat
   With that young Elian fellow
   And Stalagmus—yes, Stalagmus—your slave:
   The one who ran away
   With your little four-year-old.

HEGIO   Oh, go and rot yourself!
   You're making fun of me.

ERGASILUS [*with his hand on his belly*]   So help me Holy
   Stuffing, Goddess of Gorging,
   May she grace me with her name perennially . . .
   I *did* see him, Hegio.

HEGIO [*clutching the balustrade*]   My son?

ERGASILUS   Your son—*my* good angel.

HEGIO   And that Elian prisoner?                         *880*

ERGASILUS   Sissignore, per Baccho![22]

HEGIO   And that little twerp Stalagmus
Who ran away with my boy?

ERGASILUS   Sissignore, per Palermo![23]

HEGIO   Can I believe it?

ERGASILUS   Sissignore, per Messina!

HEGIO   He's here?

ERGASILUS   Sissignore, per Caserta.

HEGIO   You're sure?

ERGASILUS   Sissignore, per Amalfi.

HEGIO   Be careful!

ERGASILUS   Sissignore, per Pompei.

HEGIO   Why are you swearing by these foreign cities?

ERGASILUS [*arranging his lock of hair*]   Because they're
all as indigestible
As you said your dinners were.

HEGIO   Get on with you!

ERGASILUS [*pouting*]   Why should I?
You won't believe a thing I say.
[*relenting*]   This Stalagmus,
Of what race was he when he skipped from here?

HEGIO [*anxiously*]
Sicilian.

ERGASILUS   Well, he's not Sicilian now.

22 Ergasilus breaks into Greek in the original.
23 I follow Paul Nixon's example in changing the names of the (to
us) remote Greek cities which Plautus gives, into well-known towns
in Italy.

He's a Boan, stiff as a bow.[24]
With a Boanness . . . Uxorially knotted up—
He likes collecting babies, I suppose.

HEGIO [*laying a hand on his sleeve*]   Please—are you telling me the truth?                                             *890*

ERGASILUS [*solemnly*]   The truth.

HEGIO [*gripping him*]   God in Heaven! I'm a new man
   If your story's true.

ERGASILUS
   Come off it Hegio!
   You even doubt my solemn oath.
   Very well, if oaths mean so little to you,
   Go down to the port and see.

HEGIO [*flinging himself down the steps*]
   Of course! Of course!
   And you go in, dear boy, and settle things carte blanche.
   Yes, grab, ask, command . . .
   Anything you want.
   I make you butler.

ERGASILUS [*hurrying after him*]   Rot my soul and dress
   me down,
   If I don't do some pretty jugglery with dishes.

HEGIO [*rapturously*]   I'll dine with you till doomsday
   If your story's true.

ERGASILUS [*stopping short*]   Who foots the bill?

HEGIO [*beaming*]   My son and I.

ERGASILUS [*snatching his hand*]   Your word on that?

24 Plautus actually says: "Boius est, Boiam terit." This is difficult
to pun in English. The Boi were a tribe that settled in France, upper
Italy and parts of Germany: the future Bohemians. A *boia* was a
collar of leather or wood worn by slaves and criminals. The verb
*tero,* meaning to "rub" or "wear out," was the slang for sexual
intercourse. George Duckworth translates: "He's a Boan, with a
constrictor round his neck." Paul Nixon: "he's a Gaul—he's being
galled, anyhow, by that thing he's attached to." Sir Robert Allison:
"He is Bohemian, with a lady of that land." None of these attempts
succeeds in combining the idea of restriction with obscenity.

HEGIO [*raising his*]   My word of honor.

ERGASILUS   Have mine too:
   Your son has really come.

HEGIO [*running again, in the direction of the harbor*]   Do
   the best you can.

ERGASILUS [*wildly nodding*]   A pleasant walk . . . and
900   many happy returns.
                         [*Watches* HEGIO *go out of sight, takes a step
                         downstage, smiles at the audience and smacks
                         his lips*]
                               So he's gone
                         And left me master of the larder
                         Prime-minister of *haute-cuisine*.
                               What necks I'll sever!
                               What hams do in!
                         Oh the lashings of pure dripping!
                         Oh the undermining of sows' udders!
                               Oh catastrophe to crackling!
                                 And butchers bustling
                                 Porkers prattling . . .
                                       Shucks!
                         [*Breaking off*]
                               I can't go into all this now:
                         One hundred ways of stuffing a belly.
                         I'm off to the marketing-board
                                 To haggle over bacon
                                 And—oh Lord!—
                               Go to the help of ham
                                 On tenterhooks
                         Still dithering in a jelly.

         [ERGASILUS *hurries into the house. From which
         there begins to issue a great clatter: shouts of glut-
         tony, groans of consternation, and the breaking of
         dishes. After supposedly half an hour, a* BOY *runs
         out, shaking his fist at the door*]

   BOY   God blast you, Ergasilus, and your blasted greedy
         belly!
         And every parasite there is
         And anyone who ever again
910      Provides parasites with provender.

[*There is a particularly loud crash and he holds
his hands up to his ears*]
Devastation and disaster!
What a hurricane has hit the house!
I thought he'd spring on me like a hungry wolf
With that ravening look of his.
I was terrified he'd really rend me.
Yes, and when he began to gnash his teeth
I nearly died of fright.
            [*A roar of gluttony from within*]
He came bursting in:
Tore down the meat, shelf and all,
Snatched a sword and swiped the kidneys
Off three choice joints;
Smashed every vat and jar that didn't hold two gallons;
Put the cook through third-degree—
Asking for enormous crocks to boil things in;
Broke open all the cupboards
And rifled everything inside the pantry.
            [*He shouts through the door*]
Hey there, lads,
Just watch him, will you!
I'm going to look for the old man
And tell him if he wants to eat
He'll have to stock himself another larder,                   *920*
For the way this fellow here's restocking
There soon won't be—already isn't—a blessed thing.
                        [*The* BOY *goes off in the direc-
                        tion of* HEGIO's *brother's house*]


# ACT V

*From the port come* HEGIO, PHILOPOLEMUS, PHILOCRATES
*and* STALAGMUS: *all except the last in a state of elation,
talking loudly.* PHILOPOLEMUS, *still dressed as a prisoner,
is a young man of about the same age as* PHILOCRATES.
STALAGMUS *is middle-aged and wears a bitter rather frus-
trated look.*

HEGIO [*stopping for the hundredth time and putting an arm
        around* PHILOPOLEMUS] Thanks be to Jove—oh
        great good thanks

To all the gods for bringing you back home
And ending forever the horrible anxiety
That's dogged my every moment
Since you were gone.
          [*Glances at* STALAGMUS]
Yes, and for putting this creature in my power
And letting this fine gentleman prove his word.
          [*Bows to* PHILOCRATES]

PHILOPOLEMUS [*teasingly*]
Father, I've had my fill of lamentations
And quite enough of tears and pining . . .
[*smiling fondly*]   Yes, even of your elegies:
Which have been going on ever since we left the harbor.
Let's get to the point.

PHILOCRATES   Now that I've kept my promise, sir,
And restored your son to liberty,
930   What is to be my future?

HEGIO [*holding out his hand*]   Philocrates, after what
          you've done
It is quite impossible for me
To thank you half enough—
Or for my son to.

PHILOPOLEMUS [*breaking in*]   Oh but, Father, you can,
And so can I.
The gods will make it possible for us
To shower kindness on a man who's been so kind.
[*with a severe look at* STALAGMUS]   Just as you'll be
          able, my dear Father,
To give this man here his full deserts.

HEGIO [*turning to* PHILOCRATES]   Sir, words are useless.
I could not frame the syllables
Refusing you a thing.

PHILOCRATES   Then I ask you to restore me
The slave I left behind me as security.
He treated me at every turn
Much better than himself.
940   I want to pay him back for all he's done.

HEGIO   Your own generosity forwards your request.
I grant it, and whatever else you ask . . .
        [*Suddenly embarrassed*]
B-but I hope you won't be in a rage with me.
I—I lost my temper and was hard on him.

PHILOCRATES [*anxiously*]   What did you do?

HEGIO [*awkwardly*]   When I discovered how he'd duped
      me
I sent him off in fetters to the quarries.

PHILOCRATES [*wincing*]   God forgive me! . . . That man
      of sterling worth . . .
Made to suffer so . . . And all because of me!

HEGIO [*quickly*]   For that very reason
I shan't accept a farthing for his ransom.
He's all yours now: he's free.

PHILOCRATES [*breaking into a smile*]   Wonderful! Good
      Hegio, how generous!
Please summon him at once.

HEGIO   By all means.
        [*Claps his hands. There is a pause*]
Where are you all?
        [*Two slaves appear*]
Go immediately and bring Tyndarus here.                950
        [*The slaves go out on the double.* HEGIO *turns to
        the two young men*]
Will you go inside, good sirs,
While I find out from this whipping-post
What was done to my younger son . . .
Go and bathe yourselves meanwhile.
        [*Strides over toward* STALAGMUS]

PHILOPOLEMUS [*to* PHILOCRATES]
Well, Philocrates, let's go in.
        [*They enter the house together*]

HEGIO [*with a rap of his walking stick on the pavement*]
Come along now, my good man,

    Over here with you,
    My charming piece of chattel.

STALAGMUS [*hardly moving*]   What am *I* supposed to do
    When a fine gentleman like you—tells lies?
    [*seeing* HEGIO's *bewilderment*] Handsome? Charm-
      ing? . . . Yes,
    I've had my day. But a "good man"
    Or a good anything—not *me;*
    No and never will be, mark my words.
    So don't go building up your hopes.
    I'll never be less than good for nothing.

HEGIO   Well, I'm glad you see exactly where you stand.
    In point of fact, if you tell the truth
    You're not so badly off as you imagine.
960    Come on, for the first time in your existence,
    Be honest and straightforward.

STALAGMUS [*tight-lipped*]   Am I supposed to blush to order
    For something I am willing to admit?

HEGIO [*swinging his stick*]   You'll blush all right:
    I'll make you one big bruise.

STALAGMUS   Hoity-toity! So it's stripes and threats?
    As if I didn't know what *they* were!
    Come off it, man, say what you want—
    If what you want you'd get.

HEGIO [*surveying him with the utmost distaste*]   Quite a
      gift, eh!
    But I'd be obliged if you'd save it for the moment.

STALAGMUS [*shrugging*]   As you like.

HEGIO [*to the audience, shaking his head*]   How he's
      changed!
    He used to be a nice compliant boy.
    [*to* STALAGMUS *briskly*] Come on then: give me your
      attention
    And answer me exactly what I ask.

If you stick to the truth
You'll be better off.[25]

STALAGMUS   Nuts!
D'you imagine I don't know what's coming to me?

HEGIO   Well, you can escape a little of it—                    *970*
If not all.

STALAGMUS [*with a twisted smile*]   Precious little, I can
    tell . . .
There's such an awful lot. And it serves me right:
I ran away, I took your son, I sold him.

HEGIO   To whom?

STALAGMUS [*affecting a yawn*]   Oh . . . to a Mr. . . .
    Praisedbegodforbullion Goldfinger,
In Elis . . . for a hundred pounds.

HEGIO [*slapping his forehead*]   God in Heaven!
That's the father of Philocrates.

STALAGMUS [*coldly*]   Well, I knew him better than you
    ever did:
Saw him oftener.

HEGIO [*beside himself with excitement*]   Great Jove, save
    me! Me and my poor boy.
        [*Runs to the door, shouting*]
Philocrates, for the life of you, please:
I must see you at once. Come on out.
        [PHILOCRATES *emerges, somewhat spruced-up
        after a wash*]

PHILOCRATES   Yes, Hegio? Here I am at your disposal.

HEGIO [*in short bursts*]   This man asserts he sold . . . my
    son . . .
In Elis . . . to your father . . .
For one hundred pounds.

25 This line (968) is bracketed as doubtful by Leo.

PHILOCRATES [*dubiously*]   How long ago was that?

980   STALAGMUS   Almost twenty years.

PHILOCRATES [*looking at him with distrust*]   He's lying.

STALAGMUS [*unperturbed*]   One of us is . . .
In point of fact,
Your father once presented you
With a tiny boy of four,
When *you* were just a nipper too.

PHILOCRATES   What was he called?
If your tale is true
You shouldn't hesitate to tell me that.

STALAGMUS   Tiddles. That was his name.
You had it changed to Tyndarus.

PHILOCRATES   Why don't I know you, then?

STALAGMUS   Because it's the normal thing
To forget or never know
Someone who's no use to us.

PHILOCRATES [*slowly*]   Tell me:
Was the boy you sold my father
The same boy he gave me for my own?

STALAGMUS [*jerking a thumb at* HEGIO]   Yes, this man's
son.

HEGIO [*trembling*]   Is he still alive this—this—man?

STALAGMUS   They paid me up. What care *I*?

HEGIO [*with an agonized glance at* PHILOCRATES]   W-what
is your opinion?

PHILOCRATES   Why, it's Tyndarus—Tyndarus himself that
990   is your son.
This rascal here's just proved it.
We boys were brought up together till our youth—
And respectably!

HEGIO [*laughing and crying out*]
    I am a happy and unhappy man
    If what you tell me is the truth . . .
    Wretched that I've hurt my son.
            [*Wrings his hands*]
    Oh dear! Imagine it: how much I've done
    Beyond all justice—yet how far short!
    Yes, that's the torture: that the wrong
    Cannot be undone . . . If only . . .

            [*Further torn between joy and remorse, as* TYN-
            DARUS *walks heavily into view, weighed down
            with shackles and guarded by overseers*]

    Ah! Look, he's coming here—not comely—
    Not in the manner that he ought, but . . .

TYNDARUS [*forlornly shifting his crowbar*]
                In many a picture I've seen
                    The tortures of hell,
            But, dammit, there never has been
                    Quite such a hell
            As the purlieus where I've been
                    Having a spell:
                    The quarries.                    *1000*

            It's a perfect place down there
                For wringing the worry
                Out of a weary body.

            For when I arrived down there
            Like a rich little son-and-heir
            Who's given a pet to play with:
            (A duck or a quail or a daw),
            They gave me this goddam crow
                    Oh, to be gay with,
                        Oh!
                            [*Stops short and gazes at
                            the group in the street*]
    But there's my master outside the house,
    And my other master, come back from Elis.

HEGIO [*hurrying toward him*]    M-my long-lost boy . . .
    How are you?

TYNDARUS [*stepping back*]   Eh? . . . Long-lost what?
[*with an icy laugh*]   Oh, I get it: you're like a father to
me—
Introduce me to the light of day . . .
As parents do, ha! ha! ha!

PHILOCRATES [*striding toward him*]
Tyndarus!

TYNDARUS   You too?
For whom I am suffering ignominy.

PHILOCRATES [*stretching out a hand*]   No no no!
1010    Now I'm going to make you rich and free,
I promise you.
        [*Waves a hand toward* HEGIO *and* STALAGMUS]
This is your father here,
And this the slave that kidnapped you when you were
four.
You see, he sold you to my father for a hundred pounds
And gave you to me for my toy:
A little present for a little boy.
        [*Sees* TYNDARUS *is still incredulous*]
This fellow here's confessed:
We brought him all the way from Elis.

TYNDARUS [*open-mouthed*]   What? . . . Son . . . of this
gentleman?

1015  PHILOCRATES   Yes. And you have a brother there inside.

TYNDARUS   You mean, you finally restored
1016[26]   The old man's prisoner-son?

PHILOCRATES   I did indeed. He's inside, as I said.
        [PHILOPOLEMUS *comes to the door and stands smil-
        ing at his father. The family resemblance between
        all three is suddenly obvious*]

TYNDARUS [*stunned*]   It's—it's . . . such a fine . . . such a
noble
Thing to have done!

[26] Leo brackets lines 1016 through 1022. Unwarrantably, I think.

PHILOCRATES [*leading him by the hand*]   Look, here's your
    father,
  And here's your thief:
  The man who stole you away from here.
        [*Pushes* STALAGMUS *in front of* TYNDARUS]

TYNDARUS [*with a stony glance at him*]
    But now I'm big
  I'll take good care
  He gets the biggest stringing up there is.

PHILOCRATES   It serves him right.

TYNDARUS [*turning away*]   By Jupiter, it does!
  I'll see he gets what he deserves.                    *1020*
        [*Stands stock still in front of* HEGIO]
  You? . . . Oh . . . please . . .
  Tell me really: are you my father?

HEGIO [*opening his arms*]   Your father . . . My own dear
    lad!

TYNDARUS   Imagine it! . . .
  [*in a dazed whisper*]   Ah, thinking back a bit,
  I seem to hear—at last—
  As in a mist:
  The name of "Hegio," my dad.

HEGIO [*taking him in his arms*]   Yes, yes—I am he.
        [*A long embrace*]

PHILOCRATES [*breaking the solemnity*]   For mercy's sake,
    sir,
  Get yourself a lighter son
  And make this slave here
  The heavier one.

HEGIO [*releasing* TYNDARUS]   Of course! Of course!
  That's the first thing to be done.
  Let's go inside: send for a smith
  To strike these fetters off
  To deck the blackguard with.

STALAGMUS [*with a toss of his head and a wink at the audi-
        ence*]   That's ducky!
    I'll have some very
    *Private* property.

            [*Exeunt omnes, except* HEGIO *who steps downstage
            to address the audience*]


# EPILOGUE

HEGIO

                        Spectators,
                This play is most respectable:
                Not subversive, not suggestive
1030                    (no love-affair),
            No children substituted and suspectable.
                    What's more:
                No money got by crime,
                No young amorous flame
                (Behind his poor dad's back)
                    Setting loose
                    A loose dame.
                        [*Shakes his head*]
                    Oh there's a lack
                    Of plays like this:
                    Of such caliber,
                They make a good man better.
                    [*Leaning toward the audience*]
                        So,
                    If we've pleased you
                And haven't been a bore,
                    Just make that clear.
            And if you favor the reward's
                    Going to virtue,
                    Will you please
1036                    Just applaud.